ERRATUM

The publisher regrets that a typographic error has led to a number of missing apostrophes in the text. This will be corrected in a future edition.

Savage Junctures

Published and forthcoming in KINO: The Russian Cinema Series
Series Editor: Richard Taylor

Film Propaganda: Soviet Russia and Nazi Germany (second, revised edition)
Richard Taylor

Forward Soviet! History and Non-Fiction Film in the USSR
Graham Roberts

Russia on Reels: The Russian Idea in Post-Soviet Cinema
Edited by Birgit Beumers

Real Images: Soviet Cinema and the Thaw
Josephine Woll

Cinema and Soviet Society: From the Revolution to the Death of Stalin
Peter Kenez

Vsevolod Pudovkin: Classic Films of the Soviet Avant-Garde
Amy Sargeant

Savage Junctures: Sergei Eisenstein and the Shape of Thinking
Anne Nesbet

KINOfiles film companions

1. *The Battleship Potemkin*
Richard Taylor

2. *The Man with the Movie Camera*
Graham Roberts

3. *Burnt by the Sun*
Birgit Beumers

4. *Repentance*
Josephine Woll and Denise J. Youngblood

5. *Bed and Sofa*
Julian Graffy

6. *Mirror*
Natasha Synessios

7. *The Cranes Are Flying*
Josephine Woll

8. *Little Vera*
Frank Beardow

9. *Ivan the Terrible*
Joan Neuberger

10. *The End of St. Petersburg*
Vance Kepley, Jr.

SAVAGE JUNCTURES

Sergei Eisenstein
and the Shape of Thinking

ANNE NESBET

I.B. TAURIS
LONDON · NEW YORK

Published in 2003 by I.B.Tauris & Co Ltd
6 Salem Road, London W2 4BU
175 Fifth Avenue, New York NY 10010
www.ibtauris.com

In the United States of America and in Canada distributed by Palgrave Macmillan
a division of St Martin's Press, 175 Fifth Avenue, New York NY 10010

ISBN 1 85043 330 5

A full CIP record for this book is available from the British Library
A full CIP record for this book is available from the Library of Congress

Library of Congress catalog card: available

Typeset in Calisto MT by Steve Tribe, Andover
Printed and bound in Great Britain by MPG Books Ltd, Bodmin

Contents

KINO: The Russian Cinema Series
General Editor's Preface

Cinema has been the predominant popular art form of the first half of the twentieth century, at least in Europe and North America. Nowhere was this more apparent than in the former Soviet Union, where Lenin's remark that 'of all the arts, cinema is the most important' became a cliché and where cinema attendances were until recently still among the highest in the world. In the age of mass politics Soviet cinema developed from a fragile but effective tool to gain support among the overwhelmingly illiterate peasant masses in the civil war that followed the October 1917 Revolution, through a welter of experimentation, into a mass weapon of propaganda through the entertainment that shaped the public image of the Soviet Union – both at home and abroad for both elite and mass audiences – and latterly into an instrument to expose the weaknesses of the past and present in the twin processes of *glasnost* and *perestroika*. Now the national cinemas of the successor republics to the old USSR are encountering the same bewildering array of problems, from the trivial to the terminal, as are all the other ex-Soviet institutions.

Cinema's central position in Russian and Soviet cultural history and its unique combination of mass medium, art form and entertainment industry, have made it a continuing battlefield for conflicts of broader ideological and artistic significance, not only for Russia and the Soviet Union but also for the world outside. The debates that raged in the 1920s about the relative merits of documentary as opposed to fiction film, of cinema as opposed to theatre or painting, or of the proper role of cinema in forging of post-Revolutionary Soviet culture and the shaping of the new Soviet man, have their echoes in current discussions about the role of cinema *vis-à-vis* other art forms in effecting the cultural and psychological revolution in human consciousness necessitated by the processes of economic and political transformation of the former Soviet Union into modern democratic and industrial societies and states governed by the rule of law. Cinema's central position has also made it a vital instrument for scrutinizing the blank pages of Russian and Soviet history and enabling the present generation to come to terms with its own past.

This series of books intends to examine Russian and Soviet films in the context of Russian and Soviet cinema, and Russian and Soviet cinema in the context of the political and cultural history of Russia, the Soviet Union and the world at large. Within that framework the series, drawing its authors from both East and West, aims to cover a wide variety of topics and to employ a broad range of methodological approaches and presentational formats. Inevitably this will involve ploughing once again over old ground in order to re-examine received opinions but it principally means increasing the breadth and depth of our knowledge, finding new answers to old questions and, above all, raising new questions for further inquiry and new areas for further research.

The continuing aim of the series is to situate Russian and Soviet cinema in its proper historical and aesthetic context, both as a major cultural force and as a crucible for experimentation that is of central significance to the development of world cinema culture. Books in the series strive to combine the best of scholarship, past, present and future, with a style of writing that is accessible to a broad readership, whether that readership's primary interest lies in cinema or in Russian and Soviet political history.

Richard Taylor
Swansea, Wales

Preface and Acknowledgements

I am fortunate to be surrounded at Berkeley by lively and inspiring colleagues. Olga Matich and Irina Paperno not only tolerated but encouraged my slippage into the visual; my work has many times benefited from their perceptive suggestions. Linda Williams, Marilyn Fabe and Mark Sandberg make any country more interesting and have been a great source of inspiration and encouragement. Kaja Silverman and Harsha Ram responded very thoughtfully to earlier versions of this book, and Jeff Karlsen and Glen Worthey made invaluable contributions to this project as my research assistants.

I am often inspired by the work of my fellow Eisenstein scholars, many of whom have become deeply valued interlocutors: Oksana Bulgakova, Yuri Tsivian, Richard Taylor, Ian Christie, Barry Scherr, David Bordwell, Joan Neuberger and Alexander Zholkovsky are some of those whose questions and comments have improved the shape of my thinking.

I am grateful, too, to the many institutions that have given me financial or practical support over the last few years. The Social Science Research Council, IREX, the Hellman Family Foundation and UC Berkeley provided funds that enabled my research in Moscow and elsewhere. The Townsend Center for the Humanities at UC Berkeley gave me not only time but also a sense of community. The staffers of RGALI (the Russian State Archive of Literature and the Arts) proved to be extraordinarily helpful. Edith Kramer and all the amazing people at the Pacific Film Archive have my admiration and gratitude. I would like to express my thanks also to Ann Martin at *Film Quarterly*, where some of the material now in this book's seventh chapter first appeared. At I.B.Tauris, Philippa Brewster, Deborah Susman and Susan Lawson have been both patient and helpful.

In Russia, I learned an enormous amount from conversations with Naum Kleiman, whose dedication to the preservation of Russian and Soviet film history is unsurpassed. Lev and Karma Slezkine knew how to make Moscow feel like home, and Masha and Viktor Zhivov welcomed my family with open arms. My heroic mother, Helen MacPherson Nesbet, came to Moscow one summer and shepherded a volatile two-year-old all around the city while I worked in the archives. I wish she could be here now to see how the child and the book have grown.

In every person's life there are certain essential people without whom nothing would get done. Grisha Freidin has stepped in on a number of occasions to help me out of book-related difficulties. For the moral and practical support provided by him and by Victoria Bonnell, I am eternally grateful. Yuri and Natasha Goroshko made Russian our household language for a while. Lisa Little and Yuri Slezkine make me glad to live in Berkeley. Will Waters knows better than anyone how much words matter and how much better it is to revise book chapters above treeline. Roo Hooke and Sharon Inkelas have repaired my spirits many times over the last few decades, and at home Thera, Ada and Eleanor Naiman keep everything a bit off-kilter in the nicest possible way.

There are two people I would like especially to acknowledge. I think the first conversation I ever had about Eisenstein was with Russell Merritt. Russell has a wonderful way of handing over nuggets of wisdom, while insisting repeatedly (and entirely without cause) that *you* have been terribly, terribly helpful to *him*. He is the most generous person I've ever met. He is also far and away the best person to sneak off to the movies with. And of all the academics I know, Eric Naiman is probably the best reader. He lets nothing steal by. He's tough. His standards are high. How these sterling qualities got mixed up with a fondness for obscene puns, I confess I have no idea, but Eric is a great coach and a great friend, and I admire him no end. To Russell Merritt and Eric Naiman, then, my favorite teachers, this book is dedicated with equal amounts of admiration and affection.

A Note on
Transliteration

In the scholarly apparatus I follow the system used by the Library of Congress, but in the text certain names appear in spellings that have become familiar to Western readers: 'Eisenstein', for instance, rather than 'Eizenshtein'.

Frequently Cited Sources

Archival materials from the Russian State Archive of Literature and Art (RGALI, 'Rossiiskii gosudarstvennyi arkhiv literatury i iskusstva') are cited by 'fond' (collection), 'opis' ['op.'] (record series), 'edinitsa khraneniia' ['e/kh'] (file) and 'list'' ['l.'] (sheet). The Eisenstein collection is held in Fond 1923.

BTS   Sergei Eisenstein, *Beyond the Stars: The Memoirs of Sergei Eisenstein*, ed. Richard Taylor, trans. William Powell, Vol. 4 of *Selected Works* (London: British Film Institute, 1995)

EOD   *Eisenstein on Disney*, ed. Jay Leyda and Naum Kleiman, trans. Alan Upchurch (Calcutta: Seagull Books, 1986)

GA   GV Alexandrov, *Epokha i kino*, (Moscow: Izdatel'stvo politicheskoi literatury, 1983)

IP1-6   SM Eizenshtein, *Izbrannye proizvedeniia*, 6 vols., eds PM Atasheva, IV Vaisfel'd, NB Volkova, Iu A Krasovskii, SI Freilikh, RN Iurenev, SI Iutkevich (Moscow: Iskusstvo, 1964 [Vol. 1]; 1964 [Vol. 2]; 1964 [Vol. 3]; 1966 [Vol. 4]; 1968 [Vol. 5]; 1971 [Vol. 6]

SW1   Sergei Eisenstein, *Writings, 1922–34*, Vol. 1 of *Selected Works*, ed. and trans. Richard Taylor (London: British Film Institute, 1988)

SW2   Sergei Eisenstein, *Towards a Theory of Montage*, Vol. 2 of *Selected Works*, ed. Michael Glenny and Richard Taylor, trans. Michael Glenny (London: British Film Institute, 1991)

SW3   Sergei Eisenstein, *Writings, 1934–47*, Vol. 3 of *Selected Works*, ed. Richard Taylor, trans. William Powell (London: British Film Institute, 1996)

Introduction

All these mythological figures that we consider, at most, as allegorical material, at some level are figurative resumes of a way of perceiving the world... The Bororo, for instance, claim that they, although people, are at the same time a particular species of red parrot, common to Brazil. What's more, they do not mean by this that they will turn into these birds after death, or that in the past their ancestors were parrots. Categorically not. They directly claim that they actually are these very birds. And this is not about a similarity of name or some kind of relatedness, but rather the complete, synchronous identity of the two beings.[1]

SM Eisenstein

Sergei Eisenstein delighted in unlikely juxtapositions: he was apt to cite from Stalin and Walt Disney in the same breath and folded a startling mixture of mythological references, scraps salvaged from the newspapers of the day and pornographic jokes into his films and essays. Although there have been quite a number of books written on Eisenstein, most of them shy away from the heterogeneity underlying his work. This was a man, after all, who could say in all seriousness of an advertisement clipped from an issue of *Life* magazine, 'one could write a whole book about this' and go on to bring its imagery into a thematic series that included Gogol, Freud, circus clowns and the early German mystics. Although he was a passionate Marxist, Eisenstein's interpretation of dialectics (for one example) was hardly orthodox; he translated all the tenets of 'dialectical materialism' into aesthetic terms as flexible as his own intensely plastic imagination. Thus a cream separator could become the very embodiment – no mere illustration – of the transformation of 'quantity' into 'quality', and the 'negation of the negation' could be achieved with mirrors, reflective puddles and film run in reverse. In short, his approach to philosophy (and to political thought) was figurative: he mined Hegel, Engels, Lenin, Freud (and Stalin's speeches, too) for their figures, their images, which he then threw into sometimes blasphemous conjunction with images borrowed from literature, folklore, popular culture and myth.

These habits irritated his contemporaries, made uneasy by, among other things, the effect bawdy jokes had on what in another director's hands would be straightforward epic and by Eisenstein's suggestion that Soviet actors could learn a thing or two from the Bororo Indians of South America, who believed they were not just men, but also (and at the very same time) red parrots. I think it is safe to say that Eisenstein's many different audiences continue even now to be unsettled by his lack of decorum: he is never clearly one thing over another, never philosopher enough or fool enough to be easily categorized, and his political attitudes, too, resist pigeonholing even as they seem to invite it. There is not yet (nor will there ever be) a critical consensus as to whether *Ivan the Terrible*, the film Stalin first lauded (Part One) and then banned (Part Two), is really a despicably pro-Stalinist or a fearlessly anti-Stalinist tract. It is, like most of Eisenstein's work, too many things at once, and some of those things, like *Ivan*'s playful quoting of *Snow White and the Seven Dwarfs*, aren't even 'serious'. In fact, Eisenstein could be most profoundly serious at the very points where silliness or obscenity erupted. He did not merely mine philosophy for likely figures, but insisted that the figure, the image, could itself be the basis of serious, even philosophical, thought.

At the heart of intellectual thought, a scandalous, blasphemous or perhaps pornographic image: this was a basic rule of Eisenstein's essays, films and lectures. The device is most plainly bared, perhaps, in *Alexander Nevsky*, when, as he plans strategy for the battle with the Teutonic invaders, Nevsky overhears an anecdote about a vixen and a hare:

> A hare leaps into a ravine with a vixen on his tail. He makes for the forest, the vixen after him. So the hare hops between a pair of birch trees. The vixen springs after him – and sticks. Pinned between the two birches, she wriggles and she struggles, but there's no getting free. Calamity! Meanwhile the hare stands alongside her and says in a serious voice: 'If you're agreeable,' he says, 'I'll now put paid to your virginity, all of it...'

> The soldiers around the campfire laugh. Ignat [the plain-spoken armourer

who tells this story] goes on:

'... Oh, how can you, good neighbor, it isn't done. How can you serve me such a shameful trick. Have pity!' she says.

'This is no time for pity,' the hare tells her. And he pounces.

Alexander turns around and asks: 'Between two birch trees?'

Ignat replies: 'He pinned her.'

Alexander's voice asks: 'And pounced?'

Ignat replies laughing: 'He pounced.'[2]

From this story of one animal's clever capture and rape of another, Alexander Nevsky instantly develops a fail-safe scenario for victory. He splits up his forces and has his troops lure the Teutons onto the ice so that the Russians, like the hare, may 'pounce' on them.

The difference between Ignat, earthy man of the people, who tells the joke and Alexander Nevsky, who overhears it, is that while the 'little man' (and his immediate audience) sees in the joke only a joke, it is the military leader and strategist who is wise enough to recognize that obscenity and conceptual thought are by no means mutually exclusive – and may, in fact, be comrades-in-arms. The tale of the Vixen and the Hare embedded in *Alexander Nevsky* demonstrates the power of such thinking: if Nevsky, following in the footsteps of the Bororo, can accept seeing his own predicament in that of a mere rabbit, then the enemy, no matter how carnivorous, is doomed.

It is entirely appropriate that Eisenstein should have found this anecdote in a collection of pornographic folklore given him by Viktor Shklovsky.[3] We know about Shklovsky's own affection for this genre from, among other things, his seminal essay 'Art as Device' (1917), the last third of which explores the dirty joke as a model for the aesthetic function of 'defamiliarization': the 'making strange' that makes art. If, as Eisenstein suspected, art communicated with its audience by means of unexpected images and juxtapositions, then the shocks that were to precipitate the spectator in an unexpected mental direction were applications not just of force, but also of force eroticized.

These shocks had the ability to restore the full intensity and vigor of perception (and thus of life) to the spectator, but whether that renewed vision should be confused with thinking was another issue entirely. Indeed, Shklovsky had polemicized in 'Art as Device' against the notion of art as 'thinking in images', a phrase he attacked at the outset of his essay as an already long-exhausted cliché: '"Art is thinking in images.' One hears this phrase even from gymnasium students and it is also the standard point of departure for learned philologists.'[4] For Shklovsky, picture-thinking was something significantly less than art: the deterioration of poetry into the prose of illustrative examples (the image in bondage to the idea). Shklovsky wanted his readers to replace this old chestnut with art as detour and defamiliarization, so that seeing might be rescued from recognition and so that life might be rescued from the deadening effects of automatization.

Eisenstein's work, however, which absolutely insists on the power of 'thinking in images', is both an indebted homage to and a travesty of Shklovsky's revolutionary poetics. In Eisenstein's practice, images are not merely 'simpler and clearer' signs for the abstract ideas they represent (Shklovsky's objection to art as thinking-in-images): they are as complex, as 'real,' as any of the meanings they might convey. The relationship between image and idea in Eisenstein is like that perceived by the Bororo between man and red parrot: neither identity in thrall to the other. Eisenstein, in short, defends a truly image-based – figurative – philosophy as the most profound and relevant goal of modern thought.

The union of idea and image was a scandalous juncture not only for staunch defenders (like Shklovsky) of the primacy of aesthetic experience, but also for those who approached the problem from the perspective of the philosophical tradition. Still looming large over the aesthetic debate in the early twentieth century was Hegel's monument to the temptations of picture-thinking, *The Phenomenology of Spirit*, in which a mighty struggle between 'image' ('Bild') and 'concept' ('Begriff') had been revealed as the motor-powering man's ascent towards transcendent truth. As Hegel told the story, the image might help the philosophical pilgrim learn the lesson of the moment, but it must itself be surpassed, lest the seeker find himself trapped within it. The Russians struggling with these issues in the age of cinema inherited a long tradition of fascination with the paradigms presented in Hegel. In the late 1920s, Eisenstein would tackle this issue head-on, phrasing the goal of cinema as a project of combining the 'language of images' and the 'language of ideas'. For Hegel – and for his philosophical descendants – a philosophy that got itself too mixed up with the image, with art, could only be a mockery of a philosophy, a merely figurative philosophy. 'One would do better,' proclaimed Theodor Adorno in 1931, 'to liquidate philosophy entirely and to dissolve it into its various sciences than to come to its aid with a poetic ideal that amounts to nothing other than a poor ornamental cover for false thinking.'[5]

What is it about the mixing of image and idea that lends itself so to warnings about the disaster of 'faulty thinking,' that well-dressed usurper of philosophy? The image can become a stumbling block, a trap, not merely attracting the mind, but to some degree arresting it in its tracks. Another philosophical lesson – itself an image – was on the minds of those puzzling through the relationship of thought and picture in the first few decades of the age of cinema: Plato's parable of the cave from *The Republic*. Plato's exemplary spectator, trapped in a cave and watching the shadows of objects projected onto the walls, is quite thoroughly befuddled and imprisoned by these images. Barring the appearance of a rough and undeceiving teacher, the cave-man will never realize that these are merely shadows, that the fire that lights this spectacle is itself a mere shadow of the great sun outside, that outside this cave is a whole world more real than the one he knows. And if that man is taken from the cave, it will be painful for him to adjust to the new light and the new world and even if he succeeds in that, it will be very difficult indeed to convince his companions still living in darkness of the truth of their situation. This allegory of the difficulties involved in true education (Plato says one must take the shoulders of the person one is trying to educate and literally turn him to face the truth) is itself a spectacle, an image, endowed with a remarkable power to infect the mind of the reader, and thus it demonstrates both the potency and the danger of images for philosophy. Its effectiveness as a warning against the allure of mere images depends on the story's eerily proto-cinematic imagery.

In both its imagery and its conceptual concerns, Plato's allegory of the cave reminds us of the philosophical dilemmas lurking in the movie theater, if that cinema wants not just to attract and imprison its viewers, but also to change and inspire them. When the young Maksim Gorkii, covering the international exposition at Nizhnii-Novgorod in 1896 as a journalist, was introduced to the cinematograph, then making its debut in Russia, he turned to the Platonic model for his metaphors: the new medium was a 'Kingdom of Shadows', a deceptive and possibly corrupting trap.[6] For those, like Eisenstein, who understood that trapping the viewer might be an integral part of getting one's point across, the cinema-as-cave's mixture of seductive spectacle and education could not be seen as merely negative. Eisenstein was tempted to add another layer of analogy to the scenario: if the cave and the cinema could be conflated (and the value of that cave largely shifted from negative to positive), so too could this cinema-cave and that other cave-like space, that central arena of all education and propaganda, the mind of the spectator.

In early writings and in his early films, Eisenstein seems taken with the idea that the images projected on the screen would actually become the thoughts in the spectator's brain. The film serves, in a sense, in the place of consciousness – an aggressive model, certainly, but one with the advantage of limiting the chances for an audience to misunderstand what it was seeing. In this light, Eisenstein must have been pleased by the discussion of *The Battleship Potemkin* at one of the Association for Revolutionary Cinema's Thursday discussions (14 January 1926). Leo Mur spoke then of Eisenstein's montage as an action not limited to the screen:

> The fundamental method used by Eisenstein he calls the montage of attractions. This name is not entirely correct. Eisenstein does not only edit the reel, but also the cells in the brain of the spectator. Montage not of attractions, but of associations. Montage not only on the screen of the movie theater, but also on the screen of the brain.[7]

Both Mur and Vsevolod Pudovkin underscored the power over the spectator achieved by Eisenstein in this film. Mur said, 'The spectator edits [*montiruet*] the scenes in his brain the way Eisenstein wants him to' (l. 2) and Pudovkin agreed: 'Montage is the forceful direction [*nasil stvennoe upravlenie*] of the spectator. Eisenstein brilliantly controls it, leading the spectator almost to pathos' (l. 4).

Although Mur tried to distinguish between the effect *Battleship Potemkin* had on the cells of the brain and Eisenstein's own term, 'montage of attractions', in fact when Eisenstein coined that phrase in 1923, he himself insisted on the essential importance of what happened within the head of the viewer, claiming that an attraction that had no such effect could only be called a sterile 'trick': 'In so far as the trick is absolute and complete within itself, it means the direct opposite of the attraction, which is based exclusively on something relative, the reactions of the audience.'[8] The 'brain-screen' was the only proper place for the projection of an Eisenstein film.

This analogy attempting to bridge the distance between the cinema screen and the murkier arena of the spectator's brain responded not only to the desire to gain direct access to that brain (the 'educational' project), but also to a widespread, but perhaps deceptive, hunch that said that thinking was a process not unlike watching a movie. Was it, though? To what degree was thinking based on images, rather than language and what connection was there between image and word? In Eisenstein's day, the notion of thinking as 'inner speech' was very prevalent, but to what degree that 'speech' was like ordinary language was a heavily contested issue. Lev Vygotsky, a psychologist who had a great influence on Russian artists in the early part of the century, described this inner speech as a mercurial substance halfway between word and image: 'Inner speech is to a large extent thinking in pure meanings. It is a dynamic, shifting, unstable thing, fluttering between word and thought.'[9] In an essay entitled 'Cinema Stylistics' (1927), the brilliant Formalist Boris Eikhenbaum extended this unstable realm to encompass the response a viewer had to a film. 'The film metaphor is a kind of visual realization of a verbal metaphor,' Eikhenbaum claimed, but his explanation becomes complicated as he tries to explain what 'kind', exactly, of 'visual realization' might be at work and to what degree film communicated by means of some *sub rosa* reference to already existing linguistic metaphors:

> A film metaphor is, as it were, a realized metaphor, actually embodied on the screen. How can it be taken seriously? Obviously, the point here is that in cinema, first of all, we are moving within the bounds not of verbal, but of cinematographic motivation; and, secondly, the internal speech of the film viewer, which is forming itself on the basis of shots, is not realized in the shape of precise verbal formulations. We have an inverse relationship: whereas the verbal metaphor is not realized in the consciousness of the reader to the point of forming a clear visual image (i.e. the metaphorical sense shields us from the literal image), the film metaphor is not realized in the consciousness of the film viewer to the point of forming a complete verbal proposition.[10]

Striking in this description is the degree to which cinematic communication depends upon things half-formed, ghostly entities glimpsed in the process of metamorphosing from one state into another (from language into image; from image into language) and thus never entirely graspable or 'realized'. 'Internal speech' and 'film metaphor' are categories blurry enough to trouble the larger outlines of Eikhenbaum's study of 'Cinema Stylistics', dependent as that essay is on linguistic analogy.

For Viktor Shklovsky, not only the founding father of formalist criticism but also the Soviet Union's most astute film critic, cinema inhabited an intermediate realm between pure image and true language. Cinema could be seen as a kind of language, but only if one compared it to those forms of communication most difficult to characterize in their own right:

More than anything else cinema resembles Chinese painting. Chinese painting lies in between drawing and the word. The people moving on the screen are hieroglyphs of sorts. These aren't cine-images, but cine-words, cine-concepts. Montage is the syntax and etymology of the cinematic language. When for the first time the film *Intolerance* was shown in the USSR, the audience couldn't endure the montage (Griffith's) and left the screening. Now the audience reads Griffith right from the page.

The convention of spatiality, the convention of silence, the convention of colorlessness in cinema – all have analogies in language. The cinematic rule that one mustn't show how a man sat at a table, began to eat and finished eating – that is, the rule of extracting from an action its single characteristic part, the mark of that action – is also the transformation of the cinematic image into a hieroglyph. For this reason it is incorrect to say that the language of cinema is universally understood. No, it is just easily learned.[11]

Interesting in this description is the way the intermediary nature of cinema (and of Chinese painting) is characterized: what one sees on the screen, whether painted or projected, is the image caught in the process of becoming more like verbal language, with the 'hieroglyph' representing one stage in a broader process of metamorphosis.

The notion of the hieroglyph as the model for cinema communication appealed not just to Shklovsky, but also to Eisenstein, who had gained permission to return to Moscow after finishing his Civil War work by applying to study Japanese. Once Eisenstein arrived in Moscow, theater rather than Oriental languages absorbed the bulk of his energies, but he always retained an affection for 'hieroglyphs' (as he referred to Chinese characters) and would occasionally use examples taken from the language and culture of China or Japan to illustrate theoretical points.[12]

Caught somewhere between language and image, both cinema and the sort of thinking it provoked escaped easy categorization. We should probably take Eisenstein's 'montage of attractions' as, to some degree, wishful thinking: the desire to discover and employ cinematic devices that would, by definition, have a determinable effect on the very cells of the spectator's brain:

An attraction (in our diagnosis of theater) is any aggressive moment in theater, i.e. any element of it that subjects the audience to emotional or psychological influence, verified by experience and mathematically calculated to produce specific emotional shocks in the spectator in their proper order within the whole.[13]

If only cinema could work like a 'mathematically calculated' chain reaction. In all of Eisenstein's many references to 'reflexes', a topic much in evidence in the Soviet Union of the 1920s, one senses this longing: to be able to construct a real chain of cause and effect that would nullify the distance between screen and brain.[14] When Eisenstein defined the effect of art in terms of a violent but calculated sort of shock ('a brilliantly calculated blow of the billiard cue [on] the audience's cerebral hemisphere'),[15] it was partly because the violence promised to cut through the fog of the communicative no-man's-land in which cinematic image and 'internal speech' circled each other so warily. A blow on the head might not be subtle, but it did seem the quintessential example of a universal language, the universality of film language being in some doubt.

What kind of philosophy could be based upon 'shocks,' however? The shock – or even a montage of shocks – might logically be seen as antithetical to real thinking. That would be Adorno's complaint about another man seeking a way of reformulating 'philosophy' to incorporate the image: Walter Benjamin. Adorno took Benjamin to task in terms strikingly reminiscent of Eisenstein's language from the period of the 'Montage of Attractions' manifesto:

> Benjamin's intention was to renounce all open interpretation and to let meanings emerge only through the shock-like montage of the material. Philosophy was not only to overtake surrealism, but also to become surreal itself.[16]

Adorno, for whom this montage-based approach to philosophy seemed hazardous, meant to suggest that Benjamin's great project of his last years, the *Passagenwerk* that remained fundamentally an archival exploration of the nature of the nineteenth century, a great collection of quotes, images and ideas sorted by theme, could not achieve its intellectual aims because it was excessively 'surrealist' – that is to say, its contents exceeded the organizational control Benjamin could impose on them. True philosophy, warned Adorno, should not be so willing to cede agency to its raw materials.

But for Eisenstein, as for Benjamin, the nature of real thinking, of philosophy, was not such a simple thing to define. Eisenstein, like Benjamin, spent the last years of his life assembling vast collections of texts and images grouped around the fundamental issues (the *Grundproblem*, as Eisenstein called one great branch of his investigation) that seemed to him to lie at the heart of the mysteries of the human mind. He, like Benjamin, could appreciate the power of a 'profane illumination', the revelation of a juncture between seemingly disparate objects or epochs.[17] Benjamin, however, had a different relationship to temporal junctures: his 'now' was always in the process of receding into the past. For Eisenstein, who did not feel himself bound by the constraints of 'late capitalism' – though socialism undoubtedly imposed its own spectrum of constraints, some cruel indeed – the whole of world history could be surveyed with a strange absence of nostalgia, partly perhaps because the cultural history of the world was not, for Eisenstein, something located in or moving towards an irretrievable past, but rather quite vitally alive in the present.

A central part of that living cultural resource was, for Eisenstein, the kind of serious thinking historically called 'philosophy'. What is it about this old-fashioned and contested term that might allow us to appropriate it for Eisenstein's radical experiments? Some members of his generation would have argued, after all, that 'dialectical materialism' had forever displaced philosophy, that tired arena of bourgeois idealism. For Eisenstein, however, philosophy (like art, for that matter) was something that should be thought of as not only dialectical, but cumulative:

> The onesidedness of a *child s* complex thinking becomes the conscious thinking of the *adult*, having absorbed into himself also that differentiating beginning. Thus also the consciousness of a *person at the dawn of culture* becomes the *consciousness of a person of a developed cultural epoch*. Thus also philosophy out of prehistorical chaos becomes the materialistic dialectic. [Emphasis in the original][18]

Even when he was employing the most generic tools of Marxist thought, Eisenstein tended to mould them to his own purposes. Here, for instance, the use of 'materialistic dialectic', instead of the more usual 'dialectical materialism', shifts the phrase's emphasis slightly away from a pragmatic focus on materialism (the dialectic made useful) towards the more figurative potential of dialectical thinking *per se*. Eisenstein found support for his unique vision of dialectical materialism in his equally unique reading of Lenin; he cited again and again passages from a few favorite Lenin articles where the political leader managed to sound remarkably like Eisenstein himself. These writings (Lenin's conspectus of Hegel's *Science of Logic*, 'On the Question of the Dialectic,' published in the journal *Bolshevik* in 1925 and the writings published in the 12th *Leninskii sbornik*) were almost always concerned with issues of the 'dialectic' itself over and above more local or more political matters. In fact, the Eisensteinian Lenin manages to transcend history in a rather sublime way. Right after describing the 'materialistic dialectic' as something developing out of 'prehistoric chaos', for instance, in the article previously cited, Eisenstein turns to Lenin for support: 'In essence we have in this instance that "seeming return to the old" about which Lenin speaks with regard to the question of the dialectic of appearances' (IP2 386).[19] With the help of Lenin, then, Eisenstein explains that prehistory is never exactly left behind, but rather turned into a dialectical component of the present historical or aesthetic moment: even the highest, most developed image bears at least a plastic trace of its most primitive ancestry (IP2 386). The 'materialistic dialectic' is more than merely itself; it encompasses also even the 'chaos' of its distant past. As dialectical materialism is stretched to incorporate its own prehistory and as Leninist thought is released from its (materialist) ties to local history, Eisenstein's version of the dialectic encroaches once more upon the territory of that more general term, 'philosophy,' which in his definition above had at first seemed to be sundered by the passage of time into the subcategories of 'prehistoric chaos' and 'materialistic dialectic'. Brought into scandalous juncture by Eisenstein's image-based and dialectical philosophy, prehistory and the present moment could be seen to illuminate each other.

Adorno derided the Eisensteinian/Benjaminian project – philosophical thought that would 'emerge solely through the shock-like montage of the material' – as a 'surrealistic philosophy', for him an oxymoronic concept at best. But perhaps we should take this impossible object seriously for a moment: what would it mean to think of Eisenstein as a 'surrealist philosopher'? In his fondness for savage junctures, after all, Eisenstein was not so very unlike André Breton, who wrote in his 'Surrealist Manifesto' of 1924 of the illuminary power of 'juxtaposition':

> It is, as it were, from the fortuitous juxtaposition of the two terms that a particular light has sprung, *the light of the image*, to which we are infinitely sensitive. The value of the image depends upon the beauty of the spark obtained; it is, consequently, a function of the difference of potential between the two conductors. When the difference exists only slightly, as in a comparison, the spark is lacking.[20]

Breton, however, unlike Eisenstein, admitted and even insisted on the artist's lack of control over the light produced by these juxtaposed images:

> Now, it is not within man's power, so far as I can tell, to effect the juxtaposition of two realities so far apart. The principle of the

> association of ideas, such as we conceive of it, militates against it[...]
> We are therefore obliged to admit that the two terms of the image are
> not deduced one from the other by the mind for the specific purpose of
> producing the spark, that they are the simultaneous products of the
> activity I call Surrealist, reason's role being limited to taking note of
> and appreciating, the luminous phenomenon. (Breton 37)

The depiction of the artist as yet another spectator, 'appreciating
the luminous phenomenon', would be unacceptable for Eisenstein
in the 1920s. As we have seen, only a year prior to Breton's
manifesto, Eisenstein had defined the unit of theatrical communication or juncture between performance and audience, the
'attraction,' as an 'aggressive moment... calculated to produce
specific emotional shocks in the spectator'(SW1 34). Eisenstein's
combative definition, one that insists on control, analysis and
calculation at every step, aims for an active approach to the creation
(though not necessarily the reception) of the dialectical image. One
might also say that Eisenstein here wants to make very clear that
his position is not, like everybody else's, among the audience.

There was an affinity between Eisenstein and the Surrealists that
could not be admitted too readily on the Soviet side (where the
Surrealists had been deemed unsatisfactory Communists). In France
in 1930, however, when Eisenstein was taking questions from the
audience, he provided a relatively generous analysis of the
connections between himself and the Surrealists:

> *Q* What do you think of Surrealism?
>
> *A* It is very interesting because Surrealism works, I may say, in a way
> that is dramatically opposed to ours. It is always interesting to
> understand and evaluate things on diametrically opposed ground: I must
> admit that on one level we might find common ground and speak the
> same language... I must add to the subject of Surrealism that the
> extremes meet or, if you take Marx's formulation, opposite objects have
> the possibility of changing places and combining. That is probably why
> the personal sympathies between us are quite strong. But from the
> theoretical point of view we are very different: the Surrealists seek to
> expose subconscious emotions while I seek to use them and play with
> them to provoke emotion.[21]

At the end of this wonderfully evasive response, one is left wondering
to what degree Eisenstein and the Surrealists, 'opposite objects'
though they might be, could be said to 'speak the same language'.
The places where 'extremes meet' were, in Eisenstein's terminology
of the period, points of 'unexpected juncture'.[22] In any case,

Eisenstein's emphasis was to be on exploiting, rather than merely 'exposing' the subconscious: the discoveries of Freud were to be put to work in the service of Marx.

From his earliest days as a filmmaker, Eisenstein demonstrated how 'opposite objects' might be forced to produce satire. The first bit of film produced by Eisenstein was an insert into a play, *Enough Simplicity for Every Wise Man* (1923), a wild and woolly remake (with Eisenstein's playwright friend Sergei Tret'iakov) of Ostrovsky's nineteenth-century classic. The play was punctuated with circus acts and other shocks, most famously, perhaps, the firecrackers that were supposed to go off beneath the seats of the audience. The short film sequence inserted into the action at the end of the play as another 'trick' or 'attraction' among many was itself a kind of collage of film attractions, a witty take-off on the trick-films of Méliès, with a central emphasis on the theme of metamorphosis.[23]

The film ('The Diary of Glumov') is supposed to represent the contents of the hero's stolen diary. Poor Glumov, eternal groveler, is subjected by his patrons (the warmongering Joffre, the fascist Gorodulin, the anti-Soviet émigré Mamaev) to one embarrassing transformation after another: he becomes, in turn, a cannon, a swastika and an ass, in each case the appropriate embodiment of the political ideology being lampooned. The political satire is underscored by a bawdiness that probably owes something to the music-hall inspirations of Eisenstein and Tret'iakov.[24] Glumov's wedding is the planned occasion that the 'diary' interrupts and makes impossible, and at every juncture his manhood is whittled away (the cannon is classically phallic in shape, so that Glumov is being forced to embody not only political symbols, but also rude jokes). Another trick sequence shows the ability of a woman, by her mere presence, to reduce a man literally to infancy again. The wedding that the film ends with is highly parodic, involving a woman cross-dressed in a man's suit, an assemblage of clowns and rude hand gestures, a close-up of which, with the audience as target now, closes the short film. For the young Eisenstein, metamorphosis is part of the bag of cinematic tricks to which characters and audience alike can be subjected, one attraction among others. 'Opposite objects' are manipulated so that the character becomes the embodiment of something demeaning to itself, its own satire. As an attraction, this composite satirical object inspires a secondary mutation: the transformation of the spectator, who is altered by emotional and even physiological 'shocks' from which he cannot retreat.

Although in 'Enough Simplicity for Every Wise Man' the objects manipulated satirically are very much constructions of the director, Eisenstein exhibited throughout his life a particular passion for knick-knacks, curios and oddments that in some respects served his satirical purposes and in other ways undermined satire. Here again the 'extremes' of Eisenstein's cinema and French Surrealism seem to meet, in a pronounced affection for 'found objects.' In his 1937 *L Amour fou* (*Mad Love*), André Breton explores the nature of the 'found object' as instigator of philosophical thought. One of the most striking examples presented there is that of a wooden spoon Breton found one day in 1934 when strolling the Paris flea market with his friend Alberto Giacometti. At first it is not so clear to Breton what it is about this spoon, the only distinctive feature of which would seem to be the little wooden 'shoe' on which the handle rests when the spoon is set down, that draws his attention so. It is the revelatory nature of the found object that most fascinates Breton:

> The discovery of an object rigorously fulfills the same function as the dream, in the sense that it liberates the individual from paralyzing affective scruples, comforts him and makes him understand that the obstacle he had believed insurmountable has been surpassed.[25]

The found object is a response to a question that the finder may not even have formulated clearly when he comes across the object; for Breton, in the case of this wooden spoon, the analysis to which he subjects his newly discovered object reveals layer after layer of relevance to those ideas that had been occupying his mind both before and after the discovery of the object upon which, it would turn out, these ideas depended: the spoon is both 'feminine' and 'masculine' in shape; it represents Cinderella's lost slipper; it speaks of love lost and found.

In its wide-ranging, awestruck analysis of the felicitous juncture of ideas made material in this interesting object, Breton's analysis of the wooden spoon is quite similar to Eisenstein's notes of the 1930s and 1940s, as 'found objects' (which for Eisenstein could be not only objects *per se*, but also memories, texts and images from all kinds of sources, ranging from medieval manuscripts to advertisements in *Life* magazine) became a more and more central source of intellectual stimulation. This trend is not limited to the 1930s, although it becomes noticeably stronger as time goes by. Already in his films of the 1920s Eisenstein had demonstrated a fascination with objects that went beyond all ordinary parameters of diegetic usefulness; from the trick tables of *Strike*, disgorging and swallowing typewriters and cocktails, through the lavishly photographed objects that so dominate much of *October* (mechanical toys encrusted with jewels, idols from around the world) and *The General Line*'s laughing porcelain pigs, the satirical function of the object in Eisenstein's work of the 1920s was always at risk of drowning in the sheer joy of examination and collection.

By the 1930s, the found object is no longer restricted to the satirical frame and indeed one suspects that Eisenstein's reaction to the 'Cinderella spoon' would have been similar in some respects to Breton's. Breton's fascination with the infinitely regressing series of 'shoe – with a heel that's a shoe – with a heel that's a shoe...' exactly corresponds to Eisenstein's affection for the structure of *pars pro toto*, a part becoming a 'whole' of which a 'part' again becomes a 'whole' of which a 'part' etc...[26] Eisenstein also shared with the distant Breton an interest in 'bi-sex', as Eisenstein called it in his notes: the dialectical presence of male and female elements within a single image, figure, story, or object – of which the wooden spoon of *L Amour fou* was such a stunning example. The Freud that intrigued both Eisenstein and Breton in the 1930s was the author of *Beyond the Pleasure Principle*, that contradictory but fascinating essay in which love and protoplasm, death drives and Plato's *Symposium*, all found a place.[27]

All of this abundance is also, of course, excessive. One of the pitfalls the image presents to philosophy is that of leading thought astray from any central idea. Rich in possible associations, every image can also be a seductive lure into infinite byways, regressions and detours. The scandal of excess is another fundamental feature of Eisenstein's figurative philosophy and throughout this book, I try to respect (rather than repress) the indecorous nature of Eisenstein's imagination. We are perhaps freer to do so now than ever before. For earlier critics, a relatively unified, more 'congruous' Eisenstein was often a philosophical or political necessity. When in 1976 Viacheslav Ivanov introduced the world to the unexpected riches of Eisenstein's voluminous archives, he did so in a book that could not take the risk of mentioning Eisenstein's name either in its title (*Notes on the History of Semiotics in the USSR*) or in the brief summary of the book that graced its copyright page ('This book is dedicated to the analysis of the most important achievements of Soviet science in the areas of the theory of sign systems...').[28] By taking Eisenstein's later musings on anthropological and ethnographic themes seriously, Ivanov was rescuing a whole segment of Eisenstein's work from obscurity; little wonder, then, that Ivanov concentrated on those places in the notes where Eisenstein seemed to anticipate the discoveries of modern ethnography: Eisenstein as semiotician *avant la lettre*. The messiness (the indecorousness) of Eisenstein's thought had, understandably under such circumstances, to be minimized.

Writing much more recently in the USA, David Bordwell has given us a magisterial, measured and exhaustive overview of Eisenstein's work as we in the West have inherited it.[29] Bordwell is a principled scholar, well read and logical, who does not suffer foolishness gladly, and so the indecorous nature of Eisenstein's wit is not what arouses his interest and respect. When he considers the question of the degree to which Eisenstein can be taken seriously as a thinker, apart from his filmmaking, Bordwell's conclusions are gently skeptical:

> He raised central questions about film form, style and effect and he made fair progress toward answering some of them. Whatever the defects of his general theory, his intellectual energy, wide learning and immense curiosity bequeathed us a wealth of concrete suggestions about how films work. (Bordwell 198)

This appraisal may be eminently fair, but it raises questions about the way we judge experiments in thinking: to what degree does serious thought depend on the development of a unified and coherent 'general theory'? The unruliness of Eisenstein's 'immense curiosity' is evident in the vast array of materials held in the Russian State Archive of Literature and Art (RGALI), Moscow. The very list of items ('edinitsy') contained in that archive fills two thick volumes and each of those 'items' represents many pages of the most varied material: drafts of essays and scenarios, quotations copied from other sources, clippings from newspapers and magazines, pictures, scraps of paper with scribbled words and phrases. More than 50 years after Eisenstein's death, the vast quantities of written work left in his archive still remain largely unpublished.

Indeed it can be difficult to know quite how to approach the undeniable wealth of specific thoughts and images Eisenstein left behind. It seems important to remember, however, that when Eisenstein became enthusiastic about an idea or pattern he saw repeated throughout history and culture (the 'circle' for instance and its thematic ties to the womb), it was the variety of the examples that drove his collecting. He did not lose the specificity of the individual objects in the thrill of the discovery of the 'general rule'. This passion for particular instances was what saved him from becoming reductive, but it can also make his brand of picture thinking unwieldy.[30] Working with Eisenstein's materials means being confronted at once by the competing demands of 'central questions', on the one hand, and of innumerable examples and cartoons and jokes on the other, seemingly trivial details that manage somehow to be both distracting and edifying. His films are much like this, too: there is 'excess', as Kristin Thompson has termed it, not only in *Ivan the Terrible*, but in every film he ever made.[31] To ignore the distraction of images that seem to lead away from the center, to extract from the huge variety of Eisensteinian material only that which seems most serious in a conventional way, is in the case of Eisenstein to risk losing a part of what matters most of all, since for Eisenstein high and low, general rule and specific instance, were both absolutely fundamental components of serious thinking.

At the All-Union Conference of Workers in Soviet Cinematography in January 1935, Sergei Eisenstein amazed the gathered luminati of Soviet cinematography by explaining to them that the most modern discoveries of cinema had their roots deep in 'primitive' ways of thinking about the world. The Soviet actor was to be understood as the descendant of the Bororo parrot-men, who 'claim that they, although people, are at the same time a particular species of red parrot, common to Brazil'.[32] That was not all: the power of cinematic metaphor, Eisenstein declared, derived from the same force underlying the Polynesian tradition of throwing open all doors when a woman was trying to give birth. His audience was not amused. Aleksandr Dovzhenko (the Ukrainian director whose intensely poetic visual style had a history of perplexing Soviet audiences) accused Eisenstein of paying too much attention to 'Polynesian dames' when, all around him, 'living' women were giving birth 'in new ways'.[33] Sergei Vasiliev, who as half of the directorial team responsible for the epic *Chapaev* (1934) was one of the chief heroes of the conference, advised Eisenstein, rather cheekily (since he himself had been a student in Eisenstein's film seminars), to 'throw off your Chinese bathrobe and busy yourself with delving into our contemporary Soviet reality'.[34] Not having produced a film since *The Old and the New* (1929), Eisenstein was vulnerable to accusations of having become stuck in the past and his claims that contemporary artists should study the laws of 'sensuous thought' as expressed in the codes governing the lives of the Bororo, the Polynesians and so on, struck his audience as highly suspect: were modern Soviet artists really supposed to learn their trade from 'primitive' man?

One of the ironies of this occasion was that Eisenstein, who was certainly not incapable of enjoying a scandal, was in this instance perfectly serious. Eisenstein had brought the Bororo into a Moscow gathering of cinematographers to illustrate something that for him was a profoundly important idea: the power of mythology as an aspect of what Eisenstein called 'sensuous thought'. Muscovite and Bororo collided, to the obvious distress of the former, at the intersection of ancient and modern practices of image-based thinking: a savage juncture.

Eisenstein was the master of savage junctures, both by virtue of his insistence on the physicality, the potential violence, of communication and also because in those 'savage' or 'primitive' patterns of thinking that had so interested anthropologists like Levy-Brühl, Eisenstein saw the potential for effective communication of the most intellectual and profound contemporary ideas. This book explores the varied and evolving role of the juncture in the construction of what I have decided to call Eisenstein's 'figurative philosophy': the role played by the slaughterhouse in Russian modernism's remaking of the eye; the odd combination of hyperphilosophy, myth and political philosophy that underlies *Battleship Potemkin*'s attempt to create a new kind of Soviet audience; Eisenstein's pornographic gloss on Hegel's *Phenomenology of Spirit* in *October*; the dangers and allures of two kinds of accumulation, capitalist and textual, that provide *The General Line* with its incendiary underpinnings; Eisenstein's rediscovery of the power of the 'flat arts' on his trip to Mexico; the political potential of animation in High Stalinism's festivals of laughter and terror; the resurgence of the autobiographical drive in Eisenstein's final years, as the compulsion to collect 'opposite objects' from everywhere and every time accelerates. My working hypothesis here has been that the very collision between specific image and general rule that would seem to disqualify Eisenstein as a philosopher in fact does the opposite. To borrow Bordwell's language, I would argue that it is in its very 'defects' that Eisenstein's image-based thinking becomes most challenging and most productive.

Although not indifferent to the arc of Eisenstein's biography, this is not a biography. We are fortunate now to have a number of works devoted to synthetic overviews of Eisenstein's life and art, ranging from Marie Seton's passionate biography and the soberer presentations of his life by Yon Barna and Rostislav Iurenev, through the erudite and encyclopedic work of Barthélémy Amengual (unfortunately unavailable in English), to the distinguished recent monographs by David Bordwell and Oksana Bulgakowa.[35] My focus has been instead the way contexts collide in Eisenstein's written and visual work: the savage junctures that structure his thinking. These contexts range from 'local' Soviet concerns (political debates, clippings from newspapers) to realms much farther afield: the mental makeup of the Bororo or the metaphysical implications of Mickey Mouse.

I draw extensively on archival materials, but this book is also not a complete guide to those immense archives. Nor does it attempt to catalogue and analyze all of those projects Eisenstein began, thought and wrote about, but in many cases never completed, although some of those projects are central to my investigation. The aim here is rather to delve into those places where the explosive complexity of Eisenstein's 'figurative philosophy' can take us in surprising or hazardous directions.

In a polemical article from 1928, Eisenstein took to task those critics who could see nothing particularly noteworthy in the Kabuki theater then visiting Russia:

> [T]he Kabuki is dismissed with faint praise: 'How musical!' 'What handling of objects!' 'What plasticity!' And people come to the conclusion that there is nothing to be learned, that (as one senior critic spitefully remarked) there is nothing much here that is new: Meyerhold long ago 'fleeced' the Japanese!'[36]

These critics, said Eisenstein, were misunderstanding the crucial nature of the Kabuki; indeed they were demanding, as the Russian saying goes, 'milk from a billy-goat': 'Milk a billy-goat? Agricultural practice is unaware of the operation. It is said that a billy-goat provides neither wool nor milk. It has another firmly established reputation and other honorable functions' (SW1 115) No, it was not food and clothing that one should expect from the Japanese theater, but rather that 'other honorable function' upon which the reputation of the billy-goat depended: insemination. The Kabuki demonstrated the possibilities for 'transference' available to the cinema as it hovered at the threshold of sound: 'the transference of the basic affective intention from one material to another, from one category of 'stimulant' to another' (SW1 118). In other words, it was not the exploitation of the Kabuki's 'wool and meat' that should be sought and even 'celebrated', as Eisenstein exclaimed in the last line of his article, but rather the juncture of Kabuki theater and Soviet cinema. This juncture was not just a matter of similarity or coincidence, but a copulatory event.

The 'juncture' that played such a key, but diverse, role in Eisenstein's intellectual landscape was sometimes, as in the essay on the Kabuki, a kind of copula, a binding joint where two elements came together in a moment of fertilization. At other points, the juncture being explored was the often violent connection between artwork and audience: the Kabuki's 'brilliantly calculated blow of the billiard cue at the audience's cerebral hemisphere' being matched by Eisenstein's description of film's effect on the audience as that of 'a tractor, ploughing over the psyche of the spectator from a given class position'.[37] The juncture joined, sometimes violently, sometimes sexually, a film and its audience, the Kabuki and the Soviet cinema, an idea and a mind. Already, in the 1920s, Eisenstein's junctures, violent though they often were, implied a certain degree of connection, even of unity, a theme that would deepen in the 1930s, as he turned his attention to the junctures between the modern mind and patterns inherited from old mythological traditions. In cinema's transformative potential (stemming not only from its rich repertoire of technical tricks, but also from its omnivorous approach to the myths and paradigms of all of human culture), Eisenstein discovered a perfect modern home for the exhilarating and savage game of thinking, in which 'abstract' and 'concrete', like bull and matador, circle each other warily, waiting for that ecstatic, painful moment of consummate penetration when even the most intellectual idea and its figure might hope finally to achieve the 'complete synchronous identity' of the Bororo parrot-men.

1. Beyond Recognition: *Strike* and the Eye of the Abattoir

'I am the Cine-Eye. I am the mechanical eye. I the machine show you the world as only I can see it.'

Dziga Vertov, 1923[1]

35. Workers carry a pail; from the pail comes steam.
36. CLOSE-UP. A bowl. From beyond the frame soup is pouring. A potato and an ox eye.
37. The hungry faces of workers, looking down.
38. CLOSE-UP. The surface of the soup, a floating potato and an ox eye. The eye approaches the camera.
AMERICAN DIAPHRAGM. [IRIS]
39. The eye comes to life; on it appears a... lorgnette. THE AMERICAN DIAPHRAGM OPENS SLIGHTLY.

Sergei Eisenstein, 1924[2]

When *Strike*, Sergei Eisenstein's first full-length film, appeared on Soviet screens in early 1925, reactions were remarkably mixed. Even a positive review was likely to contain expressions of puzzled amazement at the dizzying speed with which images replaced each other on the screen: 'The furious montage often makes a hash of the action; episode piles upon episode; the fundamental thread is lost. It's not always clear what is going on on the screen.'[3] *Strike* was a film that made great demands on its audience; its young director, after all, was full of dreams of the power of 'carefully calculated shocks'[4] to startle, unsettle and otherwise educate an audience. Judging from the admiring but flummoxed reactions of critics at the time, the result of Eisenstein's cinematic efforts was felt to be indisputably energetic and modern, but also very nearly unintelligible:

> There's a big minus with respect to the montage: the short length of
> the separate segments and the rapidity with which they follow each
> other; you can't always manage to see and understand what's being
> presented. This decidedly weakens this very valuable film's accessibility
> for the mass viewer.[5]

Eisenstein seemed to be exploring the limits of his audience's
faculties; it was, early reviewers cautioned, almost beyond the
capability of ordinary eyes and minds to integrate the flood of
images contained in his film. In fact, while some reviewers expressed
concern that the film's ideological weaknesses were serious enough
to warrant the providing by exhibitors of some sort of accompanying
commentary, 'underscoring the film's weak aspects',[6] the greater
fear seemed to be that the worker might not be able to make anything
at all of the film: '[T]he working-class spectator will not accept *Strike*
wholeheartedly, but rather with serious criticism and, of course,
will not find himself entirely in agreement with the cinematic
thinking [*kinomyshlenie*] of the director; in some places he may
simply find it incomprehensible.'[7]

The distance *Strike*'s reviewers descried between the film's
cinematic innovations and the perceptive powers of the worker
was a particularly vexing problem since *Strike* had been made under
the auspices of the Proletkult, the organization devoted (at least
in theory) to the creation of art by the masses for the masses.[8] The
young Eisenstein had found in the Proletkult financial and material
support for his early experiments in theater and, now, cinema, but
everything about his character, that of a young intellectual with
immense creative ambitions – much more eager to educate and
transform the working classes than to identify with them – was as
if designed to highlight the class tensions within the Proletkult
itself.[9] Although *Strike* was ostensibly not only a Proletkult
production, but also a collective project, the film's reviewers
seemed to assume that in fact *Strike* was the work of one inspired
and sometimes overly feverish mind, that of its brash young
director. Eisenstein naturally agreed. It was this question of the
authorship of *Strike* that led to the break between Eisenstein and
the Proletkult, an acrimonious and noisy divorce that coincided
with the film's opening and that was inspired by Eisenstein's
insistence that he himself, rather than the anonymous 'Proletkult
collective', be given author's rights. The quarrel reached its public
apex in January of 1925, as V Pletnev, on behalf of the Executive
Committee of the Moscow Proletkult, testily explained in an open
letter to the editors of the journal *Kino-nedelia* that Eisenstein had

not 'left' the Proletkult but had 'been asked to leave' in December 1924, once the Executive Bureau of the Moscow Proletkult had determined that his demands for author's rights were 'pretentious' and the tone in which he had conveyed his demands 'unacceptable'.[10] Eisenstein and the Proletkult had then apparently engaged in a race to see who could ditch the other first:

> And only after this resolution had been passed and he found out about it did SM Eisenstein attempt to communicate by telephone his decision to resign, which was not accepted from him because an official statement cannot be delivered over the telephone. On the next day a written declaration of resignation was received from him, but that was already unnecessary since SM Eisenstein by resolution of the Executive Bureau had already been removed from the lists of Proletkult workers.[11]

Thus exploded the collective effort that had been one of the cornerstones of the film's publicity before its opening.

An article in *Rabochii zritel* in October had spelled out in rapturous terms the enormous effort devoted by the Proletkult collective over the course of 'several years' to the 'collection and processing of materials' for the project.[12] The exaggeration of such claims is apparent from a stenogram of the 'evening of reminiscences of participants of the first workers' strikes', in which some Old Bolsheviks haltingly attempted to think of something about their experience that would help the members of the Proletkult collective with their film. 'Comrades,' admitted one Comrade Shelgunov, 'I am in great difficulties as to how to propose such images as would be interesting to the spectator. And I don't, as a matter of fact, know where to begin.'[13] The most vivid memory for him was the great weight of the revolutionary 'literature' (propaganda) he had had to carry around: 'about five poods' worth', or eighty kilos.[14] Eisenstein did take some suggestions from the reminiscences – the Old Bolsheviks remembered meetings in a graveyard and in an outhouse – but only when they stimulated his visual imagination and his affection for contradictory or surprising juxtapositions, such as revolutionary activity being conducted on the toilet. The latter scene would soon be singled out by a reviewer for *Vecherniaia Moskva* as an 'unnecessary, rudely naturalistic detail'.[15]

'Rude naturalism' lay at the very heart of Eisenstein's cinematic thinking in *Strike*, however. No sequence in the film elicited as much reaction as the closing scenes, in which images from a slaughterhouse were spliced into the grisly defeat of the workers. Here is how Eisenstein would reflect upon his intentions some years later:

> In the first of my films, *Strike*, I wanted to take the terror of the finale
> to a high point. The most horrible thing in the representation of blood
> is blood itself. In the representation of death – death itself. True, this
> already is a bit of a leap beyond the bounds of artistic means. But we
> were working with a truly tragic instance: a crushed strike and mass
> shooting. And so through montage I spliced into the acted scenes of
> slaughter pieces of real blood and death. The slaughterhouse. 'They
> treat people like animals' (IP4 452).

Art, like life, was subject to the deadening effects of automatization.
Only 'real blood and death' could break through the ordinary
limitations of artistic perception, by means of montage, in this
instance the juncture of fiction and blood. The twist in Eisenstein's
use of such 'rudely naturalistic details' as outhouses and the carnage
of the abattoir, however, is that the most naturalistic image is also
the one that desires to convey the abstract lesson; the real death
and real blood should not just break through the barriers of art to
inflict a shock upon the viewer, but must also be decoded as
something more than merely 'real', as a verbal message: 'They treat
people like animals'.

Eisenstein's cinematic thinking twisted abstract meaning and
concrete image together, sometimes in counter-intuitive ways. An
ordinary metaphor compares a local thing (in this instance, the
massacre of the workers) with something more distant or more
abstract. At the end of *Strike*, tenor and vehicle seem turned almost
inside out: the real blood of the slaughterhouse is brought in to
supplement the inadequate realness of the acted massacre. Their
blood, the film tells us about the workers, was like... real blood. As
a necessary corollary to this message, the dying of the actors
becomes abstract, more formal play than simulacrum of the real.

'Montage' was supposed to be able to bring together the disparate
elements of *Strike*'s finale: the concrete shock of the slaughterhouse;
the metaphorical message and the acted scenes of the workers' rout.
Eisenstein has become so thoroughly identified with montage in
standard histories of film that it is unsettling to discover that his
first attempt at film-making was found wanting precisely in that
area. The director Lev Kuleshov, whose famous experiments in the
early 1920s had demonstrated to a new generation of Soviet
filmmakers the enormous powers of the film editor to create film
meaning, claimed that *Strike* showed that Eisenstein was someone
who knew how to work with single frames but did not yet have
proper control over editing techniques:

He is a director of the *frame* – tasteful and expressive – less of montage and of human movement: Eisensteinian frames are always stronger than everything else, they are chiefly responsible for the success of his things. It's sufficient to recall the flooding with water in *Strike*, the endless savoring of these photogenic shots, in order finally to be convinced of the good 'eye' of the director, of his particular love for the plastic formation of the framed shot.

The montage of *Strike* is significantly weaker. There's too much excess in it, there's an as-yet-unsystematized infatuation with rapid changes. Everything is too chopped up, there are places that lack all sense of connection and, what's most important, any unifying line of action, any unifying line of the *siuzhet*, is often missing. For instance, in the very weakest final section of the massacre. The associative montage – the slaughterhouse and the parallel slaughter of the workers – hardly has any right to be employed in its present form. This scene in the slaughterhouse, unprepared by a second, parallel line of action, is deficient.[16]

With the polemical undertone typical of the period, Kuleshov gets right to the central issue: what is it with Eisenstein's eye? On the one hand, Kuleshov repeats the early reviewers' criticism that the montage of *Strike* goes too far, demands too much, makes a real hash of the narrative: in other words, that this is a film almost inassimilable by the human eye. On the other hand, Eisenstein comes across here as old-fashioned despite himself, a master of stillness rather than motion, almost, one might say, more a painter than a filmmaker (such seems to be the *sotto voce* dig contained in Kuleshov's praise of Eisenstein's 'good eye').

One important component of Eisenstein's cinematic thinking, then, is a certain way of looking at the world: his eye. The scene Kuleshov points to as evidence of that eye's strengths, the sequence in which the strikers are attacked by men wielding fire hoses, is indeed, as Kuleshov suggests, highly 'photogenic', even painterly. The beautiful shots of lines of water cruelly etching out the contours of flailing and flooded workers are a kind of homage in celluloid to the pre-revolutionary experiments in the development of a new aesthetic eye on the world, in particular, the Rayonist works of Mikhail Larionov and Natalya Goncharova.[17]

Inspired by the discovery of the x-ray and radioactivity, as well as by the miraculous achievements of cinema and photography, Larionov and Goncharova used rays of painted light and color to reveal the 'luminosity' of objects in works like 'Rooster, Rayonist Study', (Larionov, 1912) or 'Green and Yellow Forest' (Goncharova, 1912).[18] The motto of Larionov's 1913 manifesto, 'Rayonist

Painting', had run, in part, 'Rayonism is concerned with spatial forms that can arise from the intersection of the reflected rays of different objects'.[19] Rayonism was also, as described by Larionov, an attempt to correct, scientifically, the naive impression created by previous artists that the eye is the true organ of sight:

> Our eye is an imperfect apparatus; we think that our sight is mainly responsible for transmitting concrete life to our cerebral centers, but in fact, it arrives there in its correct form not thanks to our sight, but thanks to other senses. A child sees objects for the first time upside down and subsequently this defect of sight is corrected by the other senses. However much he desires to, an adult cannot see an object upside down.
>
> Hence it is evident to what degree our inner conviction is important with regard to things existing in the outside world...
>
> We do not sense the object with our eye, as it is depicted conventionally in pictures and as a result of following this or that device; in fact, we do not sense the object as such. We perceive a sum of rays proceeding from a source of light; these are reflected from the object and enter our field of vision.
>
> Consequently, if we wish to paint literally what we see, then we must paint the sum of rays reflected from the object. (Bowlt 97–98)

This sense that the human eye was an imperfect organ, one in need of new education, radical transformation, or perhaps some really good prosthetic aid, was something that early Soviet culture inherited from pre-war modernism. So many advances in science and technology in the early part of the twentieth century were linked to advances in vision! As Larionov representatively gushed in 1913: 'Luminosity owes its existence to reflected light (between objects in space this forms a kind of colored dust). The doctrine of luminosity. Radioactive rays. Ultraviolet rays. Reflectivity.' (Bowlt 98)

By the time Eisenstein was beginning his cinematic career in the 1920s, however, such breathless appreciation for the new century's scientific and technological advances had acquired certain shadows: an increased sense of the fragility of the human body in general and the eye in particular, brought on by the traumas of war, revolution and civil war. The abrupt fragmentation of Eisenstein's montage in the 'slaughterhouse' sequence could be seen as reflecting not just a long history of modernist experiments, but also several years' worth of frayed nerves and fractured bodies.

The First World War had been a watershed for 'modernity' across Europe; in Russia that war had been followed and exceeded by revolution and civil war. The catharsis of revolution and the violence of war had done something to the way one saw the world; that was the assumption of artists everywhere, though of course the major discoveries of modernism – Cubism, Futurism, the Black Square; the ornate and sometimes ornamental languages of Symbolism and Acmeism; the cinema – had already arrived before the onset of war. Armed with all the prosthetic machinery available to the eye in the early twentieth century – x-ray, stereoscope, camera – modernism preached with ferocious intensity the gospel of seeing life anew. Hope must lie in the prosthesis, for the human body alone had been revealed to be a very fragile thing. Years of war had left behind a legacy of horrified fascination with the mutilations inflicted by one side on the other and in particular on the violence that disfigured faces:

> On the way into the garden, I spied on the town fields a *mass of Bolshevik corpses: the heads of these corpses had been chopped into several pieces*, so that it was difficult to make out to which individuals these bodies had belonged...

> The Cossacks disfigured the bodies of the Bolsheviks so that the relatives of the dead would not be able to identify the corpse.[20]

In the literature of the 1920s, this aspect of Civil War culture – the constant threat of comrades being rendered 'beyond recognition' by the other side – was to become a recurring motif in, for instance, Isaak Babel''s stories of the Polish Campaign of 1920 (*Konarmiia*, 1925), stories in which damage to faces and eyes is a central theme.[21] Disfigurement is something that happens most fundamentally to a figure, a face, and in the early Soviet period that disfigurement occurred in two vital modes: literally, as physical destruction visited upon faces; and figuratively, in the various attempts to move art beyond the figure into the realms of abstraction. These modes, strangely enough, intersect: in the language, for example, of Malevich's manifestoes, in which the artist's desire to transcend figural representation is coupled with virulent attacks on bodies of all kinds, especially 'female hams'.[22] The figure itself – the body as such – becomes a disgusting wound that art must move beyond.

At the center of the problem of the figure lies the face. The face is that part of the body we try most fervently to exempt from corporeality: to render, as far as is possible, *im*material. Those wounds or flaws which force us to acknowledge the face *as flesh* (a missing eye, a harelip, even a badly running nose) owe their peculiar power to horrify to the obscene connection they draw between the person (thought of most comfortably as somehow trans-corporeal) and that person's all-too-perishable and material body. Such physical abuses are a kind of vandalism performed against the *trompe l oeil* perspective of a corporeal fresco: the real depths of the human face revealed to us by violence or disease reduce the human being to flesh, which in the metaphysical sense amounts to being reduced to mere surface. And if the face is the part of the body traditionally linked to individual identity and the 'false depth' of spiritual *trompe l oeil*, then the eyes may be said to be the 'face' of the face. They are at once the most sentimentalized part of the body, that part that must remain least tainted by signs of fleshliness, the organ most like a machine (all those diagrams of clean rays traversing the lens of the eye and etching trees or stick-figures of people upside down on the retina: just a *camera obscura* like any other...) and, as Luís Buñuel would show the world in *Un Chien andalou* (1928), the place where a single pass of a razor blade, reasserting the eye's identity not just as machine or 'spirit', but as meat, is able to inspire the most horror and disgust in the viewer.

The eye, in short, is a most perplexing organ, a nexus where abstract and concrete meet, sometimes with disturbing results. This nexus is absolutely central to Eisenstein's *Strike*, a film very concerned with the paradoxical nature of the eye. In an early scenario the horrific climax of the film was to come precisely from the transformation of an eye into meat:

> The butcher moves past the camera (panning) swinging his bloody rope.
>
> A crowd runs to a fence, breaks through it and hides behind it (in two or three shots).
>
> Arms fall into the frame (film-frame).
>
> The head of the bull is severed from the trunk.
>
> A volley (of bullets).
>
> Soldiers' feet walk away from the camera.
>
> Blood floats on the water, discoloring it.
>
> (Close-up) Blood gushes from the slit throat of the bull.
>
> Blood is pouring from a basin (held by hands) into a pail.
>
> Dissolve from a truck loaded with pails of blood to a passing truck loaded with scrap-iron.

The bull's tongue is pulled through the slit throat (to prevent the convulsions from damaging the tongue).

The soldiers' feet walk away from the camera (seen at a further distance than previously).

The bull's skin is stripped off.

1,500 bodies (lie) at the foot of the cliff.

Two skinned bulls' heads.

A hand lying in a pool of blood.

(Close-up) Filling the entire screen: the eye of a dead bull.

(Title) THE END.[23]

As finally edited, *Strike*'s concluding sequence ended not with the eye of a dead bull, but rather with an extreme close-up, 'filling the entire screen' just as its ocular antecedent was supposed to, of the eyes of a living worker who enjoins us to 'Remember, Proletariat!'

Figure 1.
'Remember, Proletariat!'
(*Strike*)

These eyes are, however, haunted by their dead bovine predecessors. The eye of a dead ox, far from being an unprepared distraction from *Strike*'s line of action, is in fact the essential hieroglyph under which *Strike* takes its place in the canon of Russian modernism.

Earlier scenarios not only had *Strike* ending on a dead bull's eye, but also very nearly beginning with that image. In an early version of the prologue, the eye of the ox floats in a bowl of soup fed to workers in the factory that will soon erupt into spontaneous political activity:[24]

Shot 37. The hungry faces of the workers, looking down.

Shot 38. Close-up. The surface of the soup; on it float a piece of potato and an ox's eye. The eye approaches the camera. AMERICAN DIAPHRAGM.

> Shot 39. The eye comes to life; on it appears… a lorgnette. THE AMERICAN
> DIAPHRAGM OPENS SLIGHTLY. (IP6 34)

This rather surrealist scene would have made very visible indeed the various paradoxes underlying the nature of the eye. Whatever else an eye in a bowl of soup may do, it certainly announces its difference from a potato; perhaps the essence of that difference is that the eye, an organ which as we have seen carries the weight of our human desire to transcend the flesh, resists the transformation into meat. Even if thoroughly dead, the eye seems haunted by life. In Eisenstein's prologue, that 'undead' nature of the eye becomes reality, as the ox's eye in the soup metamorphoses into the living eye of a human being (since that human being is an unpleasant factory official, the stench of death may not totally disappear upon this transition).

The eye of the ox acquires here a second double, however: the eye is compared explicitly to the 'American diaphragm', a visual pun constructed on the notion of the 'iris', one of DW Griffith's favorite means of winking in and out of scenes. Not only does the eye approach the camera physically (or, more accurately, the camera approaches the ox's eye) – but it also approaches the camera in a more essential, if more ineffable, way. The eye of the ox is itself, strangely enough, a 'camera eye'.

The comparison between camera eye and eye of the ox has a history that predates Eisenstein. It was a fancy at one time that the last image seen by a murder victim would be imprinted on the dead person's retina and this theory was tested on the eyes of slaughtered oxen.[25] Fascination with the comparison between fleshly eye and camera eye endured and in the early twentieth century left its own indelible print on the Soviet avant-garde.

The 'cinema eye' (or 'kino-glaz') was a famous component of early Soviet cinematic theory and practice. Dziga Vertov, avant-garde proponent of the documentary, dedicated several manifestoes to the 'camera eye', and in fact at the same time Eisenstein was making *Strike,* Vertov was filming a feature-length film entitled *Kino-glaz* (*Cinema-eye*) that he would later accuse Eisenstein of imitating.[26]

Dziga Vertov subscribed wholeheartedly to the theory that the human eye was, as Larionov had put it, 'an imperfect apparatus'. Vertov (born Denis Arkadievich Kaufman in 1896) had studied at the Psycho-Neurological Institute in Petrograd before turning to the cinema, a medium that appealed to his scientific interest in human perception as well as to his enthusiasm for revolutionary aesthetics. He quickly became a great champion of the newsreel and in the 1920s engaged in a polemic with Eisenstein over the relative value of 'acted' and 'non-acted' film. Vertov's programmatic manifesto ('Cine-Eyes. Revolution', from 1923) is a dizzying, Futurist-inspired hymn to the superiority of the camera lens over the myopic human eye:

> We cannot make our eyes any better than they have been made but we can go on perfecting the camera forever[...] All the weaknesses of the human eye have been revealed. *We reaffirm the Cine-Eye.* (*Film Factory* 91)

The perfectibility of the camera eye makes it the ideal antidote to the nearsighted imperfections of the human eye, which languishes in a kind of evolutionary dead end. Vertov's new man sings the praises of a kind of cinematic centaur: 'I am the Cine-Eye. I am a mechanical eye. I the machine show you the world as only I can see it.(*Film Factory* 93) A new kind of eye is needed because there is all too much that the old 'meat' eye does not manage to see at all.

The mechanized appendage, the eye that will no longer be limited by the failings of flesh-and-blood, the eye that can see action, no matter how fast and that can construct points of view impossible for mere mortals, is an appealing object (or subject). When examined closely, however, the 'kino-glaz' turns out to be haunted by the flesh it would leave behind. What – or who – is this 'cine-eye'? Camera lens, camera operator, film editor, spectator? All at points seem to be alluded to; no single identity works all the time. Sometimes the very fervor of the polemic makes it difficult to see how ill-defined the object of Vertov's attention has become. The junction, in short, between the machine and the flesh, the concrete physical 'I' and the abstraction of an 'I' as a new point-of-view – all these joints are ragged. The stitches where the cyborg has been sewn together, like Frankenstein's monster, are blurry enough that it is unclear where machine ends and flesh begins, or how much of 'machine' or of 'flesh' is ideal in order to achieve the new vision promised by the 'kino-glaz'. The fleshly prehistory of the cyborg is revealed by the manifesto's opening lines:

LOOK AROUND YOU

THERE!

I can see

as every child can see:

THE INTESTINES ARE TUMBLING OUT.

THE ENTRAILS OF EXPERIENCE

FROM THE STOMACH OF CINEMA

DISEMBOWELED

ON THE REEF OF THE REVOLUTION,

they are dragged along

leaving a trail of blood on the ground,

TREMBLING with fear and revulsion.

IT IS ALL OVER. (*Film Factory* 90)

The hymn to the machine opens with an image of the body as something that must be sliced open in order to be remade. The price of the new kind of vision is high.

In Vertov's manifesto, the human eye is scornfully set aside in favor of the superior mechanical eye, the 'cine-eye', but the transformation into cyborg, as we have seen, is unevenly accomplished and the flesh (or the human 'I' as opposed to the machine 'eye') lingers on. It is well to remember, after all, that cinema, this brave new mechanized and 'cyborgian' mode of viewing the world, is fundamentally dependent on the failings of human flesh as much as it is on the advantages of the machine: the illusion of movement is made possible only by the inability of the human eye and brain to distinguish images shown at a rate faster than about 16 frames/second. That effect may be a kind of limp in the human perceptual apparatus, but without the limp, the cinema could not exist and Vertov's cinematic centaur would no longer be able to place you 'who were created by me, in a most remarkable room that never existed before and that I also created' (92) or to achieve any of its other tricks, for that matter.

Clearly the exact nature of the joints between machine and flesh – not to mention theoretical consistency – mattered less to Dziga Vertov than conveying his enthusiasm for the new. Certainly in his own cinematic experiments of the 1920s, Vertov delighted in putting the art of the camera through its paces and the films he produced are remarkable for their good humor as well as for their unexpected images and combinations of images. In 1924 he began his documentary *Kino-Glaz* with the claim that it would catch life '*vrasplokh*', a term meaning 'unawares' but also 'unexpectedly', and indeed, throughout *Cine-Eye* the tension persists between presenting a documentary portrayal of Soviet life and showing everyday things unexpectedly, defamiliarization being wielded here not so much for the creation of high art as for amusement ('see what a camera can do') and edification ('see what you have overlooked before'). At issue in this tension is nothing less than the nature of truth and the role of manipulation, or of play, in the production of that truth.

One of the sequences in *Kino-Glaz* where Vertov's brand of defamiliarization is most clearly demonstrated is devoted, as it happens, to the production of beef. During this section of the film, Young Pioneers wage their ongoing campaign against price-gouging in the market; we see them putting up posters encouraging people to shop in the Cooperatives rather than in the dirty, expensive markets, and we see the same earnest children confronting various unsavory-looking peasants about the quality and prices of their wares. The chief lesson is directed at the thin, beaten-down mother of one of the Pioneers (a girl known as 'Kopchushka'): disgusted by the meat for sale in the market and discouraged by its price, the mother is inspired by a poster her own daughter has pasted on the wall to retrace her steps and go this time not to the market, but to the Cooperative, where everything is modern, cheap and fresh.

Her steps are 'retraced' literally: she walks backward. The film is being run backward for us, in that most popular of early cinema tricks. The Cine-Eye wishes to show us what we cannot otherwise usually see: the proof that, as a title boasts, 'The Cooperative receives its meat directly from the slaughterhouse'. For our benefit, therefore, the next title announces, 'The Cine-Eye runs time backwards'. This is truly to be a 'defamiliarization' of a trip to the slaughterhouse and, yet more ambitious, of the moment of death, that point where the one-way direction of time in our everyday universe is most unforgiving. Dziga Vertov, however, transforms the slaughterhouse into a playroom.

He shows us swinging slabs of beef; the titles identify them as 'that which 20 minutes ago was still an ox'. (Sure enough, the very meat seems still to be quivering.) Then the games really begin: 'Let's return the ox his innards'. Gradually we realize we are to be witnesses to the most profound cinematic trick of all: death run backwards. The butchers fold the intestines back into the cow, a procedure not unlike packing a suitcase. The titles keep us moving: 'Let's put his hide back on him'. Always that tone of omnipotent good humor: see what I can do, with my 'cine-eye'! His skin is smoothed back on his body and zipped up magically by the backwards-moving knives. His parts reassembled, the ox has arrived at the center of the miracle; the ox lies dead on the floor; then his legs twitch and kick; the ox leaps to his feet and the hammer flies away from his head: 'The ox comes to life.' The knife is 'unsharpened', and the cattle move out of the slaughtering rooms and back into the holding pen (and someone steals a little last milk from a cow). Even at this point, the fantasy continues; the cattle are loaded backwards onto cattle-cars and the train takes them back into the countryside, where they rejoin their herd and motion once again begins to move forward in its usual manner. (To some degree, in fact, the film becomes stuck in the countryside; instead of returning to Kopchushka's mother's shopping expedition, the film moves on to the subject of a Pioneer summer camp and the broader topic of friendship between town and country.)

In this sequence the most perplexing questions of life, death and cinema's role in both are brought into play: Vertov, like Eisenstein, turns to a slaughterhouse for the footage that most dramatically demonstrates the power of the movie camera to triumph over the usual limitations of time and space (in order to achieve, as Eisenstein put it, a 'leap beyond the bounds of artistic means'). The mechanical magic of the camera-eye is applied as a corrective to the most fleshly flesh of a slaughtered cow. But where Eisenstein was counting on the slaughterhouse shots to shock the audience, to force it to see what previously it merely 'recognized', Vertov presents us with a slaughterhouse that turns time into a game – into 'child's play'.[27] Life is not only 'caught unawares' in *Kino-Glaz* (as the film's motto promises), but it is created from the very material of death. Both uses of the slaughterhouse (to inspire horror or to inspire delight) bring with them certain ideological hazards, however. Eisenstein's metaphorical montage 'they slaughtered the workers like oxen' puts the workers into a strikingly passive position, while Vertov's metonymic chain of backwards motion ends up in what should (spatially, temporally and ideologically) be marked as the *past*: the pastoral idyll in the country meadow, where the renascent ox can once again kick up his heels with his friends.

The *kino-glaz*, in the hands of Sergei Eisenstein, becomes, I have suggested above, the eye of a dead ox. The eyes on which the film closes – the eyes of the proletarian 'educator' – should be seen, I think, as a composite, haunted by its vanished predecessors: the eye-as-meat, the eye-as-camera, the eye that oscillates so uncannily between life and death, abstract metaphor and concrete flesh. The task of the dead bull that haunts the end of *Strike* is to make memory possible for the working classes: 'Remember, Proletariat!'

Eisenstein needed to integrate 'pieces of real blood' into *Strike*'s final montage sequence because he was worried that without the blood, the film would not achieve the necessary effect. The problem he was combating was the same peril that Shklovsky had termed 'automatization'. Shklovsky, as we have seen, proposed that human vision, in its struggle against automatization and algebraization, be renewed in order to rescue life itself from the threat of 'nothingness'. Shklovsky took his examples from Tolstoy, not only from the description of innocent Natasha's visit to the opera, but also from the numerous instances in which, through the eyes of an outsider, customs (like flogging) that seem 'normal' to their audience only because that audience has ceased to 'see' them at all are shown in all their gruesome, often absurd, detail. There are ghosts haunting all levels of this argument, however: behind the Opera and in the wings of Shklovsky's own discussion, lurks the specter of the slaughterhouse.

Of all the examples he culls from Tolstoy, the one that Shklovsky cites in greatest length is a passage narrated by the horse 'Kholstomer', from the story of that name. The defamiliarizing equine point-of-view teaches us as efficiently as Tolstoy knows how that 'people treat (not just workers, but) *animals* like animals'. In fact, in Tolstoy's story the most direct mention of those perceptual effects that will later capture the interest and attention of Shklovsky occurs in a part of the tale *not* cited by Shklovsky: poor Kholstomer learns about defamiliarization at the hands of the people who slaughter him. It is then, as he feels his blood spill out of his neck, feeling 'more surprised than afraid', that 'everything became new for him'.[28]

The death of Kholstomer could be read as suggesting that if we would see the world anew – if we hope to move 'beyond recognition' – a sacrifice must be made. The use of such blood rites to provide a sense of the 'new' has a long tradition in human culture, but the difference between the slaughter of Kholstomer and other forms of public sacrifice is that the effect is worked on a different audience. It is not the sacrificers – the slaughterers, the embedded audience – who are to benefit from this surging forth of 'real blood'; these groups, on the contrary, must treat the sacrifice as entirely routine. Rather, the miracle of defamiliarization and its renewal of life is worked on the victim itself (the slaughtered beast) and on the audience at second remove, the readers or viewers.[29]

The slaughterers themselves treat their work like any other; their sober routine marks them as part of the great machine, which, it turns out, can be seen as the necessary setting for defamiliarization – the very escape from automatization! – to occur. Tolstoy's stories of how perception can be renewed, or defamiliarized, often hinge on a close encounter with one of the two poles of human existence: birth (or the unpolluted and thus 'strange' vision of a child or child-like innocent) and death, which for everybody, horses and all, comes as something truly 'new' and not yet experienced to the point of automatization. I would suggest that one of the important shifts undergone as the twentieth century reworks the notion of defamiliarization is precisely the focus on the machine, on deautomatization as something necessary because of all of the 'automatization' one is surrounded by and yet, paradoxically, made possible by that very automatized context. In this sense, perhaps Shklovsky marks the end of the old era as much as the start of the new, for in his version of the task at hand, 'automatization' is the demonic force that overtakes us, something we must struggle against in order to be able to live again. In the Soviet 1920s, however, automation has discovered its positive, modern side: or rather, we find ourselves oscillating between the positive and negative sides of mechanization (between the inspiring and the deadening aspects of 'automatization').

Automatization and slaughter find a common language in the twentieth century. Tolstoy underscores the *usefulness* of the slaughtered horse (as opposed to the uselessness in death of most humans); this theme of the efficiency of slaughter, as precursor to industrialization *per se*, also marks the work of an early Soviet modernist, Boris Pil'niak, who in a story from the early 1920s has Arina, the woman whose strangely compelling but at first indescribable aroma turns out to have its source in the blood of the slaughterhouse she runs, explain her job in terms of efficiency:

> 'The skin is used for leather, the fats are used in soap-making, we feed the proteins to the pigs. The bones and sinews go to the glue works. Then the bones are ground to make fertilizer. We waste nothing here.' Arina's hands were covered with blood; the ground was running with blood; workmen were skinning the horse; other carcasses lay about already skinned; using a pulley, they hung the horse by its legs from a gallows. And then Nekulyev understood: the smell here was the same as Arina's smell and he suddenly felt his throat contract in a spasm of nausea.[30]

The smell that hovers around Arina has been part of her attractiveness for Nekulyev, the sign of a secret that he does not yet understand that works as the engine of their love. Love is possible only in the interval of the 'detour', that space between sight (or perception, since here the operative sense is that of smell) and recognition, that space which Shklovsky hopes to open wider by means of the delaying device of defamiliarization. Pil'niak's story describes what happens once the lover recognizes what before he only perceived: and the secret, of course, turns out to be a slaughterhouse. In fact, the scene works as a perfect counterpart to the crucial scene of Kholstomer's slaughter that, in turn, is the secret withheld by Shklovsky when he retells Tolstoy's story. Like Kholstomer, Nekulyev suddenly sees everything 'anew' – though, of course, the 'new thing' that Nekulyev sees is really only the recognition of a very old story indeed.

Even in Pil'niak's rather backward example of a rural slaughterhouse, so similar still to the nineteenth-century picture, the paradigm of slaughter as part of industrial production has come to take a very central place. It is Nekulyev who is too tender yet for the new reality, not Arina, the practical slaughterer: 'we waste nothing here'.[31]

The slaughterhouse is not a parody of industrial production; it is, instead, at least potentially the epitome of such production and thus the epitome of modernity. Like other forms of industrial production (notably that of automobiles and tractors), slaughtering and meatpacking were at their most advanced stage not in Russia, but in the United States, home of Ford, Taylor and Armour. As an early historian of the meatpacking industry in the United States, John R Commons, had already remarked in 1905: 'It would be difficult to find another industry where division of labor has been so ingeniously and microscopically worked out.'[32] One of the most important models in this context, one that brings 'modernity' and 'defamiliarization' together in the figure of the slaughterhouse is Upton Sinclair's 1906 blockbuster, *The Jungle*.

Upton Sinclair was to play a very significant role in Eisenstein's life: it was he who agreed (along with his wife) to fund Eisenstein's ill-starred film project in Mexico at the beginning of the 1930s and it was thus he (along with his wife) who was at least partly responsible for one of the great artistic tragedies of Eisenstein's career, when a cataclysmic falling-out between Eisenstein and the Sinclairs led to the loss – always felt very bitterly by Eisenstein – of what was supposed to become *Que Viva Mexico!* But in the early 1920s this disaster was still years away. Upton Sinclair was enormously popular in early Soviet Russia, his fame stemming principally from his 1906 dissection of the meatpacking industry. Not only did many translations of *The Jungle* make their way to Russia, but Upton Sinclair exported a film version of *The Jungle* to the Soviet Union in 1923; a letter exists from Upton Sinclair to Sergei Eisenstein, dated 16 February 1927, in which Sinclair, apparently responding to a proposition made in an earlier letter from Eisenstein, says that he is glad that Eisenstein likes his books and that he would indeed be very glad to work with him on a film based on one of them.[33]

Sinclair's socialist-leaning sensibilities were at once impressed by the advanced technology and extraordinary efficiency of the meatpacking plants and horrified by the abuse of the people who worked in them (and by the unhealthy conditions in which sausage, for example, was created). It was Upton Sinclair's book that made famous the quip that 'we use everything from the hog but the squeal', a sentiment Pil'niak's earthy Arina would certainly understand and of which she would approve. *The Jungle*'s description of the process by which meat production takes place is mesmerizing, at once poetry, textbook and horror story. After the hogs have walked up long chutes to the top floor of the factory, 'their weight carried them back through all the process necessary to make them into pork' (34). Here we have, more powerful even than the picture of Ford's standardized production of the all-American automobile, the unbelievable efficiency of what one might call a disassembly line:

> It was all so very businesslike that one watched it fascinated. It was pork-making by machinery, pork-making by applied mathematics... The carcass hog was scooped out of the vat by machinery and then it fell to the second floor, passing on the way through a wonderful machine with numerous scrapers, which adjusted themselves to the size and shape of the animal and sent it out at the other end with nearly all of its bristles removed. It was then again strung up by machinery and sent upon another trolley ride; this time passing between two lines of men, who sat upon a raised platform, each doing a certain single thing to the carcass as it came to him. One scraped the outside of a leg; another scraped the inside of the same leg. One with a swift stroke cut the throat; another with two swift strokes severed the head, which fell to the floor and vanished through a hole. Another made a slit down the body; a second opened the body wider; a third with a saw cut the breastbone, a fourth loosened the entrails; a fifth pulled them out – and they also slid through a hole in the floor. There were men to scrape each side and men to scrape the back; there were men to clean the carcass inside, to trim it and wash it. Looking down this room, one saw, creeping slowly, a line of dangling hogs a hundred yards in length; and for every yard there was a man, working as if a demon were after him.[34]

The slaughterhouse, then, is the very model of the efficient, modern, industrial factory (disassembly into components is an *a priori* requirement of any assembly line); and under the unmediated rule of Chicago-style capitalism (so runs Sinclair's point), to work in such a factory means to be destroyed oneself, perhaps not quite as efficiently, but certainly as mercilessly as any hog or cow.

The final parts of *The Jungle* contain the passionate pleas of what we might call a 'Socialist-*ex-machina*', a character who appears in order to read us the moral of the tale: the working classes must rescue themselves from this disassembly line. They must learn to deautomatize their own perception:

> Working-men, working-men – comrades! [cries the Socialist in one of his speeches] Open your eyes and look about you! You have lived so long in the toil and heat that your senses are dulled, your souls are numbed; but realize once in your lives this world in which you dwell – tear off the rags of its customs and conventions – behold it as it is, in all its hideous nakedness! Realize it, *realize it*!' (293)

What could be a more convincing call for the *obnazhenie priema*, the 'laying bare of the device' as the Formalists called it, than this plea to 'tear off the rags' of the world's 'customs and conventions'? It is the slaughterhouse as topos of capitalist automatization and oppression that is the device that needs baring; it is the slaughter-house as height of organized industrial production that demonstrates the enormous power and potential of industry and that may inspire, eventually, in its role as the epitome of capitalism, a turn to working-class consciousness in the workers it chews up and spits out. The great tension at work in the factories of Packingtown is that between the human being abstracted into just another part of the machine (a kind of slaughtering cyborg) and the human being concretized too far, turned like the hogs and cows into mere meat. Thus the Socialist rails against the way the exploited workers of Packingtown are being subsumed into the great capitalist machine: 'the majority of human beings are not yet human beings at all, but simply machines for the creating of wealth for others' (332). Jurgis the worker agrees that something terrible has been done to him on the meatpacking lines, but he puts it another way:

> Jurgis recollected how, when he had first come to Packingtown, he had stood and watched the hog-killing and thought how cruel and savage it was and come away congratulating himself that he was not a hog; now his new acquaintance showed him that a hog was just what he had been – one of the packers' hogs. (305)

Another defamiliarized look at the meatpacking plants tells Jurgis he has only been 'one of the packers' hogs' all along: he thought himself a human being, when he was only meat. Where in this relentless oscillation between machine and meat is there any room for the human being?

The Jungle presents many of the basic ingredients for Russian revolutionary modernism: the modern factory as a place of horror and wonder, the slaughtering of beasts as the essence of modern industry, but also as a dark and sacred thing, the call for the reader and worker to look up from the automatized world and to 'realize' (a term that is linked with 'beholding' and 'nakedness' by Sinclair and thus may paradoxically be closer to 'seeing' than 'recognizing' in the Shklovskian lexicon) what is too often merely taken for granted: ironically enough, it is the height of automatization (the organized factory line of assembly or disassembly) that can enable the worker it dominates to realize, to see, that he has been turned into meat and machine and thus to struggle to achieve a new, defamiliarized, point of view on the dilemmas of capitalism. In all these senses, *The Jungle* is an essential preparation for Sergei Eisenstein's first film, *Strike*, which goes to great lengths to make visible the dilemma of the twentieth-century human being, whose identity is pulled between two grim poles: 'meat' and 'machine'.

Throughout *Strike*, people are subjected to an uncomfortable oscillation between their role as mechanized, automatized (and oppressed) line-workers and the even more unsatisfactory identification with animals. The comparison made at the end of the film between 'workers' and 'meat', in the context of the slaughterhouse, is only the most glaring variation on the theme. Animals and people are compared throughout the film: the spies are identified by means of fade-ins of animal mugshots; the children dump a goat into the factory pond in lieu of the factory bosses. The workers, too, suffer from a comparison to animals. When isolated from the greater machine, the factory, where of course they are treated as mere machines, the workers swing too far in the opposite direction and revert to animals, as they lounge about in proximity to children, women, ducks and other too 'fleshly', insufficiently 'mechanical' or abstract beings. This quite negative valorization of animal life makes the metaphor pinned on the workers at the end – 'slaughtered like cattle' – a distinctly uncomfortable one: to be compared to an animal, especially one being slaughtered, is to be told one has attained no consciousness yet of one's own. (For this reason also – to end on the note of consciousness attained – it was essential that the film's final 'eye' be that of a living worker rather than a dead bull.)

On the other side of the oscillation, people are regularly placed in comparison with machines. The workers' bodies are framed again and again by abstract, mechanical patterns (the pile of enormous gears, the factory's huge quantity of machinery). These bodies are then subjected to the 'x-ray' exploration of the 'water-hose' sequence. When the fire-hoses are turned on the workers, the water playing off the struggling bodies maps out the contours of the human in that zone where 'concrete' and 'abstract' (figural and non-figural, meat and machine) intersect: the edge of the human form. It is this edge, Eisenstein discovers here, that describes also the intersection of beauty and pain.

Strike depicts a pre-Revolutionary factory from a post-Revolutionary perspective and so the film is further complicated by the need to distinguish between 'old' and 'new' despite certain uncanny resemblances between the two. The factory is the place where workers are oppressed by being treated as machines or beasts, but it is also the place where they are most fully and truly 'themselves', that is to say *workers*. The factory itself must not be depicted as too dreadful a place, because it cannot actually (in 1924 or 1925) have changed much, physically, since the revolution, and the work in such a factory should not be portrayed as demeaning and horrible in and of itself, for *Strike*'s audiences (at least in principle) would be returning to their own factory jobs first thing the next morning. The horrors of the pre-revolutionary factory must be located, instead, in the injustices that underlie and define wage labor. Thus the crisis in *Strike* is provoked not by a machine mangling a worker or unwholesome labor conditions, but by a manager's false accusation that a worker has stolen a tool and the worker's despairing suicide when he feels his honor has been irredeemably besmirched. Thus, too, the abstract beauty of the shots of the machine-dominated factory floor. Even when beautiful, however, Eisenstein's version of the factory leaves little room for the merely human.[35]

This oscillation between meat and machine, concrete and abstract, carries over into the film as a whole. Despite the insistence with which *Strike* exhibits its many topoi and in particular the intensity with which crowds in this movie push and push and throng in some direction, towards somewhere, through some gate, we could never make a map of the whole: the topography here is impossible and incommensurate. The spaces involved don't add up and aren't easily translated onto our everyday notions of geography; the strangeness of *Strike*'s spaces may even remind us of Vertov's fanciful conceptions of a room with a dozen walls or a street that starts in present-day Chicago and ends up in the Petrograd of five years ago.[36] We are presented with a complicated machine, or engine, whose structure on a large scale we can have no comprehension of, but through which the working masses flow with immense pressure and great determination. At every threshold (or gate) the pressure builds up, builds up, builds up and then the valve is sprung and the masses rush on and the spectator is caught up in all this energetic pushing and flowing, without however being able to reconstruct a blueprint for this factory. The factory depicted in *Strike* seems to build steam engines; and the masses flow through the spaces shown in the film following the rules of a steam machine, the pressure and release of hydraulics. Or, to put it in an equally apt, more corporeal vein, they behave like the blood flowing through a (mechanical) heart.

Strike's geographies are thus mechanical and fluid at the same time, abstract and bodily; a tension central, as we have seen, to the history of Russian modernism. This oscillation is essential to Eisenstein's 'cinematic thinking' in *Strike*, in the course of which abstract ideas are given a kind of tangible shape, while at the same time physical objects and images are made to reveal their abstract contours. Typical of Eisenstein is the way 'concrete' and 'abstract' are always infecting each other: a sort of mental mapmaking. In *Strike*, Eisenstein builds maps on many different levels, not just the maps born in the laboratories of the 'Kuleshov experiment' – maps of spaces that are made contiguous by the magic of editing – but also the metaphorical maps which make these imaginary spaces at the same time both machine (engine) and flesh (circulatory system) and which assert that humanness cannot exist if isolated on either end of that oscillating trajectory.

As icon for this whole problem, we may take the map which Eisenstein gives us in the film itself: the map of the workers' quarters over which the police chief's ink spills when he angrily pounds his fist on the table. We are shown the presumably colorful blocks of the map and then, in one of Eisenstein's most forthrightly metaphorical moments, the ink creeps slowly over the whole quarter, engulfing it in 'blood'. The map itself, at once too abstract and too concrete, is a kind of *mise-en-abime* of mapping in *Strike* as a whole. As a 'map', it seems to promise information (tantalizingly visible but resolutely unrecognizable) as to how the spaces of the quarter (and the film) are put together. In fact, however, it is abstraction itself: a mess of blocks in different shades, blocks lacking visible names and labels; not a map any real person could use in any real place, but a pure abstract representation of a 'map'. It resembles a

Figure 2.
Map (*Strike*)

constructivist painting more than a guide to any real city. Then this abstraction is flooded with a fluid that is both ink and 'blood', and the map's abstract squares and rectangles vanish under the stain, the horrifying concreteness of which is itself a constructed shock (real fluid + metaphoric leap to 'blood') designed to inform the spectator that the workers' quarter, another 'body', is about to be butchered, rendered 'beyond recognition'.

Lev Kuleshov, who so famously provided cinema with the Kuleshov Effect,[37] those demonstrations of the powers of montage, and who was so displeased with Eisenstein's use of the slaughterhouse sequence at the end of *Strike*, worked not only with the effect of montage on spaces, but, of course, on specific bodies as well. Thus one of his experiments demonstrated one of the most basic discoveries of cinema: that a body can be constructed out of the bits and pieces filmed of other bodies (eyes of one, legs of another...). The actor, thanks to montage, is revealed no longer to be in control of the 'meaning' of his gestures and expressions, for the essence of film lies at another level, inaccessible to him: 'One must seek the essence of cinematography not within the bounds of the shot, but in the combination of those shots.' (1920)[38] One of the triumphs of the cinema as described by Kuleshov in 1920 is its ability to reinvent artistic production as a kind of assembly line and the actor as a line-worker, producing his expressions without the privilege of perspective on the process as a whole.

The recombination of the film actor's body according to the plans and desires of the editor, was just one part of the program, dismemberment (in the broadest sense) being a necessary prerequisite to the montage process. The modern cinema actor, once swallowed up by the cinema machine, was to be treated like the workers of Packingtown, an impression confirmed by the charts of actors' body parts and their possible movements published by Kuleshov in the

1920s.[39] The actor, like the workers in Upton Sinclair's slaughterhouses, is turned into a creature with a body as susceptible to manipulation as that of a hog or cow, to be taken apart and put together again at the pleasure of the one who controls the process, the editor or filmmaker ('The animal has been surveyed and laid off like a map', as that early praise-singer of meatpacking efficiency, John Commons, had noted in 1905 [p. 224]).[40] Montage, then, can be seen as the incursion of the assembly line into old aesthetic institutions, as film-making becomes an industrial process, based on and in some respects similar to such paragons of industrial efficiency, the Ford factory and the Chicago packinghouse. Cinema, we are tempted to conclude, is the ideal vehicle for a modern, defamiliarized view of the world not only because it is a cyborg-art, dependent on machines, but because it is so close in some respects to butchering.

Lev Kuleshov's analysis of Eisenstein's *Strike* – like that of many of the film's other early reviewers – was, as we saw, filled with criticism of the excessively choppy nature of its montage. The excesses of the montage suggest that this film, speeding by too fast for the ordinary spectator, may have been too much the product of the prosthesis, the machine-eye, whose demands on the spectator are always tyrannical and inhuman.

But perhaps Eisenstein's eye is showing us something rather different. It may be that the very choppiness of the metaphor-based montage of the film's ending, the unsettling swings between the defeat of the workers and the slaughterhouse scenes ('unprepared', as Kuleshov grumbled), is not in itself a failing, but rather a surprisingly adequate representation of the profoundly unsettled oscillation between meat and machine which is one of the film's subjects. The mediation, fulcrum, resting point and synthesis of this oscillation are indeed difficult to find. What's more, the slaughterhouse may not, in fact, be quite as 'unprepared' a line of imagery as Kuleshov complains, for Eisenstein's bright and savage eye may be doing no more than revealing for us the slaughterhouse lurking behind the modern factory: the workers in *Strike* work on steam engines, but the distances (if one travels metaphorically) between 'steam' and 'blood', between 'engines' and 'organs', between 'assembly' and 'disassembly', are not great and the oscillations that take us from one side to the other are swift and unpredictable, particularly for the intellectual whose pressing relation to these objects and processes is aesthetic.

Eisenstein's cinematic thinking in *Strike*, however, stands in problematic relationship to 'aesthesis', indeed to any kind of spectatorial perception. As the early reviewers complained, the images go by so fast that it can be difficult to see them, much less piece together all of their metaphorical connections or follow those numerous allusive strands leading beyond the film's limits. Eisenstein's first major experiment in picture-thinking, then, seems at least in part aimed at unsettling the viewers' habits not just of recognition, but of perception as well. Perhaps it would be fair to say this was a film created not only *by* but *for* a creature that could not yet truly exist: what Dziga Vertov called the 'cine-eye'.

Vertov's own opinion of Eisenstein's first film was that all that was good in *Strike* was more or less taken from him, in particular from *Kino-Glaz* (which had premiered at the end of 1924, slightly before *Strike*). In *Gazeta-Kino* in March 1925 appeared an article entitled 'Kino-Eye on *Strike*', in which Vertov declared that *Strike* was nothing other than an attempt to 'graft several of the construction methods behind *Kino-Pravda* and *Kino-Glaz* onto artistic [i.e. non-documentary] film'.[41] The Vertov group's appropriation of ultimate responsibility for all that they saw as successful in *Strike* was, naturally, galling to Eisenstein, who responded in kind with the famous line, 'It is not a "Cine-Eye" that we need but a "Cine-Fist"' (64), recasting the cine-eye as an overly passive organ.[42]

Here, perhaps, in the switch from 'eye' to 'fist', Eisenstein provides a hint as to how one might try to resolve the relentless oscillation between 'meat' and 'machine' that powers the universe of *Strike*. In the middle of the slaughterhouse/massacre sequence that left Kuleshov so unimpressed, Eisenstein includes a shot, not obviously motivated, of numerous hands reaching in silhouette towards the sky. I have always thought of this as the moment of antidote for the rudeness of the 'workers as beasts' metaphor: remember, the shot seems to say, these are people. Hands, after all and the labor that hands can accomplish, are what separate man from the animals.

Figure 3.
Hands (*Strike*)

In the 1930s, Eisenstein would return to an image that had impressed him when he had seen it on the cover of the journal *Foto-Auge* in 1929: A photomontage by El Lissitzky (from 1924) in which the artist's hand holding a compass is superimposed over the artist's face in such a way that the eye stares out from the center of the hand. This image so struck Eisenstein that he sketched it out in his notebook (on 5 January 1934) as an example of 'regression and prelogic'.[43] In fact, it encapsulates beautifully the tensions between 'abstract' and 'concrete', 'machine' and 'flesh' that had so marked the 1920s in general and *Strike* in particular. The eye that is here subsumed into the hand looks also like a stigmata, a wound. In this image of the dialectical tension between man as meat and man as machine, the tensions are not dissipated: how vulnerable the eye looks so near the sharp point of the compass! It was this kind of dialectical representation of the painful oscillation between abstract and concrete, this kind of uncanny mapping, that Eisenstein knew how to appreciate and to create. (A few years after his rediscovery of El Lissitzky's photomontage, Eisenstein played with yet another related image, this time placing the eye-shaped genitals of a doodled woman on the palm of a hand so that eye/genitals/stigmata could all coexist: thus the oscillating eye eventually would take its place in the thematic complex Eisenstein tagged 'Bi-Sex'.[44] That, however, becomes another story.)

Figure 4.
El Lissitzky,
'Konstruktor', 1924

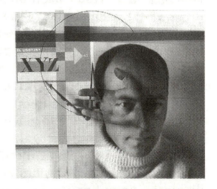

The new 'eye' of Russian modernism is a strange organ: part machine, part meat, it oscillates between these incompatible identities without finding any comfortable compromise between them. The birthplace of the modern, defamiliarizing view of the world is both the assembly line and the slaughterhouse and the bull's eye which in early scenarios opened and closed Eisenstein's first film reminds us that an ox's eye can be an 'oeil-de-boeuf',[45] a round window on the world (even, in one instance, a glass ball set on a window-sill), a lens, a *kino*-eye. Thus when we read hymns in praise of the cyborg eye, the view of the world that promises to show us what lies 'beyond recognition', we would do well to remember that other eye that watches us, too, and the ox's entrails being swept into the dark holes of the workshop floor.

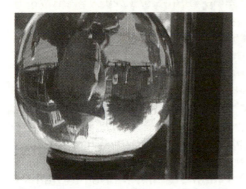

Figure 5.
Another kind of eye (*Strike*)

Strike exposes us to 'thinking' as a process dependent upon reforming and tormenting the visual apparatus. In order to rescue us from 'recognition' (that Shklovskian anesthetic), Eisenstein shocks the eye into seeing what ordinarily it would not or could not see. The film revels in its attractions, not only the gadgets and devices that seduce us with their wittiness and sense of play (the reflecting globe, the camera hidden in a watch, the table that folds open to reveal a hidden cocktail service), but also the cruel shocks towards which those contraptions lead us; as we leap by means of visual analogy from the charming juice squeezer to horses' hooves battering the skulls of the workers, we discover that such mechanical games, even if at first they seem to be no more than tangential flourishes, often enough end in bloodshed. *Strike* unsettles our usual categories of thinking and perceiving, but I suspect that for a first-time viewer, the film's unforgiving oscillations between play and pain, although intended to awaken the dozing automatized mind of the modern spectator, do not yet serve so much as 'thinking-in-pictures' as they stand in *lieu* of thinking: pictures in place of philosophy. *Strike*'s breakneck montage astounds the viewer but does not encourage or even permit the construction of any single point-of-view. This deficit, however, would be the focus of Eisenstein's attention as he worked on his second major film, *Battleship Potemkin*: now the spectator would be not merely dazzled and stunned, but remade.

2. Fourth-Dimensional Medusa: *Battleship Potemkin* and the Construction of the Soviet Cinema Audience

If, in the course of making *Strike*, Eisenstein had learned how to defamiliarize, how to unsettle his audience by thrusting them into the uncomfortable oscillations of a montage that refused to find an easy synthesis or resting place, as he began work on his next project – a sweeping anniversary tribute to the first Russian Revolution with the working title of 'The Year 1905' – he was himself unsettled by the fickle nature of an eye that was neither camera lens nor dead orb of a slaughtered ox: the eye of the spectator. The problem was, as he admitted later, that the 'pieces of real flesh and blood' he had stitched into the ending of *Strike* to make it effective, disturbing and altogether memorable, had not, in the end, had the function he had anticipated. At the premiere the effect was indeed everything Eisenstein, who had been known (as we have seen) to set off firecrackers under the seats of the audience in his Proletkult Theater days, could have wanted ('the impression produced was really horrific. Many could not watch the screen without shuddering'). (IP4 453) But when Eisenstein took the film to a working-class neighborhood, he was disappointed to discover that the grand and gory finale was the one section that left its proletarian spectators cold:

> I was crushed by this defeat until I realized that the 'slaughterhouse' can also be perceived as something completely unlike a poetic commonplace, not as a metaphor. A slaughterhouse can also be... the place where meat is produced... [For the working-class audience] upon the sight of these shots, the impression arose above all not of death and blood, but of beef and cutlets. (IP4 453)

This confrontation with the slipperiness of audience reaction (one viewer's 'making strange' is another's all-too-recognizable 'slice of life') must have been particularly galling to someone who, like Eisenstein, had made his name as a theorist of the cinema with a very confident description (in 'The Montage of Attractions', 1923) of how audience reaction could be determined, calculated and controlled:

> An attraction (in our diagnosis of theater) is any aggressive moment in theater, i.e. any element of it that subjects the audience to emotional or psychological influence, verified by experience and mathematically calculated to produce specific emotional shocks in the spectator in their proper order within the whole. These shocks provide the only opportunity of perceiving the ideological aspect of what is being shown, the final ideological conclusion. (SW1 34)

This model of the processes of aesthetic communication, with its piquant mixture of mathematical calculation and violence, bears a distinct resemblance to torture. The object of the torturer's interest in this description of the aesthetic process is the audience, which now finds itself, like Sinclair's unfortunate Jurgis, subsumed into the calculated cruelties of a sadistic aesthetic assembly line.

The slip-up with the oxen did not dampen Eisenstein's enthusiasm for violent metaphor. In his anti-Vertov polemics of 1925, as we have seen, he suggests the 'cine-eye' be discarded in favor of the 'cine-fist'. One soon notices that the 'cine-fist', too, seems to have learned its role in the labor process from the slaughterhouses of Packingtown:

> The Soviet cinema should smash into the skull... To smash with our cine-fist into skulls, to smash through to the final victory and now, under the threat of the influx of 'everyday life' and petty bourgeois philistinism into the Revolution, to smash as never before! (IP1 116)

The fist that emerges from the ocular oscillations of *Strike* is a weapon to be used against the thick skulls and blind eyes of an audience that cannot entirely be trusted.

Increasingly it is the eye that comes under attack: An early script for 'The Year 1905' (the working title of the project that became *Battleship Potemkin*) included a sequence – depicting the Bloody Sunday massacre – in which a Cossack was to strike with his saber the very lens of the camera itself.[1] This episode did not survive, but remaining as part of what Eisenstein referred to as 'the next tactical maneuver in the attack on the audience under the slogan of October'[2] is the famous sequence in which a Cossack, swinging his saber, is quickly followed by views of a woman's bleeding eye. Instead of a metaphorical ox, Eisenstein here slices into a synecdochic spectator.

This image thus marks the general escalation of hostilities in the struggle between audience and artwork, a struggle central to discussions of the role of cinema and theater in the Soviet 1920s and one thematized throughout *Battleship Potemkin*, a film obsessed with audiences and the kinds of things that can be done to them.

1. Towards an Effective Cinema

It was while making *Battleship Potemkin* that Eisenstein raised the stakes for himself by publishing an article, 'The Method of Making a Workers' Film', in which he came up with a fascinating if problematic redefinition of art's 'content':

> Class character [*klassovost*] emerges:
>
> ... In the determination of the purpose [orientation] of the film – in the socially useful effect that emotionally and psychologically infects the audience and is composed of a chain of suitably directed stimulants. I call this *socially useful effect* the *content of the film*.[3]

Eisenstein designates as its 'content' the 'socially useful effect' a given piece of art has on its audience. The ramifications of such a move are significant. The critic (or bureaucrat) is invited to turn away from the screen, to study instead, as a more material and concrete substitute for cinema poetics, the reaction of the audience. One method widely used was the audience survey, in various forms, but direct observation was also popular in the 1920s. For one Meyerhold play, audience analysts filled out large charts showing how many times the audience 'laughed', 'fell silent' or 'attempted to crawl onto the stage'.[4]

The Association for Revolutionary Cinematography (ARK) sent such an observer to the next-to-last screening of *Battleship Potemkin* at the 1st Goskino Theater, on 29 January 1926, to record audience reaction. The recorder was disappointed to see very few people in attendance (whereas 'in the first days people lined up in the street...') but rejoiced to find fate smiling on her sample: 'A mixed public... Near me: 3 adolescents – workers, 2 policemen, 2 middle-aged women in kerchiefs, an old lady in an old hat and – extraordinary good fortune – right next to me – a genuine *sailor from the Potemkin* with a little nephew and somewhat tipsy. The two latter circumstances furthered his talkative mood'.[5] Unfortunately for posterity, the genuine eyewitness, despite nephew and alcohol, mostly limited himself to exclamations of 'That's how it was', 'Right', '[Unprintable expletive]', and the occasional 'Not true. That didn't happen' when the film departed from his memory. The observer from ARK noted that the spectators left the theater 'stunned by keen impressions', a state again unfortunately not conducive to lively discussion, and concluded her report with a prim expression of surprise at the general bloodthirstiness of the audience ('I was surprised by the savage outcries when they were killing the officers: 'yessir!' 'got him!' and the cry 'nice!' [*krasota*] escaping one woman in a kerchief' (p. 18).

This kind of attention to audience reaction was very much in the spirit of (for example) Lenin's 1920 'Directives Concerning the Work of Agitational-Instructional Trains and Steamboats', in which he ordered, among other things, that officials 'Pay attention to the necessity of painstaking selection of films and the calculation of the action of each film on the public during its projection'.[6] But this calculation (*'uchet'*) would turn out to be riddled with extra variables: no matter how carefully films might be pre-selected, the final word on whether those films could be said to have a good or bad effect on the socialist audience (the effect that Eisenstein radicalized as the 'content' of the film) had to wait until the audience exposed to the film could be watched for its response, by which time it would presumably be 'too late' for that audience if the film's effect turned out to be noxious. Lenin's recipe for ideological control sounds perfectly straightforward, but in fact the second ingredient (studying audience reaction) points to the inherent weaknesses of the first part of the program: selecting the proper films. One could not know exactly 'what one had' (what the film really was) until one knew 'what it did'. This made control over content a slippery thing indeed.

The desire to apply the rules of science to audience reaction could be seen in many different arenas, including VM Bekhterev's books on reflexology.[7] Eisenstein was also attracted to reflexes and the reinterpretation of psychic phenomena as physiological or anatomical ones (this attraction he shared not just with the Marxist materialists, but also with Sigmund Freud). Eisenstein ends his 'Method of Making a Workers' Film' in this way:

> As with the attractional moment... we must never forget that the ideologically acceptable use of a neutral or accidental attraction may serve only as a method of provoking those unconditioned reflexes that we need, not for their own sakes but to train the conditioned reflexes that are useful to our class and which we wish to combine with the defined objectives of our social principle. (SW1 66)

Here we see, on the one hand, the language of reflexology, by means of which a particular action (on the part of the aesthetic object) and a particular reaction (on the part of the cinema audience) may be tied together as if by some iron rules of cause-and-effect; on the other hand, a stretching out of that chain of consequences until cause and effect are so separated by the series of 'dominos' between them that once again the relation between aesthetic object and its viewer, between film and spectator, is all too uncontrollable. Can we determine with any certainty the 'content' of our propaganda, our art? Can we ever gain control over the cause and effect chain?

The 'effect' that Eisenstein wished to create was 'class consciousness'. The audience's *klassovost* was to be the content of his films. The unpleasantness with the ineffective slaughterhouse had demonstrated that all audiences were not created equal: but what did that mean for the creation of effective revolutionary propaganda? Taken to an extreme, Eisenstein's 1925 acknowledgement, that 'the difference between an audience of, let us say, metalworkers and one of textile workers [will make them] react quite differently and in different places to one and the same work', (SW1 66) implies one might have to create a separate and distinct work of propaganda for each member of a possible audience – not a likely or cost-effective solution.

As the critic Mikhail Zagorskii phrased the question in 1924: 'Of whom does this spectator consist?' (141) ('*Iz kogo etot zritel sostoit?*').[8] His wording suggests how double-edged this problem can be. Figuring out 'who the audience is' is part of the larger project of describing a poetics of revolutionary art, or rather, as we now know to say, of an art with a revolutionary effect. Here opinions in the 1920s on the proper role of propaganda diverged dramatically: one camp focused on the audience as something to be described, studied and sorted into its various component classes; others insisted that revolutionary art should not just be sorting the sheep from the goats, but actively involved in changing or even creating those sheep.

Zagorskii's response to his own question was highly polemical: 'Above all it seems that there is no such thing as the spectator-in-general, but rather there is a range of spectating groups, hostile or close to each other according to their social nature'(Zagorskii 151). The role of revolutionary art, he goes on to suggest, is not to unify those groups – a goal he attributes to that branch of old-fashioned, Tolstoyan aesthetics 'still to be found[...] in a production at the Bolshoi or the Art Theater' (151) – but to separate them: '*There is no single spectator and no single spectacle.* The revolutionary current/ shock from the stage divides the audience hall, organizing and differentiating its positive and negative elements' (151). If 'each group sees on the stage that which its social nature dictates to it' (151), then clearly there can be no sense in trying to change the *a priori* 'social nature' of the component groups of an audience. This essentialist view of the nature of class consciousness has profoundly problematic implications in a culture where if one remained absolutely committed to the *a priori* class identifications of the population, there wouldn't remain much of a true proletariat class.

And the most important long-range goal of revolutionary art was, after all, to solidify the character of the proletariat as a class. Here (as suggested above) one could go in two directions: either one had to sort and purify the proletarian audience by unmasking and excluding those 'elements' hostile to the reigning class (a model in which *klassovost* is taken as a pre-existing content that the 'shock' of the artwork would merely serve to reveal or expose); or conversely, one might attempt to change the very nature of that audience's particular components by strengthening the class character of individual members of that audience (a model permitting some degree of reform and education). Despite his 1925 aside that in order for 'effect' to work properly, the audience may need to be pre-sorted, Eisenstein thought of effect as something that could indeed change the consciousness of the audience. In the same manifesto, after all, he warns of the negative changes inspired in an audience by the wrong sort of film, speaking of the 'sweet petty-bourgeois poison in the films of Mary Pickford that exploit and train by systematically stimulating the remaining petty-bourgeois inclinations even among our healthy and progressive audiences' (SW1 66).

The stakes, therefore, in placing such emphasis on the effect of cinema were high. In fact, the concern with the audience in the 1920s stemmed from deeper worries about the existence and composition of the proletariat class. It was essential that class consciousness be transmitted to those workers for whom the revolution, in the Marxist conception of things, had come too soon. Class consciousness – and thus the proletariat itself – was not something that could be counted on to arise spontaneously. Indeed, Marx, Engels and Lenin had stated quite firmly that class consciousness must come from outside the class in question. In his own 1902 manifesto, *What is to be Done?*, Lenin echoes Marx and Engels (the bourgeoisie, we remember, can take credit for the production of its gravediggers) in claiming that 'this consciousness could only be brought to them from without'.[9] Lenin cites at length what he characterizes as the 'profoundly true important utterances' of Karl Kautsky (122):

> The vehicles of science are not the proletariat, but the *bourgeois intelligentsia* [original emphasis]. It was out of the heads of members of this stratum that modern Socialism originated and it was they who communicated it to the more intellectually developed proletarians who, in their turn, introduce it into the proletarian class struggle where conditions allow that to be done. Thus, Socialist consciousness is something introduced into the proletarian class struggle from without (*von Aussen Hineingetragenes*) and not something that arose within it spontaneously (*urwüchsig*). Accordingly, the old Hainfeld program quite rightly stated that the task of Social-Democracy is to imbue the proletariat with the *consciousness* of its position and the consciousness of its tasks. There would be no need for this if consciousness emerged from the class struggle. (122)

In such descriptions of the development of class consciousness, a pivotal role is played by anticipation. The worker must be recognized as a candidate for enhanced proletarian consciousness before the worker could possibly sense that in himself. The working classes produced by capitalist conglomeration must be helped to anticipate their own consciousness of themselves as a class and as a social force. But until consciousness is achieved, a worker is not a true worker, a working class is not a true working class (but rather a relatively inchoate mass trapped in servitude). In order to come into conscious existence, the proletariat class has to be anticipated; it has to exist in a kind of provisional, illusory consciousness before it can acquire genuine political consciousness.

The working-class point of view, proletariat class consciousness, must be bootstrapped into existence and it must be essentially external in origin. What better candidate for the embodying of proletariat consciousness, in a post-Revolutionary period where still vivid anxieties about the strength and even existence of the proletariat must be dealt with in ways that do not interfere with the workingman's hours in the factory, than the cinema?

The Battleship Potemkin would like to be more than merely the story of the coming-to-consciousness of the Russian masses; it is a film that hopes actually to embody that coming-to-consciousness itself. When Leo Mur commented admiringly that the director of *Potemkin* 'not only edits the reel, but also the cells in the brain of the spectator', his remarks echoed Eisenstein's own hopes for a cinematic effect that could be both profound and determinable: 'Montage not only on the screen of the movie theater, but also on the screen of the brain' (as Mur put it).[10] An ideal artwork would know how to short-circuit the distance between filmmaker and spectatorial brain, so that the film editor could become a kind of surgeon operating directly on the class consciousness of his viewers.

Potemkin's intense interest in the process of spectating can be seen in the way the film foregrounds its self-reflexive side: it is largely about its audience. This audience at some points looks like an exact illustration of Andrei Bely's 1907 paean to the democratic nature of the movie hall:

> The cinematograph is a club: here there come together... all, all, aristocrats and democrats, soldiers, students, workers, girl students, poets and prostitutes. It is a place where those people are brought together who have despaired of the possibility of a *literary* loving union. They arrive tired and alone – and suddenly are united in the spectacle of life, they see how multifaceted and beautiful life is... The cinematograph returns to them their love of life.[11]

All one needs to do is substitute the *Battleship Potemkin* – and in particular, its red flag – for 'life', and one finds oneself in the middle of those famous shots of the citizens of Odessa, rich and poor alike, cheering on the mutineers. They are watching the 'Battleship Potemkin' just as we are. At this basic level we, the present audience of *Potemkin,* are invited to identify with Potemkin's audience within the fiction and to cheer with them as the red flag waves from the pole. Identification (by means of mirroring) with this other, embedded audience is but a first step, however.

According to the Leninist model, not only is the source of class consciousness essentially external, but in order to develop consciousness, the working class needs to move outside of its own situation: it cannot come to consciousness from within its own limits, whether those limits are seen as intellectual/psychological or practical and material:

> The workers can acquire class political consciousness *only from without*, that is only outside of the economic struggle, outside of the sphere of relations between workers and employers [and thus outside of their position as workers]. The sphere from which alone it is possible to obtain this knowledge is the sphere of relationships between ALL classes and the state and the government – the sphere of the interrelations between ALL classes.[12]

In other words, the workers need to develop a new and transforming point of view. There is an aesthetic component in Lenin's depiction of political education: to achieve a new point of view (to 'acquire class political consciousness') is to have achieved a transcendent renewal of one's perception (aesthesis).

2. Some Travels in Space-Time

Potemkin is a film with roots in many different contexts, many different philosophical worlds. To follow the tracks of any particular problem – in the present instance, the difficulties of instilling class consciousness into the cinema audience – requires travel in some directions that may seem at first to take us far afield. This detour, however, like Shklovsky's defamiliarizing swerve, promises in the end to bring us back to some of *Potemkin*'s most familiar and foregrounded images with our vision renewed.

In the background of *Battleship Potemkin* one finds traces of a series of interwoven debates on the role of perspective in political and aesthetic transformation. The ruminations of Marx and Lenin on the nature of class consciousness and the mechanisms of political enlightenment used language that was in some respects reminiscent of writing from a very different field indeed, namely 'hyperphilosophy', the science (and pseudo-science) of the fourth dimension. Lenin's sphere beyond and outside of 'the sphere of relations between workers and employers' can, for instance, also be understood as a kind of a 'hypersphere', the political equivalent of a 'fourth-dimensional' point of view. This 'fourth dimension' was a concept fascinating to a broad range of thinkers, politicians, artists and quacks in the late nineteenth and early twentieth centuries; Eisenstein thus found himself in this instance in both good and bad company.

The author himself – at the end of the 1920s – of an essay entitled 'The Fourth Dimension in Cinema' [*'Chetvertoe izmerenie v kino'*], Eisenstein had grown up in a culture saturated with references to the possibilities of the fourth dimension.[13] In the late 1910s, as an engineering student who spent all his pocket money on art books, he was perfectly situated to profit from the period's obsession with fertile (sometimes febrile) combinations of art and science.[14] Linda Henderson has traced the influence of 'fourth dimensional' thought on the avant-garde artists of America, France and Russia.[15] In the journal *Soiuz molodezhi* in 1913, as part of the project of introducing the ideas of French cubism to a Russian audience, Mikhail Matiushin – composer of the avant-garde experimental opera, *Victory Over the Sun* – larded his discussion of Gleizes and Metzinger's seminal book 'Du Cubisme' with parallel moments from the writings of the Russian hyperphilosopher Petr Demianovich Uspenskii. For Uspenskii the fourth dimension (which he discussed at length in two enormously popular and often-reprinted books, *The Fourth Dimension* [1909] and *Tertium Organum* [1911]) was part of a solidly mystical tradition.[16] As Matiushin grandly proclaimed at the beginning of his article, the true achievement of Cubism was 'the revelation of the human soul' and the sense of 'the advancing regal moment of the passage of our consciousness into a new phase of dimension, out of three-dimensional into four-dimensional' (368). He then turned immediately to Uspenskii's book *Tertium Organum*, 'which confirms in the highest measure many theses concerning the new phase of art, Cubism and the attributes of the fourth dimension'.

In a thick layering of embedded citation, Matiushin used a long quote from Uspenskii expanding on the beliefs of an American proponent of four-dimensional thought, Charles Howard Hinton. Hinton had written a 1904 book called the *Fourth Dimension* and had developed of a set of colored cubes, which when manipulated according to a complicated schema were supposed to enable the desired mental leap to a fourth dimensional point of view:

> Hinton's idea [writes Uspenskii, as cited in Matiushin] is precisely that before thinking of developing the capacity of seeing in the fourth dimension, we must learn to VISUALIZE objects AS THEY WOULD BE SEEN FROM THE FOURTH DIMENSION, i.e., first of all, not in perspective, but from all sides at once, as they are known to our consciousness. It is just this power that should be developed by Hinton's exercises...
>
> In this way, the development of the power of visualizing objects from all sides will be the first step toward the development of the power of seeing objects as they are in geometrical sense, i.e. the development of what Hinton calls a HIGHER CONSCIOUSNESS.[17]

How are these 'fourth-dimensional' lessons in seeing like or unlike those taught by Viktor Shklovsky in 'Art as Device'? We notice, for one thing, the emphasis of the hypervisionaries on effort, education, practice and developing new habits in our view of the world: 'We can learn to visualize objects as we know they really are' (372-3). The projected triumph of the brain over the eyes takes us far, potentially from the idea of 'defamiliarization' as a means of making people *see* rather than *recognize*. The trade-off between vision and 'higher consciousness' is difficult to resolve satisfactorily.

When Eisenstein mentioned Gleizes and Metzinger, authors of 'Du Cubisme', he did so to underscore the shift from vision as a 'retinal' activity to something dependent also on the brain:

The dominance of the retina of the eye, i.e. of the *pictorial imprint*, over the brain centers, i.e. over the *reflected image*, was an example of that trend [Impressionism]. It was precisely on the issue of this argument that the Impressionists were defeated by Cubism, which historically superseded them. Cubism (despite the considerable faults of its excessively one-sided approach) appreciated this position absolutely correctly, even though it conveyed it in forms that were more expressive of decadence than of a 'reunifying' art. Here, incidentally, Cubism was also to blame because its medium of expression – static painting – was not capable of carrying out the task which it was called upon to fulfill. To level this accusation at Gleizes and Metzinger would almost be like reproaching Leonardo da Vinci for fooling around with birds instead of using an advanced model of the Antonov-25 for his experiments in the theory of flight![18]

What 'static painting' was unable to achieve, cinema could be brought in to complete. Here, finally, was a medium of expression that knew how to involve both eye and brain:

When we say that in the fundamental structures of film aesthetics there is retained the unique nature of the cinematic phenomenon – the creation of motion out of the collision of two motionless forms – we are not dealing with natural, physical movement but with something that has to do with the way our perceptions work. This is not only the primary phenomenon of cinematic technique; it is above all a primary phenomenon of the human mind's capacity to create images.

For strictly speaking what occurs in this case is not movement; instead, our consciousness displays its ability to bring together *two separate phenomena* into a *generalized image*: to merge two *motionless* phases into an *image of movement*. (SW1 119)

The 'image of movement' is created as part and parcel of that greater achievement, 'the human mind's capacity to create images'. This skill is not merely a peripheral human talent, but in some respects central to the creation of consciousness itself (one could even say that consciousness can be seen as a by-product of the human brain's work with images). It is bringing phenomena together into a 'generalized image', into an 'image of movement', that marks the human mind's leap into higher-dimensional thinking.

Russian reception of the 'fourth dimension' as propagated by cubists and others focused largely on the potential of the fourth dimension as a new, transcendent point of view. There were many variants on this theme. One who experimented with several different approaches to this fourth-dimensional perspective was Kazimir Malevich, who had worked with Matiushin and Kriuchenykh on the *Victory over the Sun* (in fact, later he would claim that the backdrops he had designed for that opera were the birthplace of the famous Black Square). His 'Knife Grinder/Principle of Flickering' (1913), a Russian remake of Marcel Duchamp's famous 'Nude Descending a Staircase, No. 2' (1912), attempts to achieve a transcendent point of view by giving us several different moments at once. This is very much in keeping with one of the most popular ways of understanding the fourth dimension – as a way of spatializing time. The Time Traveler in *Victory over the Sun* had a very famous predecessor, after all: the hero of HG Wells's 1898 story, *The Time Machine*. This story begins with a sort of pastiche of Plato's dialogues, as 'the Time Traveler' explains the nature of space and time to a set of mystified houseguests:

> 'Clearly,' the Time Traveler proceeded, 'any real body must have extension in four directions: it must have Length, Breadth, Thickness and – Duration. But through a natural infirmity of the flesh, which I will explain to you in a moment, we incline to overlook this fact. There are really four dimensions, three which we call the three planes of Space and a fourth, Time. There is, however, a tendency to draw an unreal distinction between the former three dimensions and the latter, because it happens that our consciousness moves intermittently in one direction along the latter from the beginning to the end of our lives.'
>
> 'That,' said a very young man, making spasmodic efforts to relight his cigar over the lamp; 'that... is very clear indeed.' [...]
>
> 'Well, I do not mind telling you I have been at work upon this geometry of Four Dimensions for some time. Some of my results are curious. For instance, here is a portrait of a man at eight years old, another at fifteen, another at seventeen, another at twenty-three, and so on. All these are evidently sections, as it were, Three-Dimensional representations of his Four-Dimensioned being, which is a fixed and unalterable thing.
>
> 'Scientific people,' proceeded the Time Traveler, after the pause required for the proper assimilation of this, 'know very well that Time is only a kind of Space...'[19]

This spatialization of time – if only we could see better, we would know that all moments of time coexist, just as do all points in space – was a very popular way of understanding or representing the fourth dimension for both the scientifically- and the mystically-minded. It was also a concept that led, quite naturally, to consideration of the fourth dimensional potential of the cinema. What is a reel of film, after all, but the very embodiment of this fourth dimensional idea? Innumerable little 'sections', or frames, all coexist simultaneously in space until forced by the projector to imitate the inexorable progression of time. A venerable popularizer of modern physics, Professor NA Umov, referred quite extensively to the cinema as a comprehensible model for these paradoxical new ideas. In a 1911 paper read at the opening of the Second Mendeleev Convention, he said:

> We can represent the first three dimensions by three tape measures upon which are marked feet, yards, or other measures of length. We represent the fourth dimension by a cinematographic reel, on which each point corresponds to a new phase of the phenomena of the world... The passage from one point on this reel to another corresponds to our conception of the flow of time. Therefore we shall call this fourth dimension – time. The cinematographic reel can replace the reel of any of the tape measures and vice versa. [Cited in *Tertium Organum*, p. 104]

This section of his paper was cited with enthusiasm by Uspenskii in the second edition of *Tertium Organum*; equally fascinating, however, is another moment (not cited by Uspenskii) in Umov's lecture, where the professor again turns to the cinematograph as a model for the fourth dimension:

> On the ribbon of the cinematograph are portrayed people in various poses, watches on the faces of which the hands point to various hours: are portrayed the many different phases of the action which is to be accomplished. But while the film-strip is still, there is no movement, no time, no action... The film-strip begins to move; pictures replace each other on the screen at a determined speed and you, at rest, receive the impression of life, of action. People move, suffer, play out their drama; the clocks move. But for you the tempo of this action, the ticking of the clocks, the speed of the peoples' movements and consequently, even the speed of their thoughts, depends on the speed of the movement of the film-strip, but the people on the film-strip don't notice any change; they can't determine whether events are happening fast or slow.[20]

Cinema is therefore a perfect vehicle for understanding both the spatialization of time (as in Malevich's flickering knife-grinder) and the fundamental relativity of our conceptions of space and time (whether something is 'moving' or 'still'). Both of these fourth-dimensional ideas would be picked up by Eisenstein, who was to laud the ability of his own fourth-dimensional cinema to portray 'what is spatially unrepresentable in three-dimensional space and only emerges and exists in the fourth dimension (three plus time)'.[21] Yet another feature of fourth-dimensional thought remains to be mentioned, however. The notion of the section, the slice of a four-dimensional thing, was something not confined to a Wellsian or Cubist assemblage of moments in time. There was also a great interest in spatial sections: 'time' then being the medium allowing one to contemplate a series of these 'sections' or 'shadows' and then, mentally, to leap to some sort of grasp of the fourth-dimensional object whose shadows these are.

A favorite way of getting audiences to conceptualize the fourth dimension was to introduce a two-dimensional analogy. A three-dimensional object can produce a series of seemingly incongruous and incompatible sections of itself – can cast a very peculiar series of shadows of itself – on a single two-dimensional plane or screen. Claude Bragdon, another early popularizer and ardent Theosophist, too (he was responsible for a biography of Madame Blavatsky), produced a set of images in 1912 and 1913, inspired by Hinton, of all the different 'shadows' or 'sections' (he preferred the terms 'projections' or even 'personalities') that could be produced by sending a cube through a two-dimensional plane.

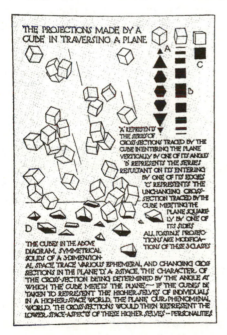

Figure 6.
Claude Bragdon,
'The Projections Made by a
Cube in Traversing a Plane',
1913

The idea behind these two-dimensional analogies was the following: just as a two-dimensional being trapped in a plane would be perplexed by the changing, shifting sections of a three-dimensional object passing through that plane, so are we perplexed by the thought of a fourth-dimensional object. If we practice hard, however, we may be able to leap to that higher perspective, from which we can see how the three-dimensional shadows all around us are actually mere sections of a fourth-dimensional hyper-object.[22]

The two-dimensional analogy was the premise of EA Abbott's 1884 hit *Flatland*, in which a square is visited in a two-dimensional universe by a mysterious growing and shrinking circle-being: a sphere, in other words. Eventually the Square is torn out of his two-dimensional world and shown what it looks like from a three-dimensional – an inconceivable – point of view:

> 'Impossible!' I cried; but, the Sphere leading the way, I followed as if in a dream, till once more his voice arrested me: 'Look yonder and behold your own Pentagonal house and all its inmates.'
>
> I looked below and saw with my physical eye all that domestic individuality which I had hitherto merely inferred with the understanding. And how poor and shadowy was the inferred conjecture in comparison with the reality which I now beheld! My four Sons calmly asleep in the North-Western rooms, my two orphan Grandsons to the South; the Servants, the Butler, my Daughter, all in their several apartments. Only my affectionate Wife, alarmed by my continued absence, had quitted her room and was roving up and down in the Hall, anxiously awaiting my return... All this I could now see, not merely infer; and as we came nearer and nearer, I could discern even the contents of my cabinet...[23]

Here it is the retina that leads the brain to a new and higher point of view; 'seeing' is much more effective than 'inferring'. Like the prisoner in Plato's allegory of the cave, the Square finds his physical displacement – his education – exceedingly painful at first: 'When I could find voice, I shrieked aloud in agony, "Either this is madness or it is Hell." "It is neither," calmly replied the voice of the Sphere, "it is Knowledge; it is Three Dimensions: open your eye once again and try to look steadily."' (Abbott 92)

Flatland is the story of the coming-to-consciousness of a Square. Although Edwin Abbott Abbott was himself a profoundly religious man who wrote many learned commentaries on the Gospels,[24] his pseudonymously-published space parable contains a great deal of biting social commentary. The two-dimensional land is governed by rules intending to perpetuate a stifling and ossified class structure: the more sides you have, the more superior you are deemed; mere triangles are forced to work as slaves and then destroyed at the whim of the higher polygons and so on. When the Square brings back to his fellow planar figures news of the Third Dimension, he is imprisoned as a madman and a rebel by a government determined to preserve the status quo. Like Lenin's worker, the square whose story is told in *Flatland* needs to travel to a higher sphere from which he might finally be able to comprehend the laws governing social history.

It is not just *Flatland* that demonstrates this sort of interest in the social ramifications of the 'fourth dimension': a similar 'class' subtext can also be found in Wells's *Time Machine*, in which the distant future descendants of class-divided human beings actually dine on each other. Again, it is by travel in a higher dimension (the fourth, in the case of Wells's time-traveler) that the hero of the tale is exposed to a new view of the social injustices and tensions at work in his own slice of space-time. Edwin Abbott Abbott's combination of social critique and a two-dimensional/four-dimensional allegory resurfaces quite dramatically in another already familiar source – Upton Sinclair's 1906 *Jungle*. The effect of the Socialist on the poor meatpacker Jurgis is described in terms which explicitly combine the acquisition of political consciousness with the achievement of a *Flatland*-inspired fourth-dimensional point of view:

> Until long after midnight Jurgis sat lost in the conversation of his new acquaintance. It was a most wonderful experience to him – an almost supernatural experience. It was like encountering an inhabitant of the fourth dimension of space, a being who was free from all one's own limitations. For four years, now, Jurgis had been wandering and blundering in the depths of a wilderness; and here, suddenly, a hand reached down and seized him and lifted him out of it and set him upon a mountain-top, from which he could survey it all, – could see the paths from which he had wandered, the morasses into which he had stumbled, the hiding-places of the beasts of prey that had fallen upon him.[25]

The ability of the two-dimensional analogy to instill in its audience an understanding of the fourth dimension is yet another place where hyperphilosophy finds its perfect illustration in the cinema. The film-strip is itself a kind of *Flatland*, whose inhabitants, as Professor Umov pointed out so colorfully, are unable to sense the limitations of their existence. By contemplating the model of the cinema properly, a modern audience may begin to be able to conceive of its own existence as a kind of three-dimensional film-strip.[26] In this context, it is truly a happy coincidence that the rebellious battleship whose story comes to dominate Eisenstein's cinematic tribute to the Year 1905 was none other than the battleship 'Potemkin', named in honor of a man who, to please Catherine the Great, perfected the two-dimensional illusion of non-existent happy three-dimensional villages.

Let us return now to our battleships. When we re-examine *Battleship Potemkin* in light of these interconnected political, artistic and metaphysical contexts within which 'hyperphilosophy' played a role, we find some evidence of Eisenstein experimenting with ways of using the cinema to create at least the illusion of a fourth-dimensional point of view. Again and again this film places extraordinary demands on its audience as it seeks to construct a transcendent, fourth-dimensional point of view. These demands are made at some points with great subtlety and at other points with furious 'Cubist' directness. One sequence combines shots of the people on the steps, the sailors on the battleship and the little yawls, taken from various angles (at first from the Odessan perspective, then from the vantage of one of the boats themselves, then from the perspective of the 'Potemkin' sailors), in order to unite civil and revolutionary views of events within the spectator's synthetic meta-perspective. On occasion the film seems to attempt to give us 'sections' of the four-dimensional hyperobject, the paradoxical three-dimensional shadows cast by a four-dimensional thing. In one famous sequence, a sailor is shown in successive, contradictory shots (or 'slices') breaking, first this way, then that, the same plate.[27] In this sequence, Eisenstein does what he does best: he creates an impossible point of view, one that would have itself considered 'four-dimensional'. The sections here are temporal, cinema's peculiar aptitude for the simulation of temporal and spatial dimensions here exploited to take the spectator on a visit to the 'mountain-top' of the fourth-dimension. It is admittedly an illusory, 'Potemkin village' fourth dimension (since even the third dimension in the cinema depends to some degree on illusion), but one that nevertheless manages to impart some of the flavor of the real thing.

3. The Lessons of Medusa

Within the limitations of our three-dimensional perspective, statues are statues. Eisenstein, in one of Potemkin's most famous tricks, uses statues of lions to point out the relativity of all conceptions of motion and stillness: he introduces us to the hyperlion they conceal. Later Eisenstein would comment that these lions marked the introduction of a new 'dimension of cinema'.[28] As has been noted often enough, these lions represent the very essence of film magic: stillness leaps into life. They are in this sense the perfect descendants of Vertov's slaughtered-and-resurrected ox in *Kino-Glaz*: animals that testify eloquently to the hyper-dimensional, time- and death-defying miracle of the cinema.

But these lions also return us to the problem of the audience – and in particular to the powerful ambivalence that I think is *Battleship*

Potemkin's engine and heart. To begin with, the lions themselves are an audience. They play out an audience reaction: they are brought to life by what they witness. At the same time they represent the unpredictability of audience reaction and the great difficulties confronting any formula that calculates that reaction. Their power is unequivocal – but their message profoundly ambiguous.

The standard way of understanding the lions has been taken from Eisenstein's 1929 essay, 'A Dialectic Approach to Film Form', as translated in Jay Leyda's early compilation of Eisenstein's essays: 'In the thunder of the Potemkin's guns, a marble lion leaps up, in protest against the bloodshed on the Odessa steps.'[29] In fact, however, this sentence is mistranslated. It should read: 'The marble lion leaps up, surrounded by the thunder of Potemkin's guns firing in protest against the bloodbath on the Odessa steps'.[30] It is the Potemkin that protests, the Potemkin that fires on the palace where the lion statue sleeps and thus 'awakens' it. Eisenstein's original intention was that the lions would be outraged on behalf of the palace and the old world it represents, not by the massacre on the steps. But Leyda's translation error cannot be dismissed as a simple 'mistake'. The up-rearing marble lion – a cinema trick of which Eisenstein was very proud – was slowly betraying its creator, just as the ox from *Strike* had earlier. Despite all of Eisenstein's hopes for controlling audience reaction, this was another place where the 'content' of his film turned out to be something quite different from what he had intended: many saw in those lions something grander than the protest of the Old World and who could blame them?

This intense ambivalence permeates all of *Battleship Potemkin*. It can be surprisingly difficult to distinguish good from evil, for instance. Both chaos and order are shown in positive and negative lights. The little boats of the helpful Odessans as they cluster around the huge Potemkin are a bright and cheerful version of the equally chaotic and life-filled little maggots that infest the sailors' meat. Conversely, the evil of the soldiers' mechanical descent down the stairs has its 'positive twin' in the extraordinary discipline demonstrated by the mutinous sailors.

Most dramatically ambiguous in this regard, however, are the images immediately surrounding the famous title that initiates the bloodbath (*vdrug* ['suddenly']). The shots that depict the crowd (watching the Potemkin) pick out some figures who disturb – very delicately at first – the general atmosphere of joy and pleasure: a woman whose dark half-veil, rolled up above the lips, but below the nose, casts a strangely disfiguring shadow over her features; a legless cripple appears on the steps; finally the sharp point of a white parasol comes forward into the camera. In other words, in this sequence the audience itself begins to become more grotesque, more frightening; even before the outside threat, the soldiers, have appeared, the film is slipping from 'dream' into 'nightmare'.[31]

This ambivalent portrayal of the audience on the Odessan steps reminds us again of the ambiguities underlying Eisenstein's attitude towards his audience. *Battleship Potemkin*, we recall, is meant as an attack on both of its audiences (the one within the film and the one in the theater), an attack that wishes to remove them violently from the limited plane they presently inhabit and force them into the higher plane, or hypersphere, of consciousness.

Eisenstein called this film his cinematic contribution to the New Economic Policy, or 'NEP', Lenin's compromise with capitalism after the economic devastation of the Civil War period:

> What characterises NEP in formal terms? It is the achievement of a particular effect by methods that are the logical opposite of the trend being followed: moving towards socialism by trading and so on.
>
> It is just the same in policy for the arts.
>
> If people ask me what I myself value in *Potemkin* I tell them it is the fact that it is the first step in the 'NEP' phase of the struggle.
>
> Because in *Potemkin* the complete review of attractions (albeit of *The Strike*) and the positive effect (the pathos) – the stern appeal to activity – are achieved by three 'negative' methods, all of them the methods of passive art: doubt, tears, sentiment, lyricism, psychologism, maternal feelings, etc.... These elements of 'right' art are dismembered and reassembled 'business fashion'.[32]

Eisenstein speaks of *Potemkin*'s concessions to bourgeois clichés, but these are concessions with a bite. Of the lovely 'mists' that mark the central caesura as the body of the murdered sailor Vakulinchuk is displayed on the pier, Eisenstein says, 'I admire them [the mists] as a sharply honed razor that will cut the viewer 100 per cent in the place that needs it at a particular moment' (SW1 68). The ideological compromises of the New Economic Policy (as well as the new capitalists, or 'NEP men' whom it spawned) were targets of immense hostility from the time of NEP's institution (1921). *The Battleship Potemkin* qualifies as a typical artifact of 'NEP' in its mixture of concession and aggression towards the forms of the past and in its extreme hostility to the audience it itself has assembled from a wide variety of classes.

The single most frightening set of shots may be the one in which the ambiguous threat embodied in the audience that is soon to become that threat's victim comes, literally, 'to a head': the swirling thrashing head of woman's hair that signals the massacre's beginning, directly following the title 'I vdrug...' ('And suddenly...').[33] Not for nothing does Eisenstein in an early shooting script describe what happens to the Schoolmistress (the one who eventually loses her eye), watching the massacre, with the words, 'she becomes a statue'.[34] At the core of *Battleship Potemkin* lies what may be its essential figure: the head of Medusa.

Figure 7.   Figure 8.
Medusa (*Battleship Potemkin*)   Mirror (*Battleship Potemkin*)

Once we spot the shadow of Medusa here, not only the dead/living statues but also some otherwise strange shots of a young man forgetting to watch the massacre in his mirror begin to make more sense. Perseus triumphs over Medusa by never looking directly at her; the *reflected* image of her horrible face cannot petrify him. The young man in *Potemkin* is instead transfixed in horror as he watches the massacre unfold; the unused mirror suggests that this spectacle may well be his doom.

Medusa, one of the most terrifying 'victims' of all time, whose head, living or dead, turns anyone who looks at it to stone, is the apotheosis of effect as art's content. Medusa has the most perfect, self-realizing point of view. She, as *Battleship Potemkin* would do, truly *projects* her own audience: anyone who sees her responds 'appropriately' (in the case of Medusa, turns to stone). Medusa's effectiveness is what *Potemkin* aspires to achieve. *Potemkin*, too, would like to contain a self-realizing point of view that does not just inspire but actually *is* a new form of consciousness. The metaphor may seem at first overly hostile, since Medusa's spectators receive as their portion not consciousness but death, but we have to remember that *Battleship Potemkin* was for Eisenstein nothing less than an 'attack on the audience under the slogan of October'.[35] Thus Eisenstein's film attempts to fulfill (by force) the ultimate task that lay before those molding and anxiously spying on the Soviet audience of the 1920s: *The Battleship Potemkin* creates an impossible point of view, thereby creating a new class consciousness and to create a class consciousness is in some respects to create a class. But *Potemkin* does its work mercilessly and it is perhaps its spectators' resulting feelings of exhilaration mixed with discomfiture – as *Battleship Potemkin* takes its audience to a transcendent four-dimensional point of view *and* turns that audience to stone – that have given the movie such enduring power.

Eisenstein was very fond of mythological references and enjoyed unleashing them in scandalous contexts. In *Battleship Potemkin*, as a further example, the mother of the famous infant in the baby carriage is struck down by historical forces she cannot comprehend and clutches as she falls at a belt buckle with a swan on it: we may read this as the proclamation that from this terrible violence, just as from Leda's rape, beauty and history will be born.

Figure 9.
Leda and the Swan
(*Battleship Potemkin*)

The two references – to Leda and Medusa – are not unrelated. Each works here as part of a meta-historical, meta-cinematic meditation (through images: 'picture-thinking') on the dialectical relationship between 'moment' and 'momentum' in history. The quandary is the following: how does the ordinary time of human existence, in which accidents happen and chaos seems to reign, get transfigured into the mystery of historical time, in which patterns can be discerned and from which the laws of myth and Marxism can be derived? In *Strike* it is a very small thing, literally and figuratively – a toddling child lost among the horses of the strikebreaking guards – that triggers the carnage of the film's conclusion, when its mother rushes to rescue her child and is struck by the guards. In *Battleship Potemkin* another infant is sent bumping down the steps as if to mark for us the cruel comparison of the iron march of history (all those steps, all those iron boots descending in heartless order) and the helpless little being weeping in his buggy because he cannot understand why he is racing along that way nor see where he's headed.

The figure of Medusa bears a particular relation to history, her terrifying, snaky locks being a part of the traditional iconography of revolution since the late eighteenth century (as Neil Hertz has traced brilliantly in his article on 'Medusa's Head'[36]). Freud, in a short article written in 1922 but not published until much later, attributed the tradition of the horrible Medusa to a complicated series of castration anxieties and compensatory petrifications, but even before Freud, the Medusa was something like the patron saint of Terror and in particular, naturally enough, of the guillotine.[37] This imagery was the stuff of childhood fantasy for Eisenstein, as he recalls one early Christmas in his memoirs:

[T]he eyes of the child glowed – probably with joy, rather than reflected candle light.

The yellow spines of two books stood out among the presents and, strange though it may seem, it was these that gave the child the greatest joy.

This was a special present. One of those on the 'list' common to middle-class families. This was not just a present – it was a dream come true. The curly-haired boy was very quick to get stuck into the yellow books, as Christmas Eve guttered and flickered in the candles and crystal.

The curly boy was me, aged twelve.

The yellow books were Mignet's *History of the French Revolution*.

And so this is the scene of my introduction to the Great French Revolution: Christmas Eve, amidst the tree, walnuts and cardboard stars...

My fascination with revolutions, especially French ones, dates from that tender age. First of all of course it was because of their romance. Their color. Their rarity.

I greedily devoured book after book. The guillotine enthralled my imagination. I saw amazing photographs of the columns toppled in the Place Vendôme. I was fascinated by the caricatures by André Gill and Honoré Daumier. I was excited by figures like Marat and Robespierre. I could hear the crack of rifles – the Versailles firing-squads – and the peal of the Paris tocsin. (BTS 59–60)

His first proto-cinematic encounters are also marked by imagery of the French Revolution, which he encounters very early in the wax renditions of the Musée Grévin in Paris:

> In the Chamber of Horrors there was even a small, unhappy Louis XVII standing by a drunken cobbler.
>
> And Marie Antoinette in the Conciergerie.
>
> And Louis XVI in a chamber being pursued by the patriots.
>
> And in an earlier tableau 'the Austrian woman' (*l Autrichienne = l autre chienne* – one of the first puns I really liked!) swooned as she looked out of the window to see a procession bearing aloft a pike with the head of the Princesse de Lamballe. (BTS 561–2, translation slightly modified)

The head of the Princesse de Lamballe becomes a transfixing and Medusan spectacle; where Marie Antoinette responds by fainting, the young Eisenstein (enjoying the spectacle of this spectacle at a safe remove) finds himself not so much horrified as 'fascinated'. So many firsts for the young Eisenstein are associated one way or another with the guillotine! First puns, first introduction to the cinema's great storehouse of visual and perceptual tricks ('the swish of the guillotine's triangular blade and even the visual impression of probably the first "double exposure" which I also saw on the screen in time immemorial – Cagliostro showing Marie Antoinette's ascent to the guillotine in a carafe of water'; *Beyond the Stars*, p. 562) and always, made up somehow out of these numerous and vivid 'moments', the sense of 'something much greater: to the first notions of historical events' (BTS 562).

The wax museum and the cinema convey not only in their revolutionary subject matter but in their formal nature the tension between things frozen or determined and things changing (in the merest instant it takes for the guillotine's blade to fall), a tension that is the central mystery of revolutionary history. Both wax museum and cinema have the uncanny ability to preserve – or, in Medusan terms, to 'petrify' – the ephemera of the moment.

The artistic ramifications of Medusa (from the blood of whom sprang forth Pegasus) feature prominently in a poem, 'The Face of Medusa', written by the Symbolist Valerii Briusov in 1905, as a response to the first Russian revolution of the twentieth century (and the one commemorated, of course, in Eisenstein's *Battleship Potemkin*)[38]:

> 1. Lik Meduzy, lik groziashchii,

2. Vstal nad dal'iu tëmnykh dnei,

3. Vzor krovavyi, vzor goriashchii,

4. Volosa spleten'ia zmei.

5. Èto khaos. V khaos chërnyi

6. Nas vlechët, kak v sryv, stezia.

7. Sporim my il' my pokorny,

8. Nam soiti s puti nel'zia!

9. V èti dni ognia i krovi,

10. Chto sol'iutsia v dikii bred,

11. Krik prokliatii, krik zloslovii

12. Zakleimit tebia, poèt! [...]

21 . Mir zavetnyi, mir prekrasnyi

22. Sgibnet v bezdne rokovoi.

23. Byt' napevom byri vlastnoi –

24. Vot zhelannyi zhrebii tvoi.

25. S gromom blizok golos myzy,

26. Drevnii khaos druzhen s nei.

27. Zdravstvui, zdravstvui, lik Meduzy,

28. Tam, nad dal'iu tëmnykh dnei.[39]

[The face of Medusa, threatening face,/Rose above the distance of dark days,/The gaze bloody, the gaze – burning,/The hair an interlacing of snakes./This is chaos. Into black chaos/The path draws us, as to ruin./Whether we argue or obey,/We cannot leave the track!/In these days of fire and blood/That flow together in wild delirium,/The cry of curses, of evil words,/Will brand you, poet!/[....] The cherished world, the beautiful world,/Will perish in the fateful abyss./To be the melody of the commanding storm – /That's your longed-for destiny./With thunder the voice of the muse is near,/Ancient chaos is her friend. Hail, hail, face of the Medusa, /There, above the distance of dark days.]

In the image of the Medusa coalesce the terrible 'chaos' of revolution and the iron determination of the 'rails' from which we cannot descend. The poet, like Medusa, must make the chaotic moment permanent; the poet, like the victim of Medusa, must submit to all the terror of history in the making. The identities of 'audience' and 'creator' are ambiguous, like the relationship between the particularities of the moment and the larger paths of history, which arise out of this chaos of particularity through mechanisms at once mysterious and fascinating. The Medusa's ability to mediate the gulf between chaos and necessity, her dreadful ability to spatialize time by freezing the moment in its tracks and in so doing, to change and to set the course of history on its inexorable rails (or down its inexorable flight of steps) reveal her unlikely kinship: to the Sphere of Abbott's *Flatland*, forcing the two-dimensional being to look down, as if removed from time, on his planar world; to the Socialist of Sinclair's *Jungle*, who tears the worker out of his limited perspective and forces him to recognize the laws and fetters governing his class; to the film that would turn its audience into a projection of itself. These are all teachers, of sorts. The Medusa and Abbott's Sphere share an affection for sudden and catastrophic pedagogy (the Medusan lesson being the more dreadful of the two: learn it and die). Both Medusa and Sphere require their students to attain a point of view that is not merely mental, but 'retinal', and radically so, since the new state of consciousness they would transmit (whether 'knowledge' or 'death') must be seen to be believed. Only such a combination of mind and eye, suggested Eisenstein, could create the 'image of movement' that marked the inauguration of human consciousness.

Mediating between these harsh pedagogues is a third figure: the sailor Vakulinchuk, lying dead on the pier. Past the little tent within which his body is displayed file the citizens of Odessa; on several occasions the film shows us these curious and grieving passers-by from the point of view of the dead man. The gaze of the dead/undead Vakulinchuk, who clearly functions here as a placeholder for the equally dead-and-yet-immortal Lenin, will soon galvanize the masses into revolutionary activity. Eisenstein calls the place held by the dead Vakulinchuk a 'caesura' and a '*mërtvaia pauza*': a 'dead pause'(IP3 48). Like the head of the Medusa, Vakulinchuk gazes at his audience from within (or beyond) death and, like the Medusa, Vakulinchuk transforms those who look at him. His death, however, is only a 'pause', in which 'the stormy activity of the beginning totally ceases, in order that it might redouble its momentum for the

Figure 10.
Mourners
(*Battleship Potemkin*)

second part' of the film (IPS 48) Thus the Medusan aim of projecting one's own audience (of determining audience reaction) can transcend even the limitations of death and petrification: instead of immobilizing the masses, *Battleship Potemkin*, like Vakulinchuk, will paralyze them only momentarily, only long enough to lead them through the 'dead pause' of the caesura to the higher consciousness and revolutionary activity that follow. More powerful than the terrifying snake-haired Gorgon of mythology, film can not only petrify but can also bring seemingly inanimate objects and images to life. As it does so, cinema also shows us the arbitrariness and contingent nature of our limited perspectives on time and space. It is only within the confines of our ordinary three (spatial) dimensions that time must limit its flow to one direction, that a Medusa can only kill her spectators instead of awakening them; a truly effective film, with class consciousness as its 'content', would presumably know how to use the Gorgon's power not just to petrify but to shape its spectator's minds and futures. In Eisenstein's *Battleship Potemkin* we are faced with that most daunting of art objects: a fourth-dimensional Medusa.

'*Potemkin* was a poster,' said Eisenstein in a 1927 interview with Louis Fischer.[40] He meant to convey by this that the two films following *Potemkin* (*October* and *The General Line*) were 'subtler', 'nearer life'.[41] The comparison of *The Battleship Potemkin* to a poster was, however, more apt than might at first glance appear. Consider, for a moment, some of the movie posters used in the 1920s to advertise *Potemkin*. The artists who made these posters manage to capture a number of *Potemkin*'s ambiguities – and even some of its four-dimensional ambitions. In Anton Lavinskii's 1926 poster, the cannons of the battleship are pointed at us. (Remember Eisenstein's claim: the *Battleship Potemkin* is an assault on the audience.) Two posters by Aleksandr Rodchenko do a remarkable job with multi-dimensional

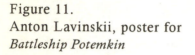

Figure 11.
Anton Lavinskii, poster for
Battleship Potemkin

Figure 12.
Aleksandr Rodchenko,
poster for *Battleship Potemkin*

imagery. One creates a wonderful optical illusion that pulsates between the second and third dimensions, between the impressions of a squashed cube and a 'thick' battleship. A second returns to the circles that in other posters would be the mouths of Potemkin's guns; here they look like the view through binoculars. But strangely, the poster presents to each 'eye' a slightly different moment from the film, in a temporal version of stereoscopy (in which a three-dimensional illusion is created by looking at two images taken from slightly different positions).[42] This is really another two-dimensional analogy of the fourth-dimensional point of view.

Figure 13.
Aleksandr Rodchenko,
stereoscopic poster for
Battleship Potemkin

The oscillation between incompatibilities (cine-eye, ox-eye) that marked *Strike* has given way to the ecstatic hazards of a leap to that impossible point beyond the horizon of our old geometries, that point where the parallel lines of time and space can be forced to meet, after all and from which, breathless and fascinated, we can watch history unfold itself like a map. The role of the fourth-dimensional visitor who tears us out of the limited perspectives of our everyday world in order to force upon us a new and nobler point of view is played by the cinema itself. The price of this acquisition of 'higher consciousness' may be very high: petrification, the loss of that individual consciousness to which we cling so tenaciously, mistaking it for life.[124] The guns of the *Battleship Potemkin*, then, are the guns of a peculiarly deadly stereoscope: it is perilous to look down their barrels, but we must – for they are sternly looking at us, their human screen.

3. Picture-Thinking:
October and the Debris of
Philosophy

The Revolution has taken into its care museums and palaces
that it does not know what to do with. Eisenstein's film is the
first rational use of the Winter Palace. He has destroyed it.

Viktor Shklovsky[1]

Scandal. I was on my way to visit someone with eight volumes
under my arm. 'Sir! Watch what you're doing with that box!'
And my threatening: 'It's not a box; it's Hegel!'

Eisenstein[2]

Writing his memoirs in the brief respite between the heart attack
that almost killed him in 1946 and his death two years later,
Eisenstein looked back on his youthful enthusiasm for radical
revolution with sympathy and humor:

It was at this very time that Alexander Kerensky was fulminating against
those in favor of erecting a guillotine on Znamenskaya Square.

I considered this a direct personal attack.

I frequently passed the Alexander III memorial and I used to imagine
that Doctor Guillotine's 'widow' stood on top of the granite pedestal...
I wanted so much to be a part of history, but what sort of a history was
it, if there was no guillotine?! (BTS 62)

For the young Eisenstein, a guillotine-less Revolution is somehow
less than real history; he longs for a history that can cut, that one can
really feel (history and film both being fundamentally indebted to
relentless editorial blades: guillotine; scissors). Eisenstein's
relationship to history is like that of the Gospel's Doubting Thomas,
whose faith could not be complete until his fingers had felt the wound

of the risen Christ. A few pages later Eisenstein remarks that during the July Days, when 'my legs carried me out of the range of the machine-guns', strangely 'it was not at all frightening' because at the time everyone was governed by 'habit!' (BTS 67). Later, however: 'These days turned out to be history. The history that I had so yearned for and that I had so wanted to touch physically.'[3]

History's habit of slipping by unrealized and unappreciated had earlier led Viktor Shklovsky to his famous cry for *ostranenie*, for 'defamiliarization'. The defamiliarizing talisman, held up to the world, could work its necessary and transfiguring magic, making the world visible by rendering it unrecognizable; as Shklovsky put it, defamiliarization can make 'stone stony' once again.[4] Eisenstein seeks, one might say, to make history Historical, with the second term capitalized: the flow of undifferentiated time within which we spin vaguely toward our deaths must be turned somehow into the History that is a story of progress and becoming. This process is governed by mysterious and paradoxical cycles, however, for the transformation of history into History also involves the aes- theticization of history. Medusa, the servant of chaos and petrification, of Revolution and of the State,[5] is still the proper figurehead here: she represents, embodies and forces her onlookers also to embody the mysterious transformation of the chaotic flow of particulars into an artistic, but arrested, historical tableau. Artist and historian, she excels at 'making stone stony'. Eisenstein, however, could not content himself with being Medusa's handmaiden: a too rigid role. In *October*, as we shall see, statues are subjected to a thaw, as the ideal forms they represent are relentlessly subverted by the particular instance or embodiment.

Unlike most of us, Eisenstein was invited (or rather, received a command, a *zakaz*) to relive the past and to relive it better: to turn the history of 1917 into the History of October as seen from the vantage point of the Revolution's tenth anniversary in 1927. Creating a better and 'realer' double for an historical period is a project with its own pitfalls, however, as Eisenstein was to discover. The history of the making of the film *October* is filled with incidents in which history and its double bumped into each other; once, like Dostoevsky's famous doubles, on a bridge, as May Day paraders in 1927 suddenly found themselves carrying slogans from the February Revolution in order to help Eisenstein's crew with a mass shot. (Security forces stunned to find the masses armed with bourgeois banners carted off Grisha Alexandrov, Eisenstein's co-director, but he was eventually able to convince them he was not a counter-revolutionary.)[6]

The crew of *October* seems to have enjoyed the chance to imitate subversive or criminal behavior. When safety fuses were needed for the late-night shooting of the bombing of the Winter Palace, Alexandrov 'staged a break-in' to get the needed fuses, since the stores were all closed:

> Then the chief of the Leningrad Militia, understanding what it would mean to break off the filming of such a scene, suggested we go on a 'crime spree'.

> An engineer-electrician, the militiaman and I raced headlong from the arch of General Headquarters, threw ourselves in a car and tore off to the largest Leningrad electronics store. The chief of police 'arrested' the watchman. The engineer and I broke the locks and collected two hundred of those blasted fuses. We threw together a report on the committed deed and triumphantly returned to the Winter Palace... (GA, p. 106)

Here as throughout the process of making *October*, the crux of the matter lies in the quotation marks: how strong are the markers that separate a 'crime' from a crime? An 'arrest' from an arrest? 'October' from October? And, especially, 'Lenin' from Lenin?

The most delicate issue of 'doubling' would indeed be the film's representation of the Revolution's central hero. As Alexandrov describes the origins of the film, the presence of Lenin in *October* was made an explicit part of the *zakaz* – the command – as presented by MI Kalinin: 'Mikhail Ivanovich [Kalinin] arose and said with particular significance: "In the film we expect to see the image of Vladimir Il'ich, leader of the socialist revolution, founder of the Soviet state"' (GA, p. 99). The news that an actor would for the first time be attempting to play Lenin in a film (as it turned out, the same actor, Vasilii Nikolaevich Nikandrov, was pulled from provincial obscurity to play Lenin in two films, Eisenstein's *October* and Boris Barnet's *Moscow in October*) provoked a remarkable quantity of critical scandalizing.[7]

The poet Mayakovsky, usually on good terms with Eisenstein, did not hesitate to make his outrage public. Already in October 1927, Mayakovsky railed against the use of Vasilii Nikolaevich Nikandrov as a 'Lenin':

> Our Sovkino in the person of Eisenstein is going to show us a counterfeit Lenin, some kind of Nikanorov or Nikandrov... I promise that at the most solemn moment, wherever it may be, I will whistle, I will throw rotten eggs at this counterfeit Lenin. This is an outrage.[8]

The word Mayakovsky uses here for 'outrage' – *bezobrazie* – is dramatically suggestive, since the root *obraz* ('image') reminds us that the heart of the matter, the source of Mayakovsky's outrage, is Eisenstein's attempt to substitute Lenin's image for Lenin himself.[9] (Alexandrov's version of the call from Kalinin contains that very word: we want to see the *obraz* of Vladimir Il'ich, says Kalinin.) Vladimir Kirshon (a RAPP playwright) used the journal *Kinofront* to deliver an almost equally radical response to Mayakovsky's attack:

> Lenin is higher than any image an actor could create. But if you approach the matter from that point of view, it quickly becomes necessary to throw rotten eggs at all the portraits and photographs of Lenin, necessary also to bespatter all the works of art with Lenin in them, for that matter also the poems of Mayakovsky himself.[10]

Mayakovsky, however, insisted that there were some representations of Lenin which transcended the category of mere 'image'. In the issue of *Kino* commemorating the tenth anniversary of the Revolution, Mayakovsky continued his polemic in favor of documentary film (as in Esfir Shub's cinema chronicles, made of found footage) and against the use of 'various similar Nikandrovs' [*raznye pokhozhie Nikandrovy*] to portray Lenin:

> It's disgusting to see a person take poses similar to those of Lenin and to make similar body movements – and behind all this externality one feels a total emptiness, the complete absence of thought. The comrade was absolutely correct who said that Nikandrov is not similar to Lenin but to all of Lenin's statues.
>
> We want to see on the screen not an actor's performance 'on the Lenin theme', but Lenin himself, who, even if only a few frames, looks at us from the cinema screen.[11]

The only cure for the *polnaia pustota* – total emptiness – of the image is the miraculous recreation not of a Lenin-*obraz* for us to look at, but a real Lenin, 'Lenin himself', who will look at us: not an object any longer, a mere copy of a statue, but a resurrected subject.

Nikandrov apparently tried very hard to do his great role justice, burying himself in the reading of Lenin's works and going to visit Lenin's wife and sister to learn 'what Il'ich was like in everyday life, *en famille*' (GA 102) – as if 'filling the interior void' that separated him, the *obraz*, so definitively from the great man he accidentally resembled. This kind of preparation was out of all proportion to the size and demands of the role (which truly asked little more than a reasonably similar statue-like 'Lenin').[12] Eisenstein wanted, however, to treat the Lenin issue with 'maximal tact' (GA 113). He was gravely concerned that something would go wrong as they messed with the old taboo against portraying Lenin: 'Yes and don't forget,' he wrote sternly to Alexandrov, 'don't let anyone have a photo of Nikandrov and especially where he and I appear together... And don't let anyone see them.' (GA 113) Where today the motivation for this might be saving a good trick or special effect for a film's grand opening, Eisenstein's worries were political and went much deeper. As Alexandrov glosses the above phrase:

> Knowing too well the journalists' long-whetted thirst for sensation and fearing as the gravest of sins the kind of idle and public chatter surrounding the filming of Nikandrov, Eisenstein called on me to exercise the utmost caution and maximal tact in relation to the name of Lenin. (GA 113)

Nikandrov was a kind of hot potato for Eisenstein; he had to protect himself against the potential *pustota* of his Lenin-substitute, an 'emptiness' which threatened to infect him, too: if a picture of someone with the real Lenin possesses a kind of apotropaic power, a picture of Eisenstein with a fake Lenin potentially can get a person into lots of trouble (like having falsified one's documents).[13] These were the dangers involved in extending the idea of 'typage' to a sacred figure like Lenin: did one really want to suggest there was a Lenin 'type'? Was sheer physiognomy enough to guarantee some kind of deeper identity? Eisenstein was always tempted by just this idea, but knew enough to distrust his own enthusiasm for physical surfaces. A few years later, he would interrupt his own lecture on the use of physiognomy as a way to construct expressive character types with the caveat that Hegel, of course, had dissected (in the *Phenomenology of Spirit*, for example) the 'dead *sistematika*' of the physiognomists and had concluded that 'One may know a person much better by his deeds than by his appearance' (IP4 371).

The most problematic character in *October*, as things turned out, would not so much be the Lenin who was 'not the real Lenin', but the Trotsky who was 'too much the real Trotsky'. In an eerie replay of the May Day parade 'sabotaged' by Eisenstein's film crews in the name of art, the Trotskyites emerged from the conspiratorial underground to 'slander and sabotage' the parades celebrating the tenth anniversary of the Revolution, 7 November 1927 – the day *October* was supposed to be shown for the first time.[14] Alexandrov claims that Stalin came by in person to see what Eisenstein and Alexandrov were up to in the editing booth, as they frantically tried to get the film ready for the showing that evening and asked them then, 'Is Trotsky in your film?'(GA 116). Stalin's terse pronouncement after being shown the offending clips was, according to Alexandrov, 'A picture with Trotsky in it cannot possibly be shown today' (GA 116), a sentiment that would send Eisenstein back to the editing room for the next three months, to try again to get History right, by cutting Trotsky where possible and recontextualizing him where need be.[15]

In *October*, therefore, we have a film in which – in the cases of Lenin and Trotsky – the image is in anxious relation (or nonrelation) with its 'signified', with History itself being at stake.

Ironically enough, the film turns out (in the history of Eisenstein's own theoretical evolution) to be all about developing a new kind of cinema – the famous 'intellectual cinema' – in which image and concept would be in such intimate contact that unfortunate interpretative accidents could be definitively prevented. One might even then consider making a film of pure ideology, a film version of, say, Marx's *Capital* (Eisenstein's famous post-*October* project, never realized but much analyzed.)[16]

Our task here is to trace some of the cracks in the foundation of what Eisenstein bravely called 'intellectual montage' or 'intellectual cinema', a project which hoped to tackle 'the problem of the transition of film language from cinema figurativeness to the cinematic *materialization of ideas*, i.e.... the problem of the direct translation of an ideological thesis into a chain of visual stimulants'.[17] As Eisenstein described the cinematic situation in 1929: 'Only *intellectual* cinema will be able to put an end to the conflict between the "language of logic" and the "language of images" on the basis of the language of the cinema dialectic.'[18]

A fascinating piece of evidence in the history of 'intellectual montage' comes to us via the French film historian Léon Moussinac, a friend of Eisenstein, who in 1963 published a letter Eisenstein had written him (in French) in December 1929:

> I think I'm ready to upend my whole system. Thematically as well as formally. I believe that in a film on 'the other side' of the acted film, beyond the film of the 'newsreel' type as well as beyond absolute film, we are going to find the secret of a pure cinematography. And what's most amusing is that this cinematography will be genetically ideological, since its content will be the screening of... (and here's a kind of coup de théâtre: the essential word of all this scribbling fails me; my explanation becomes a charade. And no dictionary at hand. Fine, take the word in German: *Begriff*.)[19]

Lacking the proper *Begriff* ('concept'), Eisenstein's explanation is reduced to a 'charade', a charade being a way of conveying messages by means of images and gestures. As it happens, the relationship between 'charade' and *Begriff* is precisely the material out of which 'intellectual cinema' is to be formed, as Eisenstein hunts for ways to translate the concepts of philosophy into the visual images of film language.

Eisenstein points in this letter to two examples from *October* which become, not only for Eisenstein, but for his many readers and critics, the first portents of the new intellectual cinema of the future: the 'Gods' sequence, in which the deity, as Eisenstein would claim later, is reduced to a block of wood (a Baroque Christ begins a series of images of 'gods', ending with simple wooden idols); and Kerensky's extended ascent of a flight of stairs in the Winter Palace (he is shown ascending the same flight of stairs again and again: thus we are informed that Kerensky is destined to get nowhere in the long run). Writing to Moussinac, Eisenstein says the 'elevation of Kerensky... serves as a ladder... towards a completely different cinema-tography'.[20] This use of Kerensky-on-the-endless-stairs as a ladder 'vers une cinématographie tout autre' works as a peculiar sort of ironicizing meta-image, since Eisenstein presumably does hope to reach the top of his ladder, the ladder that reaches up towards the paradise of the new intellectual cinema.[21]

Behind these images of staircases terminable and interminable is a remarkable book whose theme is also mankind's progress on a grand staircase with many seemingly repeating flights: Hegel's *Phenomenology of Spirit*, which as a rich source for meditations on the interrelationship of 'image' and 'concept' turns out to provide a striking gloss not only on *October* but on Eisenstein's projected 'intellectual cinema'.[22]

Hegel's *Phenomenology* is the famous 'Bildungsroman' of the world spirit, in which consciousness learns, slowly and painfully, to know itself and the world around it. It is also – and perhaps even primarily – a consideration of the complex interrelationship of *Bild* and *Begriff* ('image' and 'concept'), for as consciousness travels its long and seemingly repetitious road, it must again and again seek a new 'image' as a means of access to the 'concept' at hand and then learn to emancipate itself from the limitations of what Hegel labels 'mere picture-thinking'. So when Eisenstein, writing to Léon Moussinac, reaches into German to find the *Begriff* he needs, it is not by accident. Hegel's *Phenomenology* can be read as providing a sort of blueprint for the 'intellectual cinema'. Hegel's very hostility towards picture-thinking is, after all, thought through pictorially, and although the image is demonstrated to be nothing without a concept, the concept conversely (and perhaps despite Hegel's best intentions?) keeps finding itself needing its pictures, even if one of the principal lessons of the book is that we must learn to ask for more than mere *Bild*, that 'images' are traps for the journeying mind.[23]

Hegel will often rail against the cheap tricks of analogical explanation, only to indulge himself in a frenzy of counter-images:

> The formalism of such a 'Philosophy of Nature' [based on 'superficial analogy'] teaches, say, that the Understanding is Electricity, or the Animal is Nitrogen, or that they are the *equivalent* of the South or North Pole, etc., or represent it – whether all this is expressed as baldly as here or even concocted with more terminology – and confronted with such a power which brings together things that appear to lie apart... and which imparts to them the Notion's [*Begriff*] semblance but saves itself the trouble of doing the main thing, viz. expressing the Notion itself or the meaning of the sensuous representation – confronted with all this, the untutored mind may be filled with admiration and astonishment and may venerate in it the profound work of genius... What results from this method of labeling all that is in heaven and earth with the few determinations of the general schema and pigeon-holing everything in this way, is nothing less than a 'report clear as noonday' on the universe as an organism, viz. a synoptic table like a skeleton with scraps of paper stuck all over it, or like the rows of closed and labeled boxes in a grocer's stall. It is as easy to read off as either of these; and just as all the flesh and blood has been stripped from this skeleton and the no longer living 'essence' [*Sache*] has been packed away in the boxes, so in the report the living essence of the matter [*Wesen der Sache*] has been stripped away or boxed up dead. We have already remarked that this way of thinking at the same time culminates in a style of painting that is absolutely monochromatic...[24]

Its concepts may be founding moments in world philosophy, but it is this super-fertile imagery – tables like skeletons like a grocer's bins – that makes the *Phenomenology* such a good read.

At this point it makes sense to return to some of Eisenstein's most famous images, those comprising the sequence in which by means of proto-intellectual montage, God is turned into a stick of wood (the shots, he says, 'lead the idea of god back down to a block').[25] This is the sequence that for some commentators suggests that the *Capital* project – and intellectual cinema in general – 'could really have happened', if only the circumstances had been better, if Eisenstein had not traveled off to the Americas and so on. See for instance the comment of Noël Carroll:

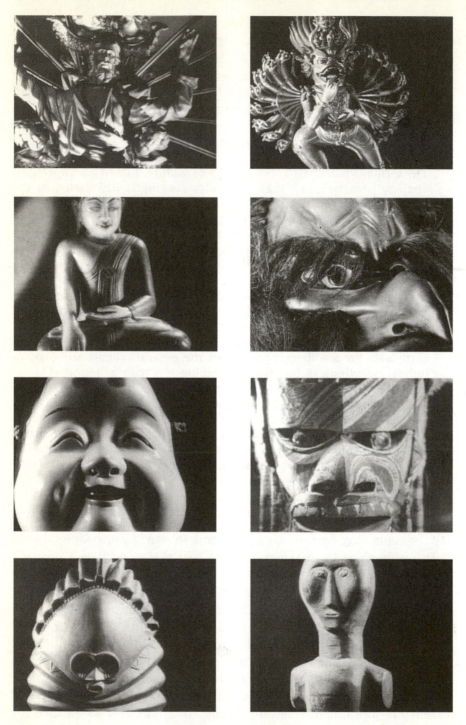

Figure 14. Gods (*October*)

The idea of a film based on *Capital* (Marx's) is mind-boggling. How does one represent the labor theory of value? Yet there is reason to believe that Eisenstein's assumption that he could film *Capital* was not unfounded. For the 'God and Country' sequence takes as its subject matter not only the depiction of a mode of alienation, but the disproof of God's existence. These matters are as 'purely' conceptual as issues in *Capital*. Thus, it is not idle to speculate about the form of *Capital* on the basis of this sequence.[26]

This logic puts a great weight on the shoulders of the 'Gods' sequence. In his autobiography much later, Eisenstein emphasizes again the way the intellectual montage of the 'Gods' sequence depends on revealing the image of god to be an empty thing, a *Bild* without *Begriff.*

> These, then, are the sources that prompted me to seize my opportunity in *October* to attack the very concept of deity by revealing its hollowness. To do this I searched for the most accurate expression of the idea about the splendor of the eternal aspect and the emptiness of content [*pustota soderzhaniia*]. The required image came of itself. It lay in the equation of the most richly gilded Baroque Christ and the crude wooden idol of the Eskimos or Giliaks.[27]

Eisenstein wants to do to God what Mayakovsky accuses him of doing to Lenin: to provide an essentially hollow image and thus allow a deadly emptiness, a resounding *pustota*, to overtake the sacred figure.

The images used in this most crucial of all sequences are not, however, nearly as empty as Eisenstein's descriptions might lead one to believe. What we find, wonderfully enough, is that Eisenstein has brought Hegel together with Freud in his project of demoting the divine phallus to a mere penis. Eisenstein's use of phallic (or, rather, 'penile') imagery in the service of intellectual montage (that is, in an attempt to take the cinema beyond mere picture-thinking), is in itself a tribute to Hegel, who – at the end of the same remarkable chapter on 'Phrenology and Physiognomy' in the *Phenomenology of Mind* that Eisenstein referred to when warning his students about the dangers of taking physiognomy too seriously – says the following:

> The *depth* which Spirit brings forth from within – but only as far as its picture-thinking consciousness where it lets it remain – and the *ignorance* of this consciousness about what it really is saying, are the same conjunction of the high and low which, in the living being, Nature naively expresses when it combines the organ of its highest fulfillment, the organ of generation, with the organ of urination. The infinite judgment, *qua* infinite, would be the fulfillment of life that comprehends itself; the consciousness of the infinite judgment that remains at the level of picture-thinking behaves as pissing.[28]

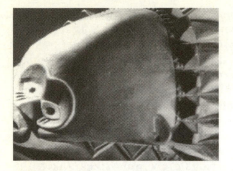

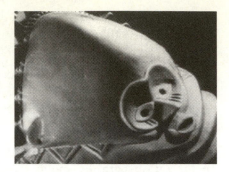

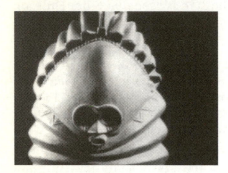

Figure 15.
A 'Hegelian' god
(*October*)

In other words, Hegel uses the example of the most oxymoronic of organs to illustrate the gulf that separates the picture-thinking consciousness from true philosophical thinking: the phallic splendor of the organ of generation is tied to philosophy and the *Begriff*, while picture-thinking is reduced to the status of the penis as organ of urination. A distinction not unlike this one is drawn by Freud in his 1922 article on the 'Medusa's Head':

> The erect male organ also has an apotropaic effect, but thanks to another mechanism. To display the penis (or any of its surrogates) is to say: 'I am not afraid of you. I defy you. I have a penis.' Here, then, is another way of intimidating the Evil Spirit.[29]

Or for that matter, God Himself, which is what Eisenstein seems to have in mind. For Freud, the 'penis' has an apotropaic effect when it is erect, when it is behaving as the organ of generation and so may be called a Hegelian phallus. He does not suggest that displaying the other organ, the urinating one, has any such magic power: indeed, it is implied here that to have only that organ (the penis from our Hegelian paradigm) is much the same as to have nothing at all, to be reduced to *pustota*, 'emptiness' (or, to shift to a slightly different terminology, to be castrated).

'I am not afraid of you. I defy you', says Eisenstein to God by demonstrating that he, Eisenstein, can reduce 'god' to mere picture-thinking, to 'pissing': there is no *Begriff* there. But then again… are the sticks of wood so very hollow? The lens treats them lovingly; the director is clearly enthralled by them, reflecting the fascination with the 'primitive' that was at that time so broadly distributed among the artistic avant-gardes of Europe.[30] It does not take much squinting to make these objects look once again like things of power; to disclose the aspect of them which is at least partly fetish. They threaten to follow the example set by the famous lions of *Potemkin*: they may, one feels, at any moment, come (back) to life (as precipitously as the 'organ of urination' may suddenly prove to be an 'organ of generation', after all).

Where in *Battleship Potemkin* the emphasis was generally on fixing the attention of the audience, in *October* it is the very tension between 'life' and 'fixity' that the film addresses – the *Potemkin* lions serving as transition point from one set of concerns to the next. *October*'s 'anti-Medusan' twist on the theme of the statue riddles the film with ambiguities. The film draws numerous comparisons, both explicit and implicit, between 'real people' and statues. Its 'Lenin', the earnest Nikandrov, seems indeed to have learned his role by studying, as Mayakovsky scornfully insisted, the numerous statues of Lenin. His portrayal is that of a statue come to life, but 'life' is a strange property. An animated statue of Lenin risks becoming a parody of Lenin, a blasphemous shell.

Eisenstein makes this situation even trickier for himself by setting into motion a series of comparisons, in *October*, between 'real people' and statues, all of which have as their intended effect the deflation of both sides of the comparison, sometimes to scandalous effect. The statues are ideals, icons: Napoleon, the young lovers Rodin entwines in an eternal and ideal kiss, the model of young motherhood, watching her offspring take its 'first steps'. When the ugly, rumpled, bulbous woman soldiers of the Tsar's 'death's head battalion' eye the smooth coolness of these marble images of Woman, they are entirely unmanned. Their rifles drop. They become wistful for the ideal from which they are separated by what seems a huge gulf indeed, the gulf separating flesh from marble, and Eisenstein laughs at both elements: the woman soldiers for being so unlike the statues that surround them and the statues for being so irrelevant to all the things that truly matter in 1917.[31] Likewise, Kerensky is a fool to think himself the embodiment of 'Napoleon', but the statues he imitates themselves represent ideals as outmoded and ridiculous as Rodin's images of womanhood. Like 'God', the statues are hollow, subjected to a thorough work of deconstruction by means of the forced encounter with the flesh, the representative sequence of this deconstructive project being, logically enough, the literal unbuilding of the statue of Alexander III with which the film opens.

Actually, the revelation of 'hollowness' is not the worst fate suffered by the statues of *October*: the most effective blasphemies are constructed by disrespecting the hallowed surfaces of all the painted and sculpted images that populate the Winter Palace, by imputing to them the presence of obscenely fleshly interiors. The marauding soldiers take pleasure in discovering the bathroom fixtures which prove that the Tsar and Tsarina were also creatures of the flesh, like anyone else, with bowels that needed moving: the Imperial Family suffers the same fate as Maternity, Love, Napoleon and, for that matter, God – brought down from the pedestal by means of comparison and forced to reveal a scandalous interior. (The scandals of 'hollowness' and of too much fleshly content – bowels – are related). Even Christ is made by the blasphemous juxta-positions of montage to lust in a very fleshly manner after a semi-naked statue: his gaze is fixed squarely on her crotch. Again an ideal is brought to life – made mortal through what we might call, thinking of Hegel, 'de-generation' – in order to be destroyed.

By means of endlessly exploding ironies, *October* undertakes the destruction of the museum: in this case, the Hermitage, the museum that is also a palace. Throughout *October*, the precious objects of the museum are taken down, examined and then used against their original purposes, used ironically. The statues of Napoleon never expected their fate would be to ridicule the very idea of imperial ambition. Yuri Tsivian has pointed to some of the film's other obscene puns: Kerensky's entrance into the anus of the fancy bejeweled pheasant (whose turning back is intercut with scenes of the door through which Kerensky must pass); the elegant enameled eggs whose appearance functions as a comment on the Tsar's testicles.[32] What is fascinating in these rude (if witty) betrayals of the objects' original roles and intentions is the way they demonstrate the uncanny flexibility of the object, of the image, which cannot be trusted to remain loyal to any one message or any single owner. When Eisenstein storms the Hermitage, its contents bend docilely to his will; as they earlier soothed the Imperial ego with their empty blandishments and jeweled reflections of the Tsar's glory, now they obediently carry out their charades of blasphemy and deconstruction. Like all traitors, however, they cannot be trusted. Pliant, they keep their own counsel. It is always difficult to be certain that they are sufficiently hollow, that they are sufficiently defused, that they are safe – and Eisenstein's very interest in them argues that they are still too alluring to be considered harmless.[33]

The *obraz*, in the end, is like nothing so much as an egg (that eternally recurring object in the history of *October*). From its exterior, one can never be sure about the contents: hollow, rotten (good for throwing at blasphemously 'hollow' images), or fertile, in which case, as Tsivian reminds us, the potency involved can be feminine or – in the case of the testicular 'egg' – masculine. In fact, the *obraz* in *October* exhibits a particularly unsettling capacity to be all of these things at once: hollow, but not safely so; rotten and all-too-fertile, or even dangerously explosive (as in the famous 'bomb' effect Eisenstein later describes proudly).[34] Such objects, such images, can never be displayed safely: Shklovsky's ironic thoughts on the fate of the museum ('Eisenstein's film is the first rational use of the Winter Palace. He has destroyed it.') may have more force than one had suspected.[35]

The museum is indeed a problem for post-Revolutionary culture. How does one prevent these unreliable, fickle images of the past from infecting the present? (In Evgeny Zamiatin's 1920 dystopian novel, *We*, the 'museum' kept by the cruelly uniform society of the far future turns out literally to be the topos of its undoing: it is there that previously dutiful cogs in the state mechanism discover sex, cigarettes and other temptations to rebellion and it is there that the tunnel to the outside world, the world beyond the 'Green Wall', begins.) The lesson of *October* would seem to be that objects and images can never be entirely tamed. But Shklovsky's claim that Eisenstein in *October* has undertaken the destruction of the museum is, though true inasmuch as object and image are co-opted for the film's greater project of deconstruction, also, in the end, inaccurate. *October* is itself a kind of museum – a very long, extremely linear museum – one whose curator, whatever he may know about the inherent perilousness of such enterprises, has been seduced by the objects and images under his care. The images and objects are presented with appropriate caution (the ironies of *October*'s deconstructive montage) and there are little 'educational displays' tucked into the halls as well (such as the sequence 'Proletariat, learn to use a rifle!' in which a rifle assembles itself, step by step), but as in any museum, the frames are never perfectly secure. It is never entirely certain that a little Giliak idol may not retain some old

power, or that 'Lenin' will not find himself 'recognized' as a fake.
(There is a wonderful moment where, in *Strike*-like double exposure,
a disguised Lenin is stripped of his disguise by the rude eyes of
observers: 'They've spotted me, the bastards!' This is one place
where Nikandrov's and 'Lenin's' anxieties overlap.)

The Museum/Palace itself also suffers from the uncertainties
of its architecture: hardly populated at all and giving no resistance
adequate to warrant the throngs of thousands which Eisenstein,
correcting history, shows fiercely fighting to conquer it, the Winter
Palace is too much a hollow egg for comfort. In Eisenstein's
obscene anthropomorphization of the palace (it is not just the
jeweled peacock who acquires an 'anus', but also the room into
which Kerensky enters, and in notes Eisenstein made as he was
planning the montage of *October*, not only do the junkers wander
through the 'Voennoi' ['Military'] Gallery, but the unladylike ladies
of the Women's Battalion are to be placed in the chambers most
appropriate to their only real function: 'in the 'Rear' Rooms'[36]),
the nature of the place is revealed: the Winter Palace is, at its
heart, a slut. Like the objects it contains, it gives itself over to
new uses almost too easily, too loosely. Why should we trust it
now? (This is the anxiety that hovers over Vsevolod Pudovkin's
rival anniversary film, *The End of Saint Petersburg*, 1927. The huge
statues and imposing architecture that dominate so many of the
film's images are unforgiving reminders that the title is a hoax:
Leningrad is still haunted by 'St. Petersburg', by all the stone traces
of the past.)

October contains its own share of 'old blueprints', set cautiously
to work for new purposes. The map from 1913 on which the
Bolsheviks carefully trace the area to be encircled around the Winter
Palace is exactly that kind of blueprint: the tool and image of the
old regime, to be used to bring that world to an end.[37] Hegel's
Phenomenology of Mind is another one of these old maps, used against
itself (against the teleological progress of the world-spirit) and yet
capable, still, of unexpected infections and eruptions, as its images
spill into the corridors of a new museum. These images and the
images of *October* – and perhaps, in the end, any image – hold more
meaning than any single *Begriff* can control.

Hegel's organs of *Zeugung* und *Pissen* (of 'generation' and of
'pissing') come as the final *Bild*, or image, in a section of the
Phenomenology about the dangers of settling for images when what
you're after is *Begriffe* (concepts) – or settling for skulls when you
seek the mind. In fact, the chapter is largely devoted to phrenology.

Eisenstein confesses in his memoirs: 'I have been attracted by bones and skeletons since childhood. An attraction amounting to a sort of malady.' (IM, p. 72) Yes: he also is attracted to graphology, to psychoanalysis, to physiognomy, to hieroglyphs and in general to the image; his 'malady' would seem to be the one diagnosed in Hegel as 'picture-thinking'. When, in his 1929 essay 'Perspectives', he digresses into a long consideration of the etymology of the word *obraz* ('image'), his interest in the twisting interconnections between 'content' and 'form' reveals a great affection for very complicated surfaces (and fantastic etymologies):

> [Y]ou have only to look in a dictionary, not a Greek one but a Russian dictionary of 'foreign words' and you will see that form in Russian is *obraz* or 'image'. 'Image' [*obraz*] is itself a cross between the concepts of 'cut' [*obrez*] and 'disclosure' [*obnaruzhenie*]. These two terms brilliantly characterize form from both its aspects: from the *individually static* (*an und für sich*) standpoint as 'cut' [*obrez*], the *isolation* [*otmezhivanie*] of a particular phenomenon from its surroundings (e.g. a non-Marxist definition of form, such as Leonid Andreyev's, which confines itself *strictly* to this definition).

> 'Disclosure' [*obnaruzhenie*] characterizes image from a different, socially active standpoint: it 'discloses', i.e. establishes the social *link* between a particular phenomenon and its surroundings.

> Put more colloquially, 'content' [*soderzhanie*] – the act of containing [*sderzhivanie*] – is an *organizational principle*.

> The principle of the organization of thinking is in actual fact the 'content' of a work.

> A principle that materializes in the sum total of socio-physiological stimulants and for which form serves as a means of *disclosure*.[38]

Perhaps there is another layer of etymological free association relevant here: the word *obrezanie*, which means 'cutting' or 'circumcision'. Circumcision, after all, is an excellent example of a 'cut' that 'discloses', that 'establishes the social link between a particular phenomenon [or person] and its surroundings'. Eisenstein's very attempts to create cinema that is philosophy reveal (disclose) that picture and concept are as imbricated in each other as phallus and penis: you can't, to be graphic about it, lop one off without lopping off the other. Nor can you keep the two in any kind of determined and constant relation: just as phallus and penis inexplicably and unpredictably tend to switch identities, the organ of generation suddenly revealing itself to be merely the organ of urination or *vice versa,* so philosophy and picture-thinking cannot do without – but tend unexpectedly to undo – each other.

In notes from 1928, on a sheet of paper that begins with the phrase 'In cinema the gods and Kerensky', Eisenstein meditates on the relationship between two kinds of dialectics: the Hegelian (idealistic) dialectic and an ironic dialectic, to which evidently the gods and Kerensky belong. These two dialectics have, themselves, a dialectical relationship: where 'idealism' reigns, there one must find also the other approach: 'On an equal footing with Hegel there actually exists another dialectic, united with him as far as method goes, but calling itself... the ironic dialectic!'[39] Eisenstein sees in this coexistence of 'ideal' and 'irony' a confirmation of Lenin's insistence on the dialectical relationship between 'theory' and 'practice':

> The nature [of this relationship] is such that theory 'strains' towards materialization (towards its putting into practice)...
>
> practice in turn tends 'towards its theoretical' basis...
>
> This 'yearning for each other' of two separate or separated elements... is the most 'lawful' of tendencies...
>
> This law of yearning for each other is one.
>
> Theory cannot 'hang' in 'airless space'.
>
> It has to 'materialize'.[40]

Abstract thinking longs to materialize itself in an image. The dialectic used here to Hegel's disadvantage (the Gods sequence revealed as an attempt to undo not just God, but also Hegel) is, nevertheless, as the same sequence reveals, a double-edged sword. These complex surfaces – form and content, image and concept, irony and idealism – are engaged in an ongoing process of call-and-response. Nothing can be counted on to be as hollow as it appears.

The Gods sequence tries to achieve a new kind of intellectual montage by revealing the slippage that occurs between image and concept, between *Bild* and *Begriff*:

> Whereas idea and image are completely synonymous in the first Baroque image, they grow further apart with each subsequent image. We retain the description 'God' and show idols that in no way correspond with our own image of this concept. From this we are to draw anti-religious conclusions as to what the divine as such really is. Similarly, there is here an attempt to draw a purely intellectual conclusion as a resultant of the conflict between a preconception and its *gradual tendentious discrediting by degrees* through pure illustration.[41]

It turns out that more than 'God' has been 'discredited' by such a procedure. As Eisenstein unlinks *Bild* from *Begriff*, he would seem to be deconstructing the very idea of intellectual montage, all hope of getting images to communicate particular concepts in a consciously controllable manner. If image and concept are fundamentally slippery, no longer held in any kind of tight correspondence, then perhaps we should see the 'Gods' sequence not as evidence that '*Capital* – the Movie' is possible (as Noel Carroll does), but as a warning that most likely such a project will prove impossible.

Since the very idea of image and concept (or 'signifier' and 'signified') being tied together in a straightforward way has been damaged by the demonstration of slippage provided in *October*'s 'Gods' sequence, we may also be right to worry again about those other troublesome signifiers, Lenin and Trotsky. Is the *obraz* of Lenin, like that of God, perhaps threatened by a sudden kind of *pustota*, or 'hollowness'? Does the image of Trotsky, no matter how carefully cut down to size, threaten to rise up unbidden and demand our attention, perhaps even our respect? (To put the problem in more 'Hegelian' terms: Is Lenin always sufficiently phallic? Is Trotsky never more than a 'pissing organ'?) The uncertainties of these dialectical transitions (like that from history to 'History') make representation – and all games with the *obraz* – dangerous, if vastly alluring. The Eisenstein who longed (Thomas-like) to touch History seems in his writings of 1928–1929 to be longing to touch the *Begriff*. But what his work, both visual and theoretical, reveals is not so much the *Begriff* in all its phallic majesty, as the concept's perhaps mortal wounds.

4. Excavating *The General Line*: The Pleasures and Perils of Accumulation

> As always the echo, the juncture, is found only at the polar extremes.
>
> *Sergei Eisenstein, 1928*

As he worked on his films of the 1920s, Eisenstein was rediscovering the erotic and intellectual potential of image-based thinking, a potential that expressed itself in collisions and explosions. Instead of the short-circuiting jump into abstraction that had brought the ire of Viktor Shklovsky down on 'thinking in images' in 'Art as Device', Eisenstein's images promised a physical as well as intellectual clash or, as Eisenstein calls it in a 1929 essay, 'copulation'. In a manner quite typical of Eisenstein's mental processes, a profound intellectual discovery – that art based on montage is nothing less than (as he says) 'a unique 'figurative' transformation of the dialectic' – is implicitly supported at a crucial moment in this article by the happy coincidence that a category of Chinese characters has a name with obscene overtones in Russian. Having dwelt for a moment on the intriguing qualities of hieroglyphs which have evolved from pictorial representation of actual objects (the essay's example is the horse), Eisenstein moves on to what strikes him as even more satisfying:

> But to hell with the horse and with the 607 remaining symbols of the *hsiang-cheng*, the first *representational* category of hieroglyphs.
>
> It is with the second category of hieroglyphs – the *huei-i*, or 'copulative' – that our real interest begins.
>
> The point is that the copulation [*sovokuplenie*] – perhaps we had better say the combination – of two hieroglyphs of the simplest series is regarded not as their sum total but as their product, i.e. as a value of

another dimension, another degree: each taken separately corresponds to an object but their combination corresponds to a *concept*.[1]

This description of 'picture-thinking' as a business made possible by copulating ideograms, the Chinese term for which sounds so beautifully like one of the rudest Russian words for the male sexual organ, synthesizes many of Eisenstein's interests in the 1920s under the new star of eroticism. The 'copulation' involved creates another dimension (a new point of view) and allows the transfiguration of object into concept (a concept that never loses the traces of its image-ancestors).

The fundamental operation on which such transfigurations depend is described in another 1929 essay as 'superimposition', a process underlying even such basic cinematic sensations as movement and depth:

> For: the idea (sensation) of movement arises in the process of superimposing on the retained impression of the object's first position the object's newly visible second position.

> That is how, on the other hand, the phenomenon of spatial depth as the optical superimposition of two planes in stereoscopy arises. The superimposition of two dimensions of the same mass gives rise to a completely new higher dimension.[2]

The superimposition made possible by 'retained impressions' – the quality of human perception traditionally called 'persistence of vision' – in Eisenstein's aesthetic universe results not only in synthesis, but in conflict:

> In the realm of art this dialectic principle of dynamics is embodied in

> CONFLICT

> as the fundamental principle for the existence of every artwork and every art-form.

> *For art is always conflict:*

> (1) according to its social mission,

> (2) according to its nature,

> (3) according to its methodology.[3]

Conflict, superimposition, synthesis, clash, copulation: these terms for that which drives art forward are themselves superimposed with explosive result.

> If we are to compare montage with anything, then we should compare
> a phalanx of montage fragments – 'shots' – with the series of
> explosions of the internal combustion engine, as these fragments
> multiply into a montage dynamic through 'impulses' like those that
> drive a car or a tractor.[4]

Art not only is 'like' dialectical thinking but actually – inasmuch as
the engine at the heart of the aesthetic machine could be
superimposed upon that driving philosophy – *is* dialectical thinking;
the name of the machine is 'montage'. Eisenstein insists with his
usual combination of seriousness and obscenity that the laws of
dialectical thought can be understood in terms not only of copulating
hieroglyphs, but also of mechanical pistons in motion.

The apotheosis of 'superimposition' can be found in Eisenstein's
film project of the second half of the 1920s, the filmic depiction of
life and change in the Soviet countryside called during most of the
period of its construction *The General Line*. Eisenstein and Alexandrov
had become interested in this project in early 1926, while still basking
in the triumph of the *Battleship Potemkin* (which was finishing its first
run in theaters around the end of January). Two instigators seemed
to have governed the choice of theme, one 'conceptual' (the
resolutions of the 14th Party Congress, held in December 1925) and
the other a real aesthetic inspiration or '*materializator*': a small book
(*Maklochane*) by O Davydov, published in early 1926, about the growth
of Soviet cooperation in the countryside.[5] This book, the title of which
means *The Inhabitants of Maklochko*, combining meticulous charts and
tables with anecdotes from the lives of the peasants living in one
small village, traced the evolution of a Soviet dairy cooperative in
the first half of the 1920s and was itself in every way an embodiment
of the platform of the 14th Congress.[6] The first literary scenario was
completed in June 1926,[7] and until the 'order' (*zakaz*) came from
Kalinin in 1927 to switch their attention to *October*, Eisenstein,
Alexandrov and Tisse worked feverishly on the agricultural project,
which in its logistics presented particular problems (traveling over
the country to find true 'peasant types', shooting away from the
studio). By the time the trio could return to work on *The General Line*
in 1928, times had changed, as had the line of the party. The film
was completed, but not before a direct intervention from Stalin
(described in Alexandrov) that led to the re-christening of the film as
'Staroe i novoe' ('The Old and the New').[8] Under its new title the
film premiered after Eisenstein, Alexandrov and Tisse had already
left for Europe and America in 1929. At that time Eisenstein described
the film in Shklovskian terms: 'The whole *General Line* is constructed

on the basis of the syncope: the traditional-automatic conception comes into collision with the new and unexpected.'[9] The nature of this clash, however, is complex: a superimposition that is also a copulation. When the elements involved are the 'old' and the 'new', 'history' and 'the present', and when those categories succeed each other at the breakneck pace at work in Soviet politics in the 1920s (so that last year's 'new' is now already 'old' and must be subsumed into the next dialectical conflict), the possibility for trouble is always nigh. An archaeological approach to *The General Line/ The Old and the New* reveals layer after layer of superimposed lines (or official ideologies); the new cannot merely liquidate the old, and the disquieting traces of the old are to be felt everywhere.

While working on *October*, during the enforced hiatus in the production of *The General Line*, Eisenstein had become more and more intrigued by the possibilities of montage not just to shock an audience into 'necessarily ideological conclusions' (as he had famously attempted to do with his inter-cutting of slaughterhouse scenes with the rout of the workers at the end of *Strike*), but indeed to convey the intricacies of intellectual thought by means of the conjunction of images. He was so taken with these ideas, which in *October* had led to the famous sequence deconstructing God, that he began, as we have also seen, to make plans for a film based on Marx's *Capital*. *The General Line* was a kind of practice ground for the future project: what he hoped to do for *Capital* in the future, Eisenstein was in a sense doing for Stalin's speeches in *The General Line*. In short, he screened the 'figures' (the 'hieroglyphs') of the ideological discourse emanating from the top of the Soviet political structure and superimposed them blithely as they changed. To analyze *The General Line* is to excavate a cinematic Troy, a city that has changed political hands several times over.

Both of the film's titles come directly from Stalin's speeches. At the 14th Party Congress, in December 1925, Stalin had thundered that there were:

> Two General Lines: one assumes that our country must remain still for a long while an *agrarian* land, that we should export our agricultural products and import machinery [...] This Line demands in fact that we simply roll up our industry. This Line leads to the conclusion that our country will never, or almost never, be able to industrialize independently... that our country should become a mere appendage to the general system of capitalism... This is not our line!
>
> There's another General Line, which assumes that we should put all our forces to work in order to turn our country, while it is still

surrounded by capitalist forces, into a country that is economically *independent*, based on its own *internal* market... This line decisively rejects the policy of turning our country into an appendage of the world system of capital. THIS is *our* line of construction, held by our Party now and one the Party will continue to hold in the future.[10]

Stalin's recipe for this General Line included voluntary agrarian cooperation, 'tractorization', the reinforcement of 'differentiation', or contrast, between classes in the countryside while underscoring the ties of progressive forces with the 'middle peasant' (*seredniak*) and the need to wage a war with 'bureaucratism' (p. 96). These were the themes Eisenstein and Alexandrov undertook to illustrate in *The General Line*.

At the 15th Party Congress, at the end of 1927, the same Congress where Trotsky's discrediting was officially completed, Stalin shifted his tropes. This is where most analysts examining the film – Yon Barna or Jay Leyda, for example – go astray when they claim that the reason for *The Old and the New s* name change is that 'Even as altered [after *October* and personal consultation with Stalin], the authorities were cool to *The General Line* and to prevent its identification with any Party policy, scaled down its release title to the less specific *The Old and the New*' (Leyda).[11] The phrase 'old and new' may sound like a rather apolitical substitute for a very political 'general line', but in fact it is another trope taken right from Stalin's speeches. At the 15th Congress, Stalin said, in a burst of poetic – if sinister –imagery:

> We will never be able, so long as there are classes, to say 'well, thank God, now everything's great'. That will never be the case here, comrades. Here there is always something in life that's in the process of dying out. But that which is dying out doesn't want to just get on with it and die, but rather fights for its existence, insists on its own outlived business. Here there is always being born into life something new. But that which is being born is not simply born, but wails and cries, insisting on *its* right to exist. (*Voices*: 'True!' *Applause*.) The battle between old and new, between that which is dying out and that which is being born – this is the basis of our development.[12]

One could say, in short, that 'The General Line' tackles the problem of Russian self-sufficiency (the Soviet renunciation of the marriage with Europe proposed by Lenin), while 'The Old and the New' picks up on the copula again, the tricky and interesting moment for both Stalin and Eisenstein being not the 'new' per se, nor the 'old', but rather the 'AND' where 'old' and 'new' collide and interact.

As Eisenstein and Alexandrov prepared the literary scenario, they collected a vast array of material potentially useful in their project. Thanks to Eisenstein's already well-developed sense of the need to preserve some sort of picture of his own development, he kept these materials in his 'archive' (as Alexandrov already called it in 1926). Here we find a real mish-mash of things, including a pamphlet containing the resolutions of the 14th Party Congress, several issues of the journal *Batrak* ['Farm Laborer'] (on one of which Eisenstein has defaced a picture of Comrade DI Kurskii, People's Commissar of Justice and Public Prosecutor of the Republic, by giving him a suit of clothes and a huge erection) and the copy of 'Molochnoe khoziastvo' ['Dairy Farming'] with the review of *Maklochane* (already praising Eisenstein in June 1926 for having chosen to make a film based on the book), articles clipped from *Pravda* and elsewhere about progress in agriculture, ads for 'milk coolers', and even brochures from the US Department of Agriculture.

From the start of the project, one of the key moments was always the milk cooperative's purchase, on government credit, of a separator, the device that would become such an eroticized symbol in Eisenstein's film. Already in scribbled plans (dated 23 May 1926) for the first literary scenario the word 'Separator' appears on the first sheet with three penciled exclamation points following.[13] Although Eisenstein would take the symbol much further, the 'cream separator' had already been marked in *Maklochane* as a central device in the transformation of the Soviet countryside. The review in *Molochnoe khoziaistvo*, recognizing the importance of this machine to the book, was entitled 'Hymn to the Separator', and the reviewer went so far as to base on the separator his hopes for a new Soviet agriculture:

> One can say it directly: where a large-scale separator has appeared, the seed of a new form of agriculture has been set in place. With the development of the marketing work of the dairy artel, the seed brought by the separator will lead to young green shoots of a new agricultural culture.[14]

Why was the 'separator' seen as the 'seed' of the future? What made the separator so richly symbolic that even in the first literary scenario of *General Line*, its entrance is the emotional center of the film?

The shining of the separator became symbolic.

The shining of the separator astounded the peasants.

THE SEPARATOR WILL MAKE IT POSSIBLE TO MAKE BUTTER.

The muzhiks opened their eyes wider.

Higher they stretched their heads.

Evdokiia poured milk into the separator.

The faces of the peasants are tense.

They await! Await! Await a miracle.

WILL IT THICKEN OR NOT?

The wheel goes around. The separator glitters. The crowd falls quiet.

DECEPTION OR PROFIT?

They wait the way the 'Battleship Potemkin' waited for a salvo [added in pencil: 'upon its encounter with the Squadron'].[15]

The milk separator was already a very important machine for the agricultural economy at the end of the nineteenth century, as evidenced by the space devoted to the topic in the Brockhaus-Efron Encyclopedia, volume 'S', 1900.[16]

Figure 16.
'The Milk Separator',
Brockhaus-Efron Encyclopedia,
1900

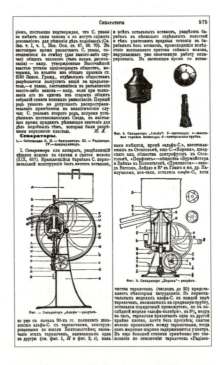

Using the principle that cream is lighter than milk and will generally rise to the top, the separator made that process much faster by spinning the milk and causing the centrifugal separation of the lighter cream from the heavier fluid. For the peasants of Maklochko, the importance of the separator lies in its speeding up of the transformation of milk, which spoils quickly, into the longer-lived commodity butter, which can be collected and sold at a profit. Even in Davydov's book, the separator's transformative process is watched with awe and narrative tension by the peasants:

> These six people managed to wheedle out of the authorities a small separator on credit. Along the mossy swamp, without good roads to follow, surprised horses pulled the shining machine for the first time... A month flew by. The inhabitants of Maklochko began to arrive, sidling up cautiously, on the veranda. They stood for hours, watching the dairy brothers churn butter; in whispers they criticized the uneven stream, trying to convince the others – but most of all themselves – that the comrades were swindling them, were pouring water into the milk. Obelit [the agronomist] quietly turned the handle of the machine, the stream was as thin and brittle as straw – and then suddenly on purpose he disrupted the measured pace of the separator, wildly flashing his palm, the milk instantly thickened – and gushed forth in a thick stream of curds. Then they understood: the flow depends on the force of revolution, the number of cycles a minute.[17]

The separator also fits wonderfully into the resolutions of the 14th Congress and responds to their figures, their tropes, as well. The Congress called for 'differentiation' in the countryside, so that the interests of the poor and middle peasants could be promoted. The separator provides exactly that, it 'separates' so that the 'cream' of the peasantry, the good, poor peasants, can rise to the top. The Separator transforms and transfigures: not only milk into cream and poverty into prosperity, but also the overly agrarian countryside into a more industrial environment (the separator is a machine).[18] In this regard it is interesting to look again at Stalin's words about the 'general line' that must be abandoned (that is, the Soviet Union as agricultural country): 'one [General Line] assumes that our country must remain still for a long while an *agrarian* land, that we should export our agricultural products and import machinery... This Line demands in fact that we simply roll up our industry.' The term Stalin uses here for 'roll up' (*svërtyvanie*) also means 'to curdle': if we remain agrarian and backward, our industry will curdle. The separator is an important element in the ongoing fight against curdling.

Not only is the separator richly figurative in its name and function, but it is also sexually evocative in its appearance, a feature which appealed to Eisenstein and which, as he turned the transformation of milk into cream into an ecstatic event, he played on amply. Not for nothing is the separator, playing its double role as Marxian and

Freudian fetish, the 'seed' of the new Soviet agriculture. The cream/ semen that bursts forth from the separator's spout to spatter the faces of ecstatic onlookers is a sign that they have, finally, found 'the Grail' (as Eisenstein labeled the Separator in later notes),[19] the key to future fecundity and prosperity. This latter point is crucial: the ecstasy experienced by the separator's onlookers represents, among all its other meanings, also quite an odd pleasure for Soviet Russia – the thrills of the accumulation of capital. It is the separator that allows the dairy cooperative to begin making real money. 'Deception or profit?' wonder the peasants in the first scenario: by 1928 (in later scenarios) that has become the less overtly capitalist 'Deception or money?'.

Figure 17.
'Profit!' (*The General Line*)

One of the things buried in the many layers of meaning in the *General Line* is this flirtation with the ecstasies of capitalist accumulation. *Maklochane* is a peculiar book because of its treatment of this issue. The narrative is overwhelmed with an obsession with profit. All the tables and charts serve to create in the reader the fierce desire to see these peasants 'enrich themselves' (as Bukharin had urged in late 1925, to immediate and furious controversy).[20] Following the narrative formula of the rags to riches story, the peasants painfully struggle towards the goal – the holy grail – of profitability. If their children must go without milk in the mean time, so be it: profit-making is an exercise in delayed gratification, as is made clear in the following passage (describing the ultimate results of the economy transformed by the separator):

> Thus Aleksandr Ivanovich Petrov for the first time milked out of his milch cow the equivalent of 15 poods 20 pounds of bread. The children of Aleksandr Ivanovich saw very little milk that year – under the curses of his wife and the teasing of his neighbors Aleksandr Ivanovich took the milk away to Zagriaz'e.

> If you count twenty-one accumulated separators, several churns and an agricultural library bought against profits of 3200 rubles, the general profit of the inhabitants of Maklochko equaled 6000 rubles. Consequently, one family in a half year of work produced almost 12 rubles of pure profit.
>
> Now I ask you, reader: would Aleksandr Ivanovich Petrov or Vasilii Ivanovich Morozov have accumulated on their three-field portion plus the extra from hiring themselves out, apart from the productive accumulation in the form of a five-field portion of land, vetch, clover, a heifer, an improved cow-shed and increased milk-yield from the healthier milch cow – an accumulation of 12 rubles in a year?... [N]o, only the revolution, thickening in that portion of land and collectively raising the qualifications of the Maklochko workforce, could have given them that 12 rubles.[21]

The Revolution, 'thickening' like cream in the countryside, brings profit to the peasant households if they are willing to trade immediate gratification – the calves they used to feast on immediately, the milk they used to let their own children drink – for the thrills of capitalist accumulation.

With its charts and tables allowing the reader to count every accumulated coin along with the peasants whose labor has enabled this accumulation, *Maklochane* becomes not just a hymn to the separator, but a hymn to profit and the heroine of this rags-to-riches story, a war widow named Evdokiia Ukraintseva, is praised for all those qualities that make a Horatio Alger hero so successful (except that she does not depend on luck): hard work, cheerfulness, savvy use of available resources. She is the first one to see the advantage of the new ways of agriculture promoted by the 'agronomist', a 'Northerner' named Ian Obelit and she is quick to add the latest agricultural improvements – in this case a 'Danish feeding trough' – to her very poor but very clean household. She is the one who suggests that the families in the dairy cooperative use their profit to buy 'breeding bulls and good fodder', 'so that our cows might be a support to us and to our State' and she weathers the laughter of the naysayers without batting an eye.

The reader is apparently intended to follow with breathless attention the slow crawl of the 'Maklochane' [the inhabitants of Maklochko] towards profit and prosperity. Then the book shifts its focus, in its final chapter, to a figure who seems at first to exemplify all of the good qualities praised in those peasants, like Evdokiia Ukraintseva, who manage to improve themselves and their households. Here is a person, Egorii Malofeev by name, who not only has increased the number of his cows and lands, but has managed to build a small factory:

> 'Our chairman then was a good one... When I began building the candy factory, I didn't have enough money, so he lent me 100 million in 1923 – a good man.'

With these words of Egorii Malofeev the author opens a final chapter from the life of the diamond-in-the-rough from Gdov:

> They come from the last months of 1925, when the farm of Egorii with the help of... the good communists had attained the following results:
>
> 80 *desiatin*[22] of land for mowing and plowing,
>
> 20 milch cows,
>
> 5 or 6 carthorses fed on clover,
>
> a horse-driven threshing machine,
>
> a candy factory,
>
> bakeries.
>
> Far beyond the boundaries of Gdovshchina resounded the heroic name of Egorii. His name fills many, many with just hopes and love – and is pronounced with great respect by the local muzhiks.[23]

The narrator 'praises' his industry and cleverness for many pages and then, suddenly, the tables turn: 'However... haven't we had enough of this joking, reader?' (p. 60). Sure enough, the next little section is titled 'The Chapter In Which the Heroes Take Off Their Masks' (p. 60).[24] It turns out that the narrator has been being ironic all along, that this fine farmer and businessman is a *kulak*, one of those terrible exploiters whose destruction is heartily to be wished.[25] The use of irony has an extraordinarily unbalancing effect here, because, in fact, the sins of the *kulak* are, the book has unwittingly revealed, indistinguishable from the virtues of the hardworking, profit-seeking peasants of the Maklochko dairy cooperative, whose attempts to make a profit and increase their riches have been the focus of the narrator's attention and praise up until this final section.

One of the deep layers of meaning buried in the *General Line* is this hymn to capital accumulation and growth (in the spirit of Bukharin's 'Peasant, enrich thyself!'). Even with the term 'profit' exiled from the later scenario of the film, the narrative of improvement follows structures whose form is by no means specifically loyal to its socialist context. Eisenstein's film puts a considerable amount of visual energy into making the kulaks unambiguously evil: they are 'unmasked' by camera angles that stress their corpulence and mark their greed and by 1928 they have become the poisoners of the bull Fomka (who previously was to have died due to mishandling on the part of the peasants); the kulaks by then are huge lazy louts whose function is that of a centripetal force, a gravity well of evil.

Other changes in the film's scenarios between 1926 and 1928 serve to repress the story's strong connection between capital accumulation and libidinal drives. Central to *Maklochane* – and still present in the 1926 literary scenario of *General Line* – was the question of how to keep men (themselves a scarce commodity after the Civil War) in the village. Evdokiia is a Civil War widow in the original text. The 1926 scenario began with the peasants besieging the house of the local landowner (whose bloodthirsty, rifle-shooting, whip-wielding daughter would reappear in one of the *Que Viva Mexico* episodes some years later) during the fight that would widow the *soldatka* (soldier's widow) and a title informs us later that once the separator and the bull have improved the lot of the peasants, 'for the first time the son did not go off to the city'.[26] Two years later, the female lead who starts off as Evdokiia, the *soldatka*, will have become Marfa, the poor, single peasant woman and she will no longer have a son to try to save from the temptations of the city.

One of the advantages of profit, then, is that it keeps men on the land. There is a sexual tinge to this lesson about the advantages of growth that survives into the later scenario even though the explicit moments (the need to keep male peasants from wandering away from the land in search of temporary work) have vanished. Progress and profit are erotic things, in *The Old and the New* as well as in *General Line*.

Almost as famous as the erotic explosions of the separator sequence is the episode of 'Marfa's dream', in which the dozing heroine has a vision of a magical bull bringing prosperity, fecundity and rain to the parched countryside.[27] *Maklochane* was a book resolutely hostile to frivolity; the dream of the dairywoman, in which sex, rain and milk are all 'superimposed', is a quintessential Eisenstein invention. In the 1926 version of *General Line*'s scenario this dream amounts to a slightly comic 'aside' on the part of Evdokiia, who awakens at the end of it to discover that while she was dozing, her compatriots have been raiding the till.

'Sun once, sun twice, sun till unconsciousness.'

The soldier's widow fell a-dozing in the dairy artel.

And up to the soldier's widow came her own scrawny cow. The cow pointed out her ribs, pointed out her skinny legs, her dry udders, her bony hindquarters – sad and tearful eyes covered with dung flies.

All the poor peasants' cows presented themselves to Evdokiia, mooed before her, got down on their knees and bowed their heads to her.

Evdokiia agreed – the cows took off at a gallop – they ran fast and struck poses as if they were at a physical education class. They looked up into the sky.

And like Mephistopheles in the clouds of steam and light appeared a Bull – ah! what a bull!

The bull surprised them with a leap. Bullish love was what they had needed.

The cows' udders filled with milk, their backbones grew straighter, their ribs disappeared. The nipples couldn't hold against the pressure of the milk – and a milky rain poured in torrents.

Laughing the soldier's widow awoke...[28]

Evdokiia's dream has a message so obvious that even the dreamer (without, we presume, ever having encountered Freud in the dairy cooperative's library) has to laugh: sex fills you up. She is punished very gently for dreaming by awakening to find the precious 'profit' in jeopardy, but she is able to save the money... and with it find a way to bring a real little bull to the hungry cows of the village.

Marfa's dream retains the wet thematics of Evdokiia's (much rainy milk), but there are certain essential differences. Marfa's dream is not, like Evdokiia's, an instance of 'falling asleep on the job': she only allows herself to dream after she (now only with the help of the Agronomist) has rescued the cooperative's money from the impatient peasants.

And when all the money was in the little chest, Marfa felt tired after all the great excitement and, happy that she had saved the money and that there would be a little bull after all, she dozed off.

And it seemed to Marfa that all the village cows were running toward the place where in the mornings dawn begins and the sun rises. And that from this very place there began to arise an enormous and powerful breeding bull.

And when his figure covered the whole sky, there gushed forth from the clouds a milky white rain, milky waterfalls poured and milky rivers began to run.

And just as snowy white, just as bright, sprouted up homes, cow barns, pigsties and houses for little chicks.

Marfa saw beautiful cows, completely unlike her own emaciated little cow. She saw pigs swimming in the river and sunning themselves on beaches.

She saw stalls as clean and bright as the halls of state banks.

Perhaps you think that this all is a dream?

Nothing of the sort.

Marfa has come to a Sovkhoz – and to a breeding farm, in order to buy, with the money that has been saved, a breeding calf for her collective farm. And when that calf had been bought, they named it Fomka.[29]

Marfa's dream turns out not to be a dream: it has no frame at the far end. Instead of the dream ending, the whole film enters into the dream... and stays there. This reflects the new impatience of the speeches of the 15th Congress (December 1927): progress has been too slow; let's just get there, to Communism, that 'meta-Sovkhoz'. In Stalin's terms, the 'new' must get on with the job of being born and the old must be thoroughly and speedily rooted out. The goal is no longer merely to change the country from an 'agrarian' land to an 'industrialized' one, but to 'catch up to and overtake the leading capitalist countries'.[30] The whole country, like Marfa, is invited to jump directly into a dream-made-real. She brings whole rivers and waterfalls of milk to the Soviet millwheel.

Marfa's dream of a utopian future without kulaks or exploitation takes her through a series of images of ecstatic, sensual abundance, to a 'real' model cooperative farm. It is ironic, however, considering the terms of Stalin's 'general line' as outlined at the 14th Congress (Russia, above all, must not be an 'appendage' [*pridatok*] to the West) that Eisenstein had to film these scenes of a utopian collective at a special farm imported lock, stock and barrel from Europe. Even the pigs are coddled English swine, about whom Eisenstein's co-director, Grisha Alexandrov, tells the following tale:

The Academician Mikhail Fedorovich Ivanov... brought over from England some Yorkshire pigs. They were provided with excellent, newly-built pigsties. The animals were really enormous, just like hippopotami. We hurried to film this novelty, too.

But there was panic on the farm: for a third day in a row the Yorkshire pigs had declined to take into their mouths the food that had been prepared for them according to a special recipe. They summoned from Moscow the Englishman who had accompanied the animals from Britain. He asked to be shown the food being given the pigs. He sniffs it, rolls the mash a bit between his fingers. Everybody insists to him,

'The food's been prepared just exactly according to the recipe.'

'But it has been prepared FILTHILY.'

The Englishman himself sets about fixing up the pigs' mash and the Yorkshire beauties don't leave their troughs until they've consumed it all.

...The Englishman continues to lay down the law. It seems that these pigs must have recreation time at the *beach*, in order to sun themselves and swim. Quickly this pleasure, too, is arranged, for the Yorkshire pigs. We film it all. All of this was so new to us! (GA 97–98)

Among the clippings Eisenstein collected as he worked on *The General Line* was a little notice in *Pravda* about a new 'bacon factory' [*bekonnyi zavod*], outfitted with Danish equipment and capable of processing 1000 pigs a week.[31] One of the stranger sequences in *The General Line* involves following the anthropomorphized sun-worshipping swine as they are processed into meat. Perhaps as a kind of antidote to *Strike*'s too-bourgeois use of the slaughterhouse as existential horror, the shots of pigs in the bacon factory are presented with unrelenting cheeriness: the scenes from the factory alternate with shots of a little porcelain piggy, twisting from left to right in seeming glee. In this world of imported utopias, imported pigs and imported tractors, the hysterically overplayed copulation between the genuinely Soviet bull Fomka and his bovine bride (a moment accompanied by colorized fireworks in original prints) functions, like the laughing piggy, as a kind of figurative and allegorized antidote, in this instance a veiled replay of Zeus's rape of *Europa*: 'Take that, Europe!' There is Stalin's 'General Line' – an end to our subordination to the West! – thought out for us in images.[32]

But since one of the ways Eisenstein reanimates 'picture-thinking' is by working with images that are invariably at least as complicated as the 'message' they are to convey (in other words – images very resistant to any single reduction), Fomka's reenactment of the Rape of Europa is not the only story being told here. Fomka's own origins are well worth excavating. In the 1926 scenario for *The General Line*, Fomka is described as the product of Sovkhoz genetic experiments,

experiments that begin with the arrival by airplane of a mysterious little box in which is contained a fly from Texas. On this Texan fly (more properly, on its numerous descendants), are performed all sorts of miracles:

> The scientists, though receiving little by way of salary, did great work. They created descendants of the Texas fly with four wings instead of two and instead of four feet, some had six or even twelve. They caused the fly to grow fur. They perfected this fur with regard to softness and length... And then the lessons learned on the flies were tried out on animals. These Soviet scientists caused sheep that from time immemorial had only produced two lambs to give birth at once to eight. Two udders couldn't satisfy eight lambs and so these Soviet 'magicians' created ewes with four udders... A rejuvenated chicken already in its fifth year laid eggs like a two-year-old. The 'magicians' [and here it's obvious Eisenstein and Alexandrov were uncomfortable with this inadequately scientific term, *fokusniki*; it's crossed out] sat in laboratories, looked through their microscopes at the flies and every day brought miracles. Chickens, cows, rams, seals, horses, pigs, rabbits, cats – all were perfected the way an automobile is perfected.[33]

Note that Fomka is produced as an automobile – or for that matter a tractor – is produced and, as notoriously in the case of Soviet tractors, the question of ultimate origin, Sovkhoz magicians or no, is an awkward one. Like the assembly line and the tractor, the miraculous modern Sovkhoz and its wonders of genetic engineering are haunted by the specter of foreign (and in particular American) paternity. When the peasants in search of little Fomka come to the Sovkhoz to pick him up, they find themselves in a fairyland where 'the very rams were Americans – Merinos and Lincolns'.[34] (Among the materials collected by Eisenstein as he prepared to make *General Line* is an issue of the *American Sheep Breeder and Wool Grower*, June 1926, containing an article entitled 'The Proper Way to Shear a Sheep'.)

Very interesting in this regard are Eisenstein's 1929 thoughts on how *The General Line* might be turned into a sound film:

> *In general*. The conflict of the agrarian theme (negative), localized in sugary Slavic melody and the industrial theme (positive), in the style of contemporary western music... The lapidary nature of the leitmotifs. Their development: for example the theme of the bull, developed out of the theme of Industry and so on...[35]

Fomka, the industrialized, Westernized animal, is needed to 'bring up the blood-lines' of the Russian countryside: here is an illustration not so much of Stalin's 'General Line' from the 14th Party Congress as of Lenin's suggestion to the capitalist West in 1920 that if Western technology, particularly tractors, could be combined with the rich, but fallow Soviet land, hunger could be defeated the world around:

> In the sovkhozes of the Don region there are up to 800,000 *desiatin* that we are unable to cultivate and for the cultivation of which is needed an enormous quantity of livestock or whole detachments of tractors, which we can't produce, but certain capitalist countries, including some in desperate need of food – Austria, Germany, Bohemia – could send those tractors and receive superb wheat in a summer's campaign. To what degree we'll be able to realize this proposal, we do not know. At this time we have two tractor factories working, in Moscow and Petrograd, but as a result of difficult circumstances they can't produce a large number of tractors. We would be able to alleviate the situation with the purchase of a greater number of tractors. Tractors are the most important means for a radical break with old agricultural methods and for the increasing of our arable land. With these concessions we can show a whole series of countries that we are able to develop a world-class economy of gigantic proportions... The Soviet Republic is coming forward and saying: 'We have hundreds of thousands of superb lands that could be improved with tractors and you have tractors, you have fuel and you have trained technicians and here we offer to all people, including the people in capitalist countries, the chance to lay the cornerstone for a renaissance in agriculture and the salvation of all nations from hunger.'[36]

Lenin's sub rosa presence in the 'Fomka' story is underscored by the 1926 scenario's remark that the peasants name the best of the young calves fathered by the industrializing bull 'Stalin'. Fomka, appropriately (making room for his heir), dies shortly thereafter, the victim in the book *Maklochane* of his owners' ignorance (they let him eat the wrong grasses) and in the final post-*October* versions of kulak treachery. Actually, Fomka has double successors: not just the calf 'Stalin', about which we know nothing more than that he exists (in the final film the calf comforts Marfa, but is not named), but also the tractor finally wrested from the bureaucratic labyrinths of the city: the 'Fordson' (or, more affectionately, 'Fordzosha')[37] who is the real heir to Fomka's place at the center of the village's hopes for the future.

In the 1926 scenario the tractor claims its preeminence by a nonchalant 'crashing' of a mythological tableau. The Komsomolets Vas'ka races to show he can reap as fast as the best of the prior generation, a peasant with the suggestive nickname of *Gigant* (at some points *Velikan* – both meaning 'Giant'): a title labels the situation for us as 'THE OLD STORY OF DAVID AND GOLIATH'.[38] Then 'a mechanical noise interrupted their work' (l. 43); the peasants look up in shock to discover that they have totally misunderstood the nature of socialist competition. A tractor from the Sovkhoz is harvesting grain at a rate mere human beings could never hope to imitate; in fact, the whole concept of agricultural labor is suddenly different: 'The tractor driver was smoking and sat in the shade of the umbrella – the harvester worked on agilely.' (l. 44) Their sweat, their competition, their generational struggles (that 'OLD STORY') are suddenly all shown to be nonsensical. It is perhaps not too surprising that the early scenario's emphasis on the tractorist's easy life vanishes in the later version of the film; perhaps the lesson it seemed to be teaching ('What's the point of effort anyhow?') was felt to be too much of an 'old story' in its own right.

In the film there is a charming montage sequence depicting a tractor 'assembling itself', a piece of trick-film worthy of Dziga Vertov; this serves as a fig leaf hiding the question of origins which, if troubling in the case of Fomka, are blatantly problematic in the case of the 'Fordzosha'. Soviet production of tractors (as Lenin hinted in 1920) was extremely limited – perhaps as few as eleven in 1924 – and remained so into the mid-twenties.[39] The Fordson – no longer named in a title in the film, but clearly identified by a shot of its nameplate – is a symbol of Soviet technological progress, but it is also a symbol of lingering backwardness. In the latter half of the 1920s the Soviet performed a cautious dance around a set of dangerous contradictions, managing to embrace 'Fordizm' as an essential part of – rather than hindrance to – the idea of 'Socialism in one country'.[40]

The multiple identities brought into play here do not fit easily together: Fomka the bull, bovine offshoot of the 'theme of industry' and distant offspring of a 'Texan fly', represents not only Lenin and/or Stalin, but also the industrial influence of the West; the flower-bedecked cow he tackles is not just Europa, but also the as yet inadequately fertilized agrarian backwardness of Russia (in which case, we have another interpretation: what Stalin, say, is doing to the countryside is more or less what Zeus did to Europa).[41] It is the explosive potential not only of the 'copulating ideograms' here but of the multiple and colliding paradigms those ideograms represent that makes for scandal. The Rape of Europa becomes also, paradoxically, an incestuous attack on a parent (the West) one is loath to acknowledge.

The history of *General Line* is one of scandalous junctures between 'old' and 'new'. In 1928, as he was taking up work on the film once again after the hiatus of 1927, Eisenstein wrote an article about the

Kabuki theater, an essay that became famous in the English-speaking world as 'The Unexpected' when it appeared as part of *Film Form* in 1949. In that later incarnation, however, as part of the collection designed to make Eisenstein's name as a serious thinker, the essay was bowdlerized, deprived of half of its title and almost all of its scandal. The original title was 'An Unexpected Juncture' (*Nezhdannyi styk*) and the earlier version is framed by the sort of vigorously animated figure of speech of which Eisenstein was very fond: 'Milk a billy-goat? Agricultural practice is unaware of the operation. It is said that a billy-goat provides neither wool nor milk. It has another firmly established reputation and other honorable functions.' (SW1 115) As we have seen earlier, the billy-goat's 'honorable function' is that same sort of *styk*, or 'junction', which is also the special field of Fomka the bull: insemination. The proverb's slightly wicked association of milk and semen is completely in the spirit of *The General Line*, as is the general subject of the essay, which is all about the potential for reciprocal influence between the Kabuki theater of Japan and Soviet 'montage'-based sound cinema.

The billy-goat of 'Unexpected Juncture' is the Kabuki theater, the 'contrapuntal' techniques of which make it not only a potentially powerful inseminating force, but also (in that bisexual logic so prevalent in *General Line*), ripe for appropriation. The Kabuki has 'instinctively' grasped those rules and techniques which lie at the basis of Eisenstein's dreams for the future of sound cinema, in that the Japanese have created a truly 'monistic ensemble' (as opposed to 'the theater that is denoted by that nasty word "synthetic"'): 'Sound, movement, space and voice *do not accompany* (or even parallel) one another but are treated as *equivalent elements*.' (SW1 117) The elements brought together in the 'sensual thinking' (picture-thinking no longer limited solely to visual images) based on this kind of juncture do not 'synthesize' into some seamless whole, nor is one half of the juncture annihilated by its encounter with the other element, for in Eisenstein's version of the dialectical image the collision/copulation continues into the 'new'. In other words, a metaphor or figure of speech is never made perfectly hollow: the billy-goat persists even after he has delivered his message. Eisenstein's encounter with the Kabuki inspires him to make some particularly dramatic junctures; consider, for example, the description-by-comparison of the Kabuki as football match:

> The first association that occurs to us in our perception of the Kabuki is *football*, that most collective ensemble sport. Voice, rattle, mime, the

narrator's cries, the folding sets seem like innumerable backs, half-backs, goalkeepers, forwards passing the dramatic ball to one another and scoring a goal against the astonished audience.

In the original, the strangeness of this comparison is accentuated by the foreign words (*khavbeki*, *golkipery* are 'halfbacks' and 'goalkeepers' in Cyrillic disguise) as much as by the brazenness of the comparison. The reader is probably just as astonished as the spectator.

At the end of his article, Eisenstein claims that the most effective (if hazardous) junctures are those orchestrated between seeming opposites, those that are the most 'unexpected':

> As always the echo, the juncture, is found only at the polar extremes. The archaic non-differentiated sense of the Kabuki's 'stimulants' on the one hand and, on the other, the acme of the development of *montage thinking*.

> Montage thinking, the peak of the differentiatedly sensed and expounded 'organic' world, is realised anew in a mathematically faultless instrument, the machine.

> We recall Kleist's words that are so close to the Kabuki theatre that derives 'from puppets': 'The perfection of the actor lies either in the body that has no consciousness at all or has the maximum consciousness, that is, in the puppet or the "demi-god".'

> The extremes meet...

> There is no point in grumbling about the soullessness of the Kabuki or, even worse, in finding in Sadanji's acting a *'confirmation* of Stanislavsky's theory'! Or in looking for something that Meyerhold 'has not yet stolen'!

> Broadly speaking, that's... milk from a billy-goat.

> *The Kabuki can only celebrate its juncture with the sound film*! (SW1 121, translation modified for accuracy)

Even in his use of Kleist's famous marionette theater, Eisenstein exaggerates the contrariness of his comparisons: the Kabuki may be the equivalent of a puppet and 'montage thinking' like a Kleistian 'demi-god', but that god-like consciousness is itself... a machine. In *Strike*, the mind was required to oscillate madly between contradictory poles, but here the contradictions exist simultaneously: they accumulate. Kabuki and the sound film, organic world and perfect machine, puppet and god: it can be hard to be certain just what components are being joined together, but clearly Eisenstein is willing to celebrate this juncture with the same mixture of seriousness and farce with which his dairy farmers presided over the polysemous wedding of Fomka and his bovine bride.

In the clashes, copulations, collisions, conflicts and super-impositions that form the basis of Eisenstein's picture-thinking in the late 1920s, one finds an explosive combination of sex, violence and humor, the rape that inseminates being his operating model for intellectual thought as well as history (as we are reminded also by the reference to 'Leda and the Swan' in *Battleship Potemkin*). *The General Line* is filled with these 'junctures', some more unexpected than others, between city and countryside, Russia and Europe, technology and agriculture; the scandal erupts when the layers of meaning accumulate (since the old is never merely annihilated) to such a degree that they begin to chafe against each other. Lenin or Stalin as bulls? Stalin inseminating – or, for that matter, raping – the countryside? Lenin's and Stalin's speeches shown to be in collision? With his turn to copulative paradigms, Eisenstein also seems to be reminding us that one meaning of the French verb from which 'montage' is derived (*monter*) refers to the planned copulation ('mounting', 'covering') of domestic animals. In *The General Line*, cinematographic montage finds its metaphor – and point of origin – in animal husbandry.

The transformation of milk into cream is, Eisenstein liked to point out, a transformation of 'quantity' into 'quality', like the 'gigantic qualitative leap in the area of social progress, from individual landownership to collective agriculture', that the separator both instigates and symbolizes.[42] Accumulation cannot help but transform, eventually, the world in which it takes place. Such 'qualitative transformations' are a dangerous magic, however, for it can be hard to know when exactly – at which turn of the crank – quantity will explode into something entirely new: when does a successful peasant suddenly become the kulak Erofeev? When do too many references to too many 'general lines', past and present, become something suspiciously akin to political satire? ('Persistence of vision' may make the phenomenon of cinema possible, but it could prove an unhealthy habit when applied too assiduously to the accumulated speeches and platforms of the Soviet leadership.) Ironically enough, in the case of *The General Line*, it is by taking political discourse literally – or, rather, by taking its figures seriously – that Eisenstein gets himself into potential difficulties. For now, the consequences are minor (it would be a little 'pretentious' still to claim the film represents the Party's 'General Line', suggests Stalin in 1928 [GA 119]), but the pattern is set and the unexpected juncture of adulation and devastation will be the hallmark of Eisenstein's political picture-thinking from this point on to the end of his life and career.

5. Savage Thinking:
The Sublime Surfaces of
Eisenstein's Mexico

A human skeleton astride the skeleton of a horse...

What could it be? A madman's delirium, or a modern version of Holbein's *Danse macabre*?

No! These were photographs of the Day of the Dead, in Mexico City...

This impression lodged in me like a splinter.

My desperate longing to see this in reality was like a chronic sickness.[1]

Eisenstein, 1940s

What was it that drew Eisenstein to Mexico? As he recalled years later, it was the picture of death that haunted him 'like a splinter' or even 'like a chronic sickness', giving him no peace until he could find his way to this place that seemed on such intimate terms with death. A German magazine's images of the 'Day of the Dead' were reinforced by photographs Diego Rivera brought to Russia in 1927,[2] and again by the acerbic woodcuts of José Guadalupe Posada. The 'splinter' had a double identity: on the one hand, of course, death, a theme which had always held a central position in Eisenstein's imagination, but just as important, I suspect, was the medium, the picture. The late 1920s had been dominated by dreams of depth and transcendence (the search for the eruption or collision that would serve as a springboard into the fourth dimension). Eisenstein's epic journey to Mexico became a journey back from fourth-dimensional aspirations to a new appreciation of the power and potential of the 'flat' two-dimensional image, the picture within the frame.

1. Pictures and Museums

Eisenstein had wanted to travel for a very long time. In 1925–6, he had planned with Sergei Tret'iakov (with whom he had already worked in his theater days) a sweeping Chinese saga to be titled *Dzhungo (China the Chinese Way)*.[3] Tret'iakov's literary scenario provided a panoramic vista of Chinese history, with glimpses of the brutalities of colonialism, the heroism of revolutionary movements, progress in industry, a vista whose crowning moment was the 'ovation' given by Revolutionary Chinese to a group of visiting Soviet representatives.[4] The greatest appeal for Eisenstein in this material seems to have been the chance to travel to China. (He also was very fond of a particular street scene, which he sketched a number of times, in which an exotic tower competes with a sprawled body and an overpowering moon for attention.)[5] Tret'iakov wrote up an elaborate proposal for a cinematic expedition to China to be funded by Goskino: he proposed the making of a three-part film (*Dzhungo*), a medium-length 'buffonade' using devices taken from Chinese popular theater, a newsreel documenting their expedition, plus a series of 'up to ten film lectures of a scientific-educational type' (about which he noted, 'special material for these films is unnecessary; it will be provided by the negatives of the newsreels and features').[6] Little did Eisenstein suspect that this pragmatic recycling of footage that he and Tret'iakov used to bolster the chances of their Chinese cinema expedition being approved would resurface, with exquisite irony, as the fate of his Mexican film, the never-finished *Que Viva Mexico!*.

Eisenstein had traveled to Berlin in 1926 for the premiere there of *Battleship Potemkin* and at the end of the 1920s he was very eager to go West again. As Eisenstein, Alexandrov and Tisse were shifting their attention, in 1928, away from *October*, finally completed, back to the still waiting *General Line*, they were more and more preoccupied with the looming entrance of sound into film. Russia was not the place to learn about sound techniques. Having met some visitors from the Americas (Douglas Fairbanks, Diego Rivera), Eisenstein hoped to make the journey to Hollywood to see the new developments in show business at first hand. As Alexandrov describes the next series of events, Stalin called Eisenstein and Alexandrov in for another chat; this time as well as christening the agricultural film (as 'The Old and the New' – see Chapter 4) and approving (as his representatives had already done) the proposed trip abroad, Stalin indulged in some rather contradictory pronouncements on the status of film now and in the future:

'Learn all you can about sound film. It's very important for us. When our heroes master speech, the effective force of the cinema will become enormous... Abroad there are very few books with communist content. They hardly read our books there at all, because they don't know the Russian language. But everyone watches Soviet films with interest – and everybody understands them. You, workers in the cinema industry, can't even imagine how vital a responsibility you bear... Before you head off to America, you need to travel around the Soviet Union, look at everything again, think about things, come up with your own views of everything.' (GA 119)

Even after taking this anecdote with the usual ample dash of salt required by Alexandrov's stories, one is left marveling at Stalin's oxymoronic approach: on the one hand, (silent) Soviet cinema is important because, unlike Russian books, it can be understood by the whole world and on the other hand, the acquisition of sound is absolutely vital (never mind that Russian films will then be less intelligible to the outside world). So Eisenstein's big journey abroad started with travel around the Soviet Union, in order to admire and appreciate the technological advances of the late 1920s. Then it was off to seek, ostensibly, the grail of sound.

Eisenstein's thoughts on sound in the 1920s were, like his thoughts about everything, prejudiced in favor of the complex and contrapuntal. With Alexandrov and Pudovkin in 1928 he formulated a manifesto on the subject of sound, which decried the horrible dullness of 'talking pictures', or indeed any use of sound that would weaken montage by replacing counterpoint with mere harmonious juxtaposition.[7] Sound could be seen as a threat to montage, or it could be mined for yet more strands to be worked into the complex patterns of conflict and collision. The antidote to blandness was insistence on sound being kept, at first, in 'sharp discord with the visual images' (SW1 114). A year later, Eisenstein described to an interviewer possible techniques for working with sound, to be 'shot *separately* from the non-sound part',[8] and then combined with the images: in other words, to be treated just like any other (visual) shot destined to enter the montage laboratory. In his refusal to acknowledge the differences between cinematic materials, Eisenstein was perhaps indulging in stubborn utopianism. In any case, these statements were purely hypothetical, because Russia was, as usual, far behind in the advances that would lead to a flourishing sound cinema. That meant that Eisenstein would have to go abroad to find the knowledge he was seeking.

In the autumn of 1929, Eisenstein, Alexandrov and Tisse left for the West.[9] They would not return until 1932, years that would prove as momentous for the travelers as for the country they left behind. On their way to California the Soviet trio visited Germany, France, Switzerland and England. In Hollywood the Russian trio was welcomed warmly (as curiosities?), but none of the projects they worked on – Dreiser's *American Tragedy*; a version of Blaise Cendrars's *Gold* about the tribulations of John Sutter; a moody allegory, *The Glass House*, to be set in a transparent apartment building – got beyond the scenario stage. Writing his memoirs in the late Soviet era, Grisha Alexandrov salted his impressions of Hollywood with anecdotes suggesting the trio spent much of their time fending off ideological attacks and attempts at political seduction. One story has Trotsky calling up to offer a scenario ('Secrets of the Kremlin') and Eisenstein saying sharply: 'Put down that phone!' (GA 151). Ivor Montagu, the British filmmaker and critic who had come to know Eisenstein at a conference of independent filmmakers in the castle La Sarraz in Switzerland, helped to arrange some contacts for Eisenstein in Hollywood and (with his wife, Hell), came along as part of the team. He paints a different picture of the director's Hollywood experience: steam baths with Douglas Fairbanks, party games with Charlie Chaplin and the gang, the little group (Eisenstein, Alexandrov, Tisse, Montagu, Hell) 'scraping by' on $900 a week.[10] Eisenstein earned a reputation for polyglossia and wicked wittiness – he offended Charlie Chaplin by being awarded a perfect '10' for 'charm' in the course of one parlor game.[11] Yet he couldn't manage to get a film treatment going that satisfied Paramount (source of the nine hundred a week).[12]

One of the occasions where Eisenstein unleashed his wit was at a meeting of the Technicians' Branch of the Academy of Motion Picture Arts and Sciences, on 17 September 1930. His lecture, 'The Dynamic Square', was ostensibly about the debate over the proper size and shape for movie screens, an argument that Eisenstein entered from a perhaps unexpected angle, as defender of the square screen.[13] This is a text that Eisenstein critics have not been particularly comfortable with, partly because of its rough-hewn nature ('warts and all' is how Richard Taylor describes the version of it that appeared in *Close Up*; both he and Jay Leyda tidy it up for publication), but also, I suspect, because it is extremely hard to know how much of it should be taken seriously.

Eisenstein starts his lecture with an attack on the wide screen, the latest threat to creative film-making since 'the incorrect handling of sound' (SW1 206).

> The card inviting you to this meeting bears the representation of three differently proportioned horizontal rectangles, 3 X 4, 3 X 5 and 3 X 6, as suggestions for the proportions of the screen for wide film projection. They also represent the limits within which the creative imagination of the screen reformers and the authors of the coming era of a new frame shape revolve. (SW1 206)

Eisenstein bemoans the narrowness of vision that this obsession with the horizontal rectangle actually disguised; in a Whitmanesque eruption, he sings the virtues of the vertical: 'It is my purpose to defend the cause of this 50 per cent of compositional possibilities which have been exiled from the light of the screen. It is my desire to intone the hymn of the male, the strong, the virile, active, *vertical* composition!' (SW1 207) In order to do proper justice to the vertical and at the same time to acknowledge the 'nostalgia for infinite horizons' and its call for the horizontal, Eisenstein suggests that movie screens be square. Then, depending upon the nature of the particular shot, whether it was a primarily vertical or primarily horizontal composition, the square could be masked so as to create the necessary rectangle. (The vertical rectangle has to be able to rise above the upper limit of the horizontal, not just be a subset of that latter design and hence the need for a square, within which neither the vertical nor the horizontal would be primary.) Not only does Eisenstein sprinkle this lecture with ribald references ('Indeed, from the methodological similarity of different arts it is our task to seek out the strictest differentiation in adapting and handling them according to the organic specifics that are typical for each. To impose the adoption of the laws that are organic to one art upon another is profoundly wrong. This practice has something of adultery in it. Like sleeping in another person's wife's bed...' [SW1 210]), he also contradicts himself, both locally (after the comparison to adultery, he – are we surprised? – himself goes on to wander from art form to art form, considering everything from medieval miniatures to stage design to Japanese scrolling prints) and more 'globally' (as part of his polemic against the horizontal wide screen supporters, he criticizes continued allegiance to 'the golden section', although a few years later, he would become a big fan himself of the 'golden section' in *Nonindifferent Nature*).[14]

Despite all the emphasis in this lecture on the vertical, however, I think the striking thing about this talk is the way it marks a move from the search for transcendental, higher dimensions, to a renewed interest in the possibilities of the pictorial (and of framed flatness). Each shot becomes a picture in a gallery, and the question the square screen is brought in to answer is, 'what's the best way to frame each of these pictures?' Eisenstein himself uses as argument against the horizontal rectangle his personal observations of pictures in museums:

> But as I set about summoning up my pictorial recollections gathered through all the museums that I have so lately visited during my rush through Europe and America and recalling the heaps of graphic works and compositions studied during my work, it seems to me that there are exactly as many upright standing pictures as pictures disposed in horizontal lines. And everyone will agree with me. (SW1 210)

This interest in framing (and, more generally, in the frame, the shot, the picture) was not something that emerged from nowhere: Eisenstein had loved graphic art long before he had even considered a career in film; he had been, already as an adolescent, an eager collector of art books and he had never abandoned this interest, even in his most fervent days of promoting the newness, the uniqueness, the conflict-based transcendent dimension of cinema (think of his interest in the framing of shots and pictures as described in 'The Cinematographic Principle and the Ideogram'). If in *October* the film-strip became a museum, in the sense of a repository (like the Hermitage) for precious, fascinating, possibly hazardous objects, in the 'Dynamic Square' we find intimations of a new, less antagonistic relationship to the museum. In a sense the praise of the 'vertical' may be a bit of a red herring distracting us from the greater shift from the transcendent fourth dimension to a new, richer sort of flatness (or horizontality on a greater scale). Only a couple of months after this lecture, Eisenstein was on his way to Mexico, where he would discover the full potential of a 'two-dimensional' approach to life and thinking.

2. The Screen: Moebian Mexico

Eisenstein's life in Hollywood, though busy and quite happy, did not result in the making of any films. The sensibilities of the Soviet visitors produced scenarios which, though dramatic, did not inspire confidence in the Paramount executives, who were also feeling the effects of some campaigning against the 'Red dog Eisenstein' spearheaded by Major Frank Pease and Representative Hamilton Fish.[15] The final straw came when Jesse Lasky of Paramount pulled the plug on *An American Tragedy* and announced that the studio's connection with Eisenstein's group was at an end (Montagu, pp. 120–1). Eisenstein quickly set his sights on greener pastures ('greener' only in a figurative sense!): if they could not make movies in the USA, then perhaps they could finally travel to Mexico, the place he had been longing to see for so many years.

This dream was made possible by Eisenstein's connection with the leftwing author of *The Jungle*, Upton Sinclair, with whom the Soviet film-making trio had socialized occasionally since their arrival in Hollywood. Sinclair and his wealthy wife were glad to finance the Mexican project of so distinguished a filmmaker as Eisenstein. (This connection with the Sinclairs did not materialize out of thin air; in the 1920s, as the reader will recall from Chapter 1, there had already been correspondence between Eisenstein and Sinclair on the possibility of a film based on Sinclair's books.) At the end of November 1930, Eisenstein signed a contract with Upton Sinclair and his wife for the making of a film about Mexico and Eisenstein, Tisse and Alexandrov crossed the border on 9 December 1930. As he went to meet the real Mexico, he carried a large amount of mental preparation – or preconceptions – with him: his talks in Moscow with Diego Rivera, the reproductions he had seen of the Mexican muralists' work, the prints of Posada and a sense of the uniqueness of Mexican culture and history derived from books like Anita Brenner's 1929 *Idols Behind Altars*.[16]

Eisenstein found in Mexico what all his varied sources had taught him to expect and yet still it was a revelation to him. Here was a place where flatness reigned, though not, certainly, in the sense of dull monotony nor even of geographical blandness: Mexico, rather, was a relentlessly pictorial place. Central characteristics of Eisenstein's Mexico were the coexistence of all things and times on a single plane, the punctuation of this plane by the savage thrills of bullfighting and other sacrifices and the ecstatic opening up of individual interiors into all surface.

As Eisenstein later described his reaction to Mexico, one of the fascinating features of the place was the way all the layers of history were flattened out and coexisted (unlike the sedimentary accumulation of, say, *The General Line*, within which history's swerves and secrets become landmines). Eisenstein phrased this in terms of the move from the vertical to the horizontal that had been foreshadowed, however obliquely, in his call for the square screen:

> Finally *Que Viva Mexico!*, this story of the evolution of cultures given not by the vertical (in years and centuries), but according to the horizontal, in the tradition of the geographic coexistence of different stages of culture, something that makes Mexico so surprising.[17]

To describe this horizontal contiguity that seemed so uniquely Mexican, Eisenstein (and his sources before him) resorted to a number of images that could be enlisted to stand both for 'Mexico' and for the film that Eisenstein wanted to make about Mexico, the film that would in a certain sense not only represent but be Mexico. Mexico was like a 'serape', wrote Eisenstein to Upton Sinclair in English:

> Do you know what a 'Serape' is? A Serape is the striped blanket that the Mexican indio, the Mexican charro – every Mexican wears. And the Serape could be the symbol of Mexico. So striped and violently contrasting are the cultures in Mexico running next to each other and at the same time being centuries away. No plot, no whole story, could run through this Serape without being false or artificial. And we took the contrasting independence of its violent colors as the motif for construction of our film; six episodes following each other – different in character, different in people, different in animals, trees and flowers. And still held together by the unity of the weave – a rhythmic and musical construction and an unrolling of the Mexican spirit and character.[18]

Anita Brenner, whose book Eisenstein perhaps enjoyed so greatly because, amply illustrated and including chapters dedicated to many of the major Mexican artists, it was just as resolutely 'pictorial' as Eisenstein himself, adds some other images to Eisenstein's 'woven blanket':

> Without the need for translation or a story sequence, Mexico resolves itself harmoniously and powerfully as a great symphony or a great mural painting, consistent with itself, not as a nation in progress, but as a picture, with certain dominant themes, certain endlessly repeated forms and values in constantly different relationships and always in the present, like the Aztec history-scrolls that were also calendars and books of creed.[19]

Brenner's point, made not only here but throughout her book, is that in Mexico life is art (just as history and calendars become a picture). As it was for almost every cultural tourist to Mexico in the 1920s and 1930s, the epicenter of art-oriented Mexico for Brenner and Eisenstein was the work of the great muralists: Diego Rivera, David Alfaro Siqueiros, Jose Clemente Orozco. In later years Eisenstein would, in describing his ideas for *Que Viva Mexico!*, claim that each segment of the movie would have been dedicated to a different muralist or artist. Like many of Eisenstein's claims, this statement says, perhaps, more about the grand intentions Eisenstein always had for every idea than it does about the actual mechanics of designing *Que Viva Mexico!*. The movie (like the country it portrayed) was indeed inspired by preexisting images and in particular by murals, but if Brenner could depict Mexico as a single great mural, Eisenstein's inspiration was a whole series of them, unrolling on an architecturally sophisticated two-dimensional surface (as if one were to construct a museum on a Moebius strip, that famous geometric construction – most often represented by a paper loop with a half twist – with *only one side*). The specific model for this surface was, I believe, the Ministry of Education in Mexico City, a building decorated with a whole series of murals largely by Diego Rivera. When Diego Rivera had visited Moscow in 1927, he had shown Eisenstein photos of these murals, the painting of which had started in 1923. When Eisenstein, Alexandrov and Tisse arrived in Mexico, they did some very thorough sightseeing of the art scene and the Ministry of Education was one of the places they visited.[20]

As a new kind of museum, the Ministry of Education changes the patterns of, say, the Hermitage in St. Petersburg. Instead of potentially poisonous relics of the past (see Chapter 3), the Ministry of Education looks, by its very nature, to the future and it wears its lessons on its sleeves, in the form of the murals that cover the walls, not hidden inside a series of nested treasure boxes (such had been the structure of the Hermitage in *October*, the emphasis there being the obscene deflowering of privy chambers). Though not 'flat' in the ordinary sense, the Ministry of Education's Moebian surfaces permit a rethinking of architecture as something that can also be splendidly two-dimensional, all surface.

The Ministry of Education provided Eisenstein with a map of Mexico. Like Eisenstein's Mexico, every time and place coexisted there on a flowing, architectural, two-dimensional surface. The Mexico that Diego Rivera put on the walls of the Ministry of Education was the Mexico that Eisenstein set out to 'discover' and to capture on film. Both objects, Ministry and film, have as their ambition to be Mexico and in many instances Eisenstein's images reflect directly the murals in the Ministry of Education (not just in the segment, 'Maguey', that Eisenstein suggested later was supposed to be dedicated to Rivera).

The film was to be structured as follows.[21] A 'Prologue' would depict the Yucatan and the timeless monumental art of the ancient Mayas: 'In the realms of death, where the past still prevails over the present, there the starting-point of our film is laid.'[22] The first major section of the film was to be set in 'tropical Tehuantepec', where 'time runs slowly under the dreamy weaving of palms and costumes and customs do not change for years and years' (*Mexico*, p. 53). To the tune of a sensual Oaxacan song in waltz-time

('Sandunga'), a young girl (Concepción) is married off within a matriarchal society to the boy she loves.

Next would follow a dramatic story ('Maguey') set during the dictatorship of Porfirio Diaz in the state of Hidalgo, at the pulque-producing plantation of Tetlapayac, where Eisenstein spent his happiest months in Mexico. The new bride of the peon Sebastian is raped by a guest of the cruel landowner; when the peons try to take revenge, the shootout leaves the landowner's daughter dead and in fury he buries three peons in the ground and has horses trample them to death among the maguey plants. The central song for this episode was to be 'El Alabado', a hymn to the Virgin.

The next segment, entitled 'Fiesta', also takes place under Diaz; this part of the film highlights memorials of the Spanish conquest, various sadomasochistic rituals, including pilgrims walking on their knees to churches at the top of hills... and bullfighting. A matador meets his love on 'boats adorned with flowers. Their boat sails by the floating gardens along the dreamland canals of Xochimilco, the so-called Venice of Mexico' (*Mexico*, p. 98).

Finally, in 'Soldadera' Eisenstein wished to depict the Revolution of 1910 embodied in a woman who moves from one faction to another and who would thus symbolize the bringing together of the various groups. The song for this section was to be 'Adelita', which the brass band would only prove able to play well after the Revolution: 'The civil war is over. Revolution has triumphed. There is no need now of Mexicans fighting Mexicans. The brass band discovers a new source of strength that enables it to play Adelita stoutly, solemnly and triumphantly. Like peals of thunder roll the triumphant shouts above the heads of the soldiers. The armies are fraternizing.' (*Mexico* 132) A lively epilogue presented the achievements of Modern Mexico ('Factories, railroads, harbors with enormous boats; Chapultepec, castle, parks, museums, schools, sports-grounds'; *Mexico* 137), followed by celebrations of the Day of the Dead, 2 November, in which laughing children wear skeleton masks and capitalists are shown to be the 'living dead'.

There are images in each of these sections borrowed from the 'Mexico' of the Ministry of Education and in general, Eisenstein's survey of the chronology and geography of Mexico dovetails neatly with Rivera's. The Ministry of Education unfurls the history of Mexico in picture after picture: There are pictures of pre-Columbian Mexico, of pyramids and statues and a series of images of the women of Tehuantepec[23] and images of shootouts set in places that resemble the scenery of Tetlapayac, images of the ceremonies that commemorate the Conquest (as in the 'Fiesta' section of the unfinished film) and of flowers on canals like the gardens of Xochimilco and scenes also of the 1910 revolution, of modern Mexico's factories (shots dedicated to this theme survive in the footage held at MOMA, but when Grisha Alexandrov put his version of Eisenstein's film together in the 1970s, he left out the factories – perhaps the enthusiasm for industry seemed to him somehow dated!) and of the cheerful skeletons of the Day of the Dead.

The dominance of the Ministry of Education runs somewhat counter to the more elegant idea of dedicating each section to a different artist; although Siqueiros, Orozco and Posada did influence Eisenstein's imagery, it was Rivera's grand visions that provided not only specific images, but also the overall structure of the film. Eisenstein himself preferred, whenever possible, to credit far-flung cultural influences rather than local inspirations and so in his own analysis of his Mexican project, he plays down somewhat the influence of Diego Rivera and in particular the Ministry of Education, in favor of more dramatic genealogies. Nowhere is this search for exotic precursors and inspirations so amusing as when he traces back the image of the 'fireworks bull', the 'Torito', on the shoulders of a young man in the Maguey segment to a childhood memory of a photograph of Venice, complete with 'the Lion of St. Mark, silhouetted against the sky' (BTS 746) combined with Max Ernst's surrealist montage in *La Femme 100 tetes*: 'a portico with skeletons, which was the backdrop to a tall lamp with butterflies. Again that compositional pattern: a portico and something with wings! (Incidentally, the composition of this illustration coincided almost completely with mine.)' (BTS 747). Although Eisenstein says blandly that these images all came together 'opportunely', it is also true that in the Ministry of Education there is a panel, 'Torito', painted by Diego Rivera's assistant Amado de la Cueva, that contains exactly the same image Eisenstein uses in his film and was almost certainly more of a direct inspiration than Venice and Max Ernst. (As influences 'after the fact', however, Eisenstein's mixture of childhood memory and Surrealist vision creates a suggestive and rather wonderful composite.)

But more than just history was spread out across the sublime surfaces of Mexico; this was a place where the human psyche, too, could find itself rescued from the usual pattern of deep secrets and vertical striations:

Figure 18.
'Torito', Amado de la Cueva
(left); 'Torito' (*Que Viva Mexico*)

> Upon my very first contact with Mexico I was gripped by the feeling
> that the reality before me was like something arising as a result of an
> exterior projection of all of those tendencies and attractions that
> wandered and still wander in me.[24]

He summarized this with awkward eloquence in English, in those
same notes from 1943, as 'Mexico, as *outspreading of my innermost*'.[25]
This is an extraordinary image, as it was an extraordinary
experience: for once Eisenstein was released from the ingrown knots
of a personality with 'depth'. In Mexico not only history, but the
human psyche, could become all surface, as psychological
topography is transformed from the roiling, hidden ocean of the
Romantic/Freudian unconscious to surfaces where nothing is so
hidden it cannot be 'outspread'. In this sense, Eisenstein's voyage
to Mexico introduced him to an entirely novel perspective on himself
– the same perspective that the gentlemanly Square, in EA Abbott's
nineteenth-century classic, *Flatland*, gained on his own two-
dimensional world when pulled out of it into a higher dimension
by his mysterious spherical visitor.[26] All that previously was interior,
hidden, painful, becomes part of the liberating openness of the
pictorial second dimension: an exterior unconscious. Perhaps there
is another way to think of this: the psyche could be embodied,

become part of the body surface. While looking down upon the entangled sleeping bodies of Mexican peasants and soldiers, another image that struck him as an exterior embodiment or projection of things within him, Eisenstein was most impressed by the freedom from shame and inwardness of those naked bodies:

> Washed by moonlight, the regularly breathing abundance of bodies of the *soldaderas* and their husbands – soldiers – held in close embraces seemed another external embodiment [...] The bodies breathed regularly and in unison; the very earth seemed to be breathing; here and there a white blanket showed up, modestly thrown over a pair lying among the others, black in the moonlight, bodies covered by nothing; bodies not knowing shame; bodies for whom what is natural is natural and naturally needs no concealment.[27]

There are different ways of turning psychological interiorities into things of the exterior, of course and Eisenstein would explore a number of those. One method that particularly intrigued him was the *vnutrennii monolog*, the 'interior monologue'. Despite its name, the 'interior monologue' in fact makes exterior with respect to the film audience the inward thoughts that it supposedly represents, making the 'thoughts' as accessible as the visible surfaces of the actor, of the actor's environment. This was a connection that Eisenstein was pondering that snowy day in 1943 when he described Mexico as 'outspreading of my innermost': 'Mexico as my interior monologue'.[28] When Eisenstein met with James Joyce in early 1930, '[t]hey talked of the future development of their mutual pre-occupation – the "internal monologue" – how the processes of the mind could be made visible and comprehensible through the film medium'.[29]

By the time Eisenstein arrived in Mexico, he had been considering a pet project for several years (since 1926); to be called 'The Glass House', the film was supposed to expose the hollowness of modern capitalism by depicting an apartment house made of glass, where all venalities are potentially visible to all.[30] Eisenstein's reaction to Mexico reveals an interesting shift in emphasis from his plans for the *Glass House*. In the earlier project the reigning mood was one of exposed secrets and voyeurism. There was something obscene about the things exposed in the transparency of the glass apartment house and satire involved in the exposing of them. This apartment building, made of glass though it be, has 'innards', has exterior and exposed interior spaces. The topography of Mexico is different. There, all is surface and as such liberated from the threat of being opened up, from the pain inherent in three-dimensional enclosed spaces.[31]

The project perhaps nearest to Eisenstein's heart during his stay in Hollywood had been a screen version of Theodore Dreiser's *American Tragedy*. Eisenstein saw this film as a chance to indict American capitalism for its heartlessness and its devastating influence on the younger generation. Eisenstein's planned use of the interior monologue in that film was intended to illustrate the tragedy of the isolated individual, Clyde Griffiths, oppressed by every aspect of his society – and to show how such oppression could work to divide the mind ('Kill – kill!' thinks Clyde as he's in the boat with his pregnant girlfriend, the great barrier between him and his former dreams of success; but also 'Don't kill – don't kill'), so that his motivation turns out to be a kind of inner secret, not even understood by himself.[32] The interior monologue in this instance gives only a clearer view of profoundly murky psychological territory. Again, this could not be farther from the freedom from such psychological knots offered by the Moebian surfaces of two-dimensional Mexico.

As the external embodiment of Eisenstein's 'interior monologue', Mexico was a kind of flat screen onto which his 'innermost' could be projected. What kind of thinking could be said to be going on here? Projection meant release from the endless inward mulling over of things; instead, one's hopes, fears, secrets and ideas could spread freely across the landscape of Mexico. The psyche then would no longer be a personal liability but could rejoin a much larger picture: thinking was, in a sense, collectivized (it rediscovered its communal roots). Mexico, as screen, was the perfect analyst and Eisenstein, for once in his life, was free to play the role of spectator, not only of this lovely, fascinating, uncannily familiar yet foreign country, but also of himself. One of the side effects of Eisenstein's Mexican 'analysis' was his rediscovered passion for what he would later refer to as 'the 'lost and newly regained paradise' of drawing' (BTS 578). Under the influence of Mexican art and 'the actual, astonishing, linear structure of the stunning purity of the Mexican landscape' (BTS 581), Eisenstein began to produce drawings remarkable for their line, the speed in which they were produced and their sheer quantity: 'they were drawn almost automatically. But how obscene they were!!'[33] Where the Surrealists had called for automatic writing, Eisenstein responded with automatic drawing. In some respects, however, he was closer to the Surrealist cast of mind during his stay in Mexico than at any other time, for here he basked for a time in what André Breton had called in 1924 'the light of the image', and for once came close to simply reveling in 'reason's role being limited to taking note of and appreciating, the luminous phenomenon' (Breton).[34]

Much of that illumination was provided by the art that pervaded every aspect of Mexico and in particular 'those primitives which I spent fourteen months greedily palpating with my hands, eyes and the soles of my feet' (*Mexico*, p. 581). In France at the beginning of 1930, Eisenstein had been reading Lucien Lévy-Bruhl's 1922 *La Mentalité primitive* and he found himself absolutely enthralled by the powerful paradigms of 'savage thinking', of primitive art and metaphor. The shift from inward-looking philosophy to exterior projection was part and parcel of Eisenstein's rediscovery of the primitive; it was the reverse of the evolutionary process described by Freud in *Totem and Taboo*:

> The projection outwards of internal perceptions is a primitive mechanism, to which, for instance, our sense perceptions are subject and which therefore normally plays a very large part in determining the form taken by our external world. Under conditions whose nature has not yet been sufficiently established, internal perceptions of emotional and intellective processes can be projected outwards in the same way as sense perceptions; they are thus employed for building up the external world, though they should by rights remain part of the *internal* world... [O]wing to the projection outwards of internal perceptions, primitive men arrived at a picture of the external world which we, with our intensified conscious perception, have now to translate back into psychology.[35]

The 'translation' experienced by Eisenstein in Mexico went in the opposite direction: from psychology back towards the 'external world'.

Eisenstein's passion for the primitive was not so much a new characteristic for him as it was the open acknowledgement of an interest that he had had (and in some respects had repressed) for some time. There had indeed been something totemic about the series of idols that had been the chief support of Eisenstein's witty deconstructing of 'God' in *October*: in that sequence he had constructed a ladder leading from ornate Christian representations of Christ all the way 'down' to the simple wooden idols of the Eskimos. In *October* those idols had been asked to make the very idea of 'god' seem foolish and savage, but by the time Eisenstein reached Mexico, the mental hierarchies represented by that ladder down into primitivism had been reversed. 'Primitive thinking' was no longer merely a tool for ironic destruction of contemporary pieties, but could now take its rightful place as a basic component of art and philosophy.

3. The Frame: Lessons in Dying

Eisenstein's obsession with surfaces and with the primitive was not unique to him. The new exteriority that for Eisenstein became possible (or at least imaginable) in Mexico was also the focus of a wide spectrum of Soviet artists and thinkers seeking in the 1930s to unravel the most painful knots of individuality. In a 1937–8 essay called 'Forms of Time and of the Chronotope in the Novel', Mikhail Bakhtin (another Soviet savant who did not hesitate to claim all of human civilization as his field of interest) looked back with notable nostalgia to that utopian period of the human past, when private life did not exist and so could not be brought painfully to an end:

> In ancient times the autobiographical and biographical self-consciousness of an individual and his life was first laid bare and shaped in the public square... Here the individual is open on all sides, he is all surface, there is in him nothing that exists "for his sake alone," nothing that could not be subject to public or state control and evaluation.[36]

The chronotope of the public square may strike a contemporary reader as rather more terrifying than comforting, more 'dystopian' than 'utopian', but this distant time, when 'man was completely *on the surface*, in the most literal sense of the word' (Bakhtin, p. 133) and 'utterly exteriorized, but within a human element, in the human medium of his own people' (Bakhtin, p. 135), holds a most peculiar charm to someone writing from the perspective of the late Soviet 1930s: *death is not a problem*. As Bakhtin notes in an aside, 'in public self-consciousness [death's] role had been, of course, reduced almost to zero' (Bakhtin, p. 145). The tragedy of individual existence becomes a human problem only with the end of the chronotope of the public square, when man 'was literally drenched in muteness and invisibility', when '[t]he personal and detached human being – 'the man who exists for himself' – lost the unity and wholeness that had been a product of his public origin' (Bakhtin, p. 135).

As part and parcel of that 'loneliness', death acquires a power and a threat which it never wielded in the agora: 'The motif of death undergoes a profound transformation in the temporally sealed-off sequence of an individual life. Here this motif takes on the meaning of an ultimate end.' (Bakhtin, p. 216) In the dark individualism of 'following epochs', one can merely seek out those trends which go counter to the general 'muteness and loneliness'. One such counter-trend, according to Bakhtin, is to be found in the exuberant and bawdy universe of Rabelais:

> Rabelais, in destroying the old hierarchical picture of the world and in putting a new one in its place, was obliged to reevaluate death as well, to put it in its own place in the real world and, most importantly, to portray it as an unavoidable aspect of life itself, to portray it in the all-encompassing temporal series of life that always marches forward and does not collide with death along the way, nor disappear into the abyss of the world beyond, but remains entirely *here*, in this time and space, under this sun [...] This means he must portray the material aspect of death within the triumphant life series that always encompasses it (without, of course, any poetic pathos, which is deeply alien to Rabelais) – while at the same time portraying it as something that occurs 'just in passing', without ever overemphasizing its importance. (Bakhtin 193–194)

Bakhtin describes Rabelais as succeeding in portraying life and death as part of a single surface, a surface without abysses (whether of Nothingness or of 'the world beyond'). In other words, he presents us, once again, with the marvelous topography of the Moebius strip.[37]

One of the great sources of relief, then, associated with the transformation of the self from an ingrown, knotted character to someone 'entirely on the surface' is the release from the solitary individual's obsession with death. Certainly death was one of Eisenstein's greatest interests in Mexico and the film he worked on there reflected that fascination. Its very structure used the theme of death as the pedal note tying the film together: the Prologue of *Que Viva Mexico!* was to have as its theme the ancient Mexico where 'death' reigned; the Epilogue, dedicated to the new Mexico, was to focus on a culture that, as the Day of the Dead demonstrated, had learned to laugh in the face of death (both of these Mexicos, old and new, coexisted however in the place's timeless horizontality). In between those bookend treatments of death, the spectator is treated to regular doses of bullfighting, shootouts and the horrifying, erotic martyrdom of the peons in the *Maguey* episode, who are buried up to their chests among the maguey plants and trampled to death by the landowner's horses (thus the martyred peons are 'replanted' into the ground: the seeds of future revolution).[38]

The proper relationship between death and revolution was an interest Eisenstein shared with many other Soviet cultural icons, although perhaps few of them could claim the same degree of passionate interest in things macabre. In the early years of the Soviet Union, how death was to be represented in art and literature had proved provocatively interlaced with crucial philosophical and political issues: what should 'death' mean under Communism? Aesthetic interest in this question of death was not limited to the earliest years of Soviet history, but tended instead to reach an especially high pitch during those periods when (to paraphrase Bakhtin on Rabelais), Soviet culture, 'in destroying the old hierarchical picture of the world and in putting a new one in its place, was obliged to reevaluate death as well' (Bakhtin 193). Thus the question of death seems to have been addressed with particular intensity during the early part of NEP, as literary culture emerged from the Civil War years and then again at the end of NEP, as hierarchies were once more overturned in the interests of collectivization and the Five-Year Plan.

The Soviet world, like Eisenstein in Mexico, sought a new way of death more commensurate with socialist ideals. One of the earliest literary role models was provided by the Chinese character Sin-Bin-U of Vsevolod Ivanov's 'Armoured Train 14.69' (1922); his heroism consists in his talent for untroubled self-sacrifice. When it becomes necessary for someone to sacrifice his life to keep the enemy's train from passing through, the Chinese revolutionary fighting alongside his Russian comrades obliges without fuss: 'Sin-Bin-U took out his revolver, not raising his head, brandished it in his hand as if wanting to throw it into the bushes and suddenly shot himself in the back of the skull. The body of the Chinaman pressed itself closely to the rails.'[39] Pared down to the essence of simplicity, freed from inner torment and exclamation points, this description of understated heroism is perhaps clouded slightly by the troubling point that it is a 'foreigner' who is best able to fulfill the duty of the true Soviet proletariat, marking his calm death as somehow 'alien' to the Russian way of things, whether it should be or not. This aspect of Ivanov's tale did not go unnoticed at the time: 'The story of the death of the Chinese man on the rails is exceptional in its freshness, simplicity and tragedy. The reader catches a whiff of distant thousand-year-old Asia, a land where people are used to dying in a way incomprehensible to us, wisely, simply and as a matter of course.'[40] Just as in the previous century Lev Tolstoi, member of the nobility writing for an educated audience, had turned to the peasant as one who naturally (unlike 'us') knows how to die,[41] Ivanov and his critics sought the answer to that question elsewhere, in the foreign and exotic. This was surely part of the allure of Mexico for Eisenstein, who had felt himself called to that country, after all, by 'pictures of death': in Mexico, too, one might hope to find the 'other who knows how to die'.

At about the same time that Eisenstein was exploring the superior approach to death of Mexico, the Ukrainian filmmaker Aleksandr Dovzhenko was exploring similar themes in his films. Dovzhenko had burst onto the Soviet cinema scene (as a major figure) in 1928 with his brilliant *Zvenigora*, a kind of hallucinatory combination of Ukrainian mythology with Civil War history and politics. In the next two years Dovzhenko was to produce two films of extraordinary beauty and intensity: *Arsenal* in 1929 and *Earth* 1930. In these films Dovzhenko presented his audience with deaths drawn from a very wide range of generic paradigms. *Earth* begins with a death that is fully embedded in a nature unnervingly beautiful and round and alive. After shots of sunflowers, trees heavy with fruit and close-ups of the round, round surfaces of those fruits, we are given a shot of an old man reclining amidst all this abundance. Then there's a laconic conversation between the old man lying down and another old man: 'You dying, Semion?' 'I'm dying, Petro'. More peaceful shots follow, this time of the family members watching (but each inhabits its own frame and each shot has the same full stillness of the shots of fruit earlier) and then the second old man says, 'So. Then go ahead and die'.

The 'natural death' is a cliché with a long and familiar history. 'Peasants', whether portrayed by Dovzhenko or by Tolstoy, often subscribe to it. This ability to face the end of life as if it were nothing more than nature's change of season, as if life and death were all part of one surface, is really a 'naive' natural death since it is so often observed – often with a certain amount of disbelief and envy – by a witness whose role is sentimental in the Schillerian sense: one who is all-too-conscious of what he does, who is exiled from and nostalgic for the unselfconscious genius of those admirable 'others' who are simpler and wiser and less troubled by the thought of loss of self.

It is extremely hard (perhaps impossible) to relearn how to die a natural death, but attempts in this vein, as a way of marking a definitive break with bourgeois individualism, had been a widespread aesthetic experiment in the fiction produced right after the Civil War. In these experiments one sees the reflection of a hope that death might in some sense be normalized, that it should no longer function as a defamiliarizing device, but rather transcend that role and be refamiliarized. In many cases, the 'refamiliarization' of death in early Soviet prose meant in practice a studied attempt to flatten affect throughout a text, as in the description of an old man's reasoned response to his incurable stomach cancer in a 1922 excerpt from Boris Pil'niak's *Golyi god* [*Naked Year*]. Remarking to his son that death is a very simple thing ('After all, you die – and there won't be anything, everything will end. *Nothing* will be'), Ivan

Spiridonovich Arkhipov decides, without histrionics or senti-
mentality, not to prolong his increasingly painful life and simply
shoots himself in the mouth as the last of a simple list of actions:

> Ivan Spiridonovich thought about how in sleep he felt nothing at all
> and passed those hours from evening to dawn completely without terror,
> as a single instant. Then he stood up and went into the kitchen, took
> down his revolver from the corner shelf, on the way glanced at himself
> in the mirror, noticed his frowning and serious face, returned to his
> room, put out the candles, sat down on the couch and shot himself in
> the mouth.[42]

The subject divests himself of affect (any emotion here is flattened
out and translated onto the reflected image in the mirror) and then
divests himself just as easily of consciousness. This shedding of
self *should* be made possible by the triumph of the collective over
individual consciousness (as the hero of Sergei Semenov's 1922 story
'Typhus' anxiously repeats, 'I am not afraid, not afraid, of death
because I am just a single particle in a million').[43] The ability to die
well thus becomes a test of how successfully one has left one's
bourgeois baggage behind, how thoroughly one has learned to think
as 'a single particle *in a million*' rather than a 'single particle' all on
its own. But this lesson is very difficult. So difficult, in fact, that by
the time of Dovzhenko's *Earth* such 'natural deaths' are left largely
to peasants and other others, while the more intellectual characters
stride on to other kinds of dying, less natural than ecstatic.

The ecstasies of martyrdom make for an extremely legible death,
from the generic point of view. We know how such a death should
look from hundreds of years' worth of religious, patriotic and
Revolutionary portrayals. Soviet literature, needless to say, over-
brims with examples of heroes and heroines singing the Marseillaise
or the Internationale as the firing squad takes aim. Here sheer
enthusiasm helps the individual make that all-important leap to the
higher purposes which make death somehow more palatable, a leap
which we may properly term 'sublime', since it conforms neatly to
the Kantian description of 'a pleasure that arises only indirectly
[...] produced by the feeling of a momentary checking of the vital
powers and a consequent stronger outflow of them'.[44] The martyr
does not blend into the natural landscape but rather stands out, a
kind of erotic object onto which enormous amounts of socio-
political meaning and energy can be cathected.

By sheer force of will and enthusiasm, the sublime hero is propelled
by his convictions beyond life's natural or unnatural limits, beyond

the frame. In Soviet representations of death, enthusiasm and lack of affect are related inasmuch as they achieve the same effect. Whether one is 'possessed' (to borrow enthusiasm's etymology for a moment) by something greater than oneself or merely succeeds in purging oneself of individual emotion, the result is similar: the transcendence of individual limits, of mortality and the meaninglessness which death threatens to inflict on an isolated subject.[45]

These heroes seek aesthetic 'loopholes' (a term Bakhtin used in the early 1920s to refer to attempts to 'save myself from being no more than a natural given').[46] In order to face death with aplomb, they may seek to transcend their own boundaries and leave those boundaries behind, in the ecstatic mode of self-sacrifice, or conversely they may long to become 'no more than a natural given', so that their lives and deaths escape the traumatic loop of personal significance. The martyred peons of the 'Maguey' section of Eisenstein's *Que Viva Mexico!* are interesting because they exhibit characteristics taken from both these generic paradigms. Like any Soviet hero in the 'sublime' mode, they are proud and steadfast as they are led to their deaths and the bravest and proudest of them shakes off the hands of the landowner's men and insists on hopping under his own power into the hole made for him (a classic 'sublime' movement; the equivalent of baring one's chest before the firing squad – here, however, the chests are already bared). Their deaths are a performance, played not only for us, the film's spectators, but also for a spectator hiding amongst the maguey, another peon, whose staring eyes record the scene and who will undoubtedly spread the martyrs' fame far and wide (he learns from their courage...). On the other hand, being peons rather than landowners, these martyrs are susceptible to the 'otherness' of Tolstoy's peasants – they die without histrionics, 'naturally', almost – they are *planted* in the soil and their blood and bones will fertilize the revolution to come.

From death as a 'natural given' to death as a moment where sublime transcendence is possible, the slippery slope (away from the 'natural') continues to encompass a death that in fact transcends not just the psychological limits death places on the self but also the physical limits. A particularly famous – and particularly unnatural – example comes at the end of Dovzhenko's 1929 *Arsenal*, when Timosh, who has already proved he can incapacitate would-be executioners merely by staring at them, faces a barrage of enemy bullets: the title and moral of the sequence is 'There's something in here that nothing can kill', and by Timosh's continuing to stand, unharmed, the legend proves itself literally true. This is a dramatic leap beyond merely feeling one is part of something larger than oneself; now the 'something inside that nothing can kill' is actually the self itself. As a way of portraying death in a generically satisfying manner, 'ecstatic un-death' presents certain problems from a pedagogical point of view, since it offers little by way of practical advice for those unlikely to find their bare chests able to stop bullets. No less a pedagogue than Eisenstein took up this problem with a class in the mid-1930s; he terms the figure of Timosh in *Arsenal* a 'classic example' of how the need for a hero adequate to his epoch may require the creation of a *Sverkhchelovek*, a Nietzschean Superman, a 'figure transcending the boundaries of everyday limitation', one that from the personal 'totally metamorphoses into the general':

> Under such circumstances a hero is naturally drawn beyond the limits of the real (as in the shooting scene), because it is impossible to collect in a real, living person all the aspects of the epoch. A normal person won't incorporate all those features. This can work only in a character that has grown into a generalized image. And Dovzhenko acts completely properly when he translates him onto an unreal plane, one approaching the symbolic. (IP 345)

It is completely 'natural', says Eisenstein, to have to sacrifice the real in the interests of the fantasy, the truly collective hero, the Superman. This is actually a tricky moment for Eisenstein, however, because it brings dangerously close together two terms which he is at great pains to keep separate during these lectures: *simvol* (symbol) and *obraz* (image). Eisenstein works with the *obraz*, which he defines as the 'unity of form and content', a unity marked in particular by its *dinamika* (IP4 668). The 'symbol', on the other hand, is marked by its 'immobility' (*nepodvizhnost*) and stands for all that the *obraz* is not: 'the complete rupture between form and content and the conditioned (fixed) functioning of one dependent on the other' (IP4 669). Naturally he finds that Dovzhenko (whom he treats much as Schiller treats Goethe, as a kind of 'naive genius') fills his films with symbols where Eisenstein would instead have *obrazy*.

But as Eisenstein's own suggestion that at the summit of the 'generalized image' [*obobshchennyi obraz*] we may find ourselves, like Dovzhenko, 'approaching the symbolic' implies, the drawing of straightforward distinctions between *simvol* and *obraz* is not so easy.

Dovzhenko's films are filled with things that look like 'symbols', and certainly he is also a master of 'immobility' (especially in *Earth*). But when one considers the effect of that lingering stillness, one finds oneself confronted with extraordinarily persistent surfaces (whether of grain fields or apples) that the camera dwells on until that surface itself is charged with a 'meaning' of its own, a kind of *trompe l oeil* depth.

Thus we may accept, for instance, that a Dovzhenkan apple symbolizes nature's fertility. But Dovzhenko gives us apple – apple – apple until we are drunk on the surfaces of apples, so that our own perception, thanks to the shots' very *nepodvizhnost* (immobility), is set into motion, looping between image and meaning, where that meaning has now become binocular (if illusorily so), comprising (1) the meaning of 'apple' and (2) the 'meaning' of the surface of an apple.

What happens now if we return to the ecstatic surfaces of Dovzhenko's *Earth*? We notice, for one thing, that *Earth* takes its loopholes very seriously. The film begins, as we have seen, with a peasant dying 'naturally'; by the end of the film, however, death has become an occasion for ecstasy. This sequence comes during the 'new-style' funeral of Vasil', murdered by the *kulak*-son Khoma. Vasil's father has particularly requested that the funeral contain 'new songs about the new life'. What he gets is an absolutely fantastic and ecstatic scene, in which the *kulak* is isolated by the very framing of the shots from the collectivized masses and a Party orator's words alone are enough to lay the desperate murderer low: 'With the Bolshevik steel steed [tractor] Vasil' overturned thousand-year-old boundaries...' Then Khoma (alone in the frame, but presumably looking towards this crowd) yells through his cupped hands, 'I killed him at night!' The next shots give us an impression of the crowd watching the orator with rapt interest. Khoma shouts again, 'At night, when all was asleep!' And then the titles slow down as Khoma becomes mad from the effort to get the crowd to pay attention to his confession: 'And he' – 'went' – 'down the street' – 'and danced'. And in a surreal juxtaposition, we are shown a shot of Khoma beginning to dance himself, almost in slow motion, in front of crosses sticking up from the hill and then in the next shot the orator, completely unaffected by Khoma's virtuoso mad scene: 'and with his warm blood he signed the death warrant of the class enemy'. Sure enough, in the next shot Khoma falls to the ground, flattened, it seems, by the very words of condemnation themselves.

With the *kulak* destroyed, the orator turns his attention to more sublime issues by addressing Vasil's father. 'And you, uncle, our Panas, don't be sad/the glorious name of our Vasil' will fly around the whole world.../Like that Bolshevik airplane!' The orator looks

up into the sky; the crowd looks up into the sky; we are given shots
from two other angles of this great crowd of people looking up, up
and all turning their heads in unison as if tracking this wonderful
airplane that we, the audience, cannot see. And then we are back
once again in the natural world: grain-fields, fruit.

As the crowd looks fervently for loopholes together, *Earth* moves
into the realm of pure, distilled ecstasy, which in this case looks
something like mass psychosis. The power of *Earth* lies in the
enthusiasm with which it performs the psychotic *non sequitur* taking
us from the opening question, 'are you dying?' ('is death an issue?')
to the final blissful statement of faith: '*aèroplan*!!!!!' As with the apples,
stare hard enough and one begins to see something: 'airplane' – even
if invisible – becomes through sheer conviction a kind of answer.

Earth raised a storm of controversy when it first opened, a hue
and cry inspired not by its loopholes, deaths, or airplanes, but rather
by the infamous sequence of the *golaia baba* (naked lady) – as she
was referred to by critics at the time, among them Eisenstein – who
flings herself about a room in what is apparently an excess of grief
at Vasil''s death. Eisenstein has a concise summary for what went
wrong with Dovzhenko's 'naked lady': he says such an image works
in *Earth* as a *chuzhorodnoe telo*, a kind of 'foreign body' (IP3 75).
This is absolutely true, but for more reasons than Eisenstein is willing
to give. First of all, this 'foreign body' is precisely and insistently a
body, what's more, a female (and thus perhaps particularly bodily)
body. Flesh-and-blood bodies belong, after all, to a very different
genre of 'death' than that which can effortlessly make the leap from
dying to invisible airplanes. Eisenstein suggests that the 'naked
woman' would have been more effective if her surfaces had been
shot in the super-abstracting mode of the close-up. Another way to
phrase the problem: 'Why can't a woman be more like an apple?'
Her frantic motion and all-too-fleshly, ordinary body make her truly
alien, a visitor from the everyday marring the polished stillness of
Dovzhenko's world. Her surfaces block rather than enable the leap
to false depth that marks most of *Earth*'s shots. The naked woman
writhing about gets in the way of our ecstasy; like a 'foreign body'
in the eye – a speck of dirt in the eye of *Earth* – she obstructs our
ability to look for loopholes. In this way she becomes the reminder
(or perhaps remainder) of something that's neither *image* nor *symbol*
– of the kind of death all of the 'lessons in dying' Dovzhenko
presents would have us forget, of the death that far from being 'put
in its proper place' (as Bakhtin says of Rabelais) instead puts us in
ours. Not all frames are conducive to sublime transcendence.

4. Eurydice

It was, Eisenstein tells us in notes written in 1943, a pleasant day in Switzerland 13 years earlier when he made the acquaintance of what would be one of the reigning icons of his intellectual life:

> There came a day when I both rose to the highest limits to which a person can hope to rise and descended to the lowest depths out of which a person emerges. It was on the same sunny day in Zurich. In the morning I flew with the now deceased Mittelholzer on the snowy whiteness of the Alps. In the afternoon we piled into the no less crystalline whiteness of one of the best women's clinics of Switzerland... Here for the first time, on a napkin, I saw a little living being, dying in my hands in about ten minutes after its premature appearance in the world. This stage of life interested me very much.[47]

The fetus was to leave a very definite mark on Eisenstein's interests. He had himself photographed with it, in several different poses and the expression on his face in those photographs is one of softened curiosity: Eisenstein's most maternal moment.

Figure 19.
Eisenstein in Switzerland

Eisenstein's tender encounter with the dead Swiss fetus occurred during the filming of the film *Frauennot-Frauenglück* (*Women's Misery /Women's Fortune*) in Zurich in August and September of 1929. This film, contrasting the horrors of abortions performed by ignorant lay midwives with the wonders achieved in a sterile, well-equipped gynecological clinic, was a project undertaken by Eduard Tisse as a means of funding the Soviet trio's travels around Europe. Work on the film took place between August 23 and September 17, with a break in the first week of September so that Eisenstein, Alexandrov and Tisse could attend the Congress of Independent Filmmakers in La Sarraz.[48] Although Eisenstein was clearly involved in the filming (as the autobiographical note above and remarks by Alexandrov assure us),[49] it is unclear what his involvement amounted to. Grisha

Alexandrov's single anecdote about the filming of *Frauennot-Frauenglück* has Eisenstein fully in command:

> All was prepared for the filming of a Caesarean section. But in the clinic there was no laboring woman in need of this kind of operation. We didn't have time to wait. Eisenstein decided to film at least some establishing shots. 'Lie down – play the part of the birth mother,' he said to me. I lay down on the operating table. They covered me with sheets... The 'professors' stood around my body. The lights went on. Eisenstein gave the command: 'Action!' The 'professors' took up their instruments. And the nurse, who didn't know that a masquerade had taken over the operating room, asked me the traditional question: 'How many times have you given birth?' From sheer surprise I snorted with laughter. The shot was ruined – everybody was laughing. I had to 'give birth' again.[50]

The film is a bit of a hodge-podge, both technically and thematically: there are silent sections, with titles and scenes of recorded dialogue. There are melodramatic vignettes from the lives of poor women faced with unwanted pregnancy: one worker's bride watches in horror as her husband is first electrocuted, complete with scratchy special effects to represent the electric current and then thrown (by the current) to his death from the heights of the construction project – and she had just announced her pregnancy to him over a picnic lunch! And there are animated sequences using plaster models and painted 'blood' to demonstrate the many ways a women's internal organs can be devastated by an improperly performed abortion. The moral of the film is that obstetrics and gynecology should be practiced not by dirty midwives but by clean (male) doctors in a sterile setting filled with as much machinery as possible. The shots of the clinic's technical and scientific equipment are by far the most interesting and inspired images in the film: petri dishes held up to the light make lovely circular patterns as we are invited to admire the devotion to hygiene they represent; a stunning geared mechanism that raises a bed receives an affectionate close-up; a blood transfusion is recorded in all its gory detail and the clinic achieves its moment of greatest glory in the caesarean section (not starring Alexandrov, after all), performed for the camera as if to show us the ideal modern birth: the woman unconscious, her body hidden under sheets, the baby being liberated from her belly head first by the competent scalpel-wielding doctors. One senses that the aspect of *Women s Misery / Women s Fortune* that Eisenstein found boring was its interest, precisely, in *women*; in Switzerland Eisenstein was much more interested in the fetus dying in his hands than in the woman (not even mentioned) from whose body that fetus had emerged. He could not, alas, take the embryonic being that had enthralled him so away with him, but in honor of that first fascinating specimen of prenatal life, he later acquired a related souvenir in Moscow:

> Visitors to my Moscow apartment are usually frightened by one trifle that peeks out from the piles of tumbled books. This trifle swims in a solution of formaldehyde. It has a pale gray transparent color and in general is a... fetus, one that has just taken on the features of a human being.[51]

Eisenstein seems to have been rather proud of the effect his 'souvenir' had on guests to his apartment, including the comic writers Il'ia Il'f and Evgenii Petrov, who paid a visit to Eisenstein before they left on their own American journey:

> This fetus and its jar have even entered into literature. Il'f and Petrov spotted it between the 'candelabra' and 'Mexican carpets' and put it into the first chapters of their *One-Storied America*, just as Dreiser included my 'boundlessly wide bed' in his book on the Soviet Union![52]

In Il'f and Petrov's description, Eisenstein and his apartment come across as delightfully – even cozily – mad:

> Eisenstein lived in a big apartment among church candlesticks and enormous Mexican hats. In his study stood a good grand piano and an infant's little skeleton under a bell-glass. Under such bell-glasses in the waiting rooms of famous doctors one finds bronze clocks. Eisenstein met us in green striped pyjamas. For a whole evening he wrote letters, told us stories about America, looked at us with radiant, childlike eyes and offered us jam.[53]

'In any event,' as Eisenstein confides to his notebooks, 'the fetus is dear to me.'[54]

Gradually Eisenstein was shifting away from his earlier emphasis on the abrupt, violent change that shifts the course of history, towards an interest in the early protoplasmic forms of life, in the shapes and forms of things before identity is determined.

His interest in the form of life in the womb coincided with the renewed obsession with drawing that was a marvelous side effect of his stay in Mexico. In November 1932, after returning to the Soviet Union, Eisenstein mused on the form his recent drawings had taken:

> [T]he figures 'hover' in space; that is, the atavism in them belongs to the period before being set upon solid ground, to the amoebic-plasmatic stage of movement in liquid. This is the graphic equivalent to the

> sensation of 'flight' among ecstatics: an identical uterine sensation of gyroscopicness and the identical phylogenetic pre-stage – the floating of the amoebic-protoplasmatic state in a liquid environment. (EOD 70)

These figures 'hover' not only in space, but also in time: they represented the contour in a state of liquid flux.

Another influence on these drawings was the work of Walt Disney, whom Eisenstein met in 1930 in Hollywood and admired greatly for his ability to imbue drawings with all the force of metamorphosis, a 'principle of transformation' that Disney, according to Eisenstein, had inherited from age-old literary traditions: '[P]oetry's principle of transformation works comically in Disney, given as a literal metamorphosis... Metamorphosis is not a slip of the tongue, for in leafing through Ovid, several of his pages seem to be copied from Disney's cartoons' (EOD 40). Years after his scandalous comparison of Soviet film-making to the ancient ways of sensual thought, Eisenstein invoked the parrot-men of South America once more as he pondered the meaning of Disney for himself: 'Mickey *plastically* truly embodies the "ideals of the Bororo" – he is *both* human and a mouse!' (note of 5 January 1944, EOD 96). Thus Mickey Mouse epitomizes the laws of sensual thought, that way of perceiving the world in which metamorphosis is made tangible.

The fetal obsession, the reemergence of the miracle of the animated contour, the Lamarckian flexibility of 'plasmatic' figures to shape and reshape themselves, all these things were not solely on the side of life. The fetus described so tenderly by Eisenstein was on the brink not only of new form, but also of death: the souvenir in the jar in his room later was a preservation in *death* of the moment when human life is all potential. The pictures Eisenstein was producing with such renewed vigor might be composed of flowing lines, a reminder of the infinite plasmatic possibilities of the building blocks of life, but the images they depicted were often violent: series devoted to Christ on the cross, to piercings of all kinds, to various martyrs and to the bullfight. In Mexico, Eisenstein was exploring the meaning of death and the nature of things changing and eternal. The scenario for the film (*Que Viva Mexico!*) that Eisenstein hoped to make in Mexico begins and ends on these themes: the Prologue was to be set among the 'heathen temples, holy cities and majestic pyramids' of the Yucatan ('In the realms of death, where the past still prevails over the present, there the starting-point of our film is laid.'),[55] while the Epilogue, which was to depict modern Mexico, came back again to the overarching theme of Eisenstein's Mexico:

The same faces –

but different people.

A different country,

A new, civilized nation.

But, what is that?

After the bustle of factory machines.

After the parading of modern troops.

After the President's speeches and the generals' commands –

Death comes along dancing!

Not just one, but many deaths; many skulls, skeletons...

What is that?

That is the Carnival pageant.

The most original, traditional pageant, 'Calavera', death day.

This is a remarkable Mexican day, when Mexicans recall the past and show their contempt of death.

The film began with the realm of death.

With victory of life over death, over the influences of the past, the film ends.[56]

In Ovid's *Metamorphoses* one of the most striking stories is that of the artist Orpheus, who descends into the underworld to seek his dead love Eurydice. When Eisenstein traveled to Mexico, he too was, in one sense, journeying to the land of death and, like Orpheus, he sought there inspiration for his art: a journey from life into death and back again as a way of exploring the mysterious boundaries between those realms. Mexico was a place where, on the one hand, metamorphosis still was a living force, where the flow of identity between people and things was still in flux but where, on the other hand, the metamorphic flux was matched by the timelessness of a place where every stage of human life coexisted.

The fetus brought out of the mysterious depths of the womb, like Eurydice out of Hades, died before Eisenstein's too-curious eyes and somehow that death was an intrinsic part of the mystery (as in the preserved fetus that Eisenstein kept in his apartment). The moment of metamorphosis from life to death – and from death to life – was the fascinating aspect not only of the fetus, but of another of Eisenstein's passions: the bullfight. In the bullfight Eisenstein found a most enticing combination of eroticism and violence:

> We can see why the bullfight is still alive today in Spain.
>
> For the image of the matador, who in the simultaneous attempt of the bull and the man to rush at each other, pierces with his sword like a flash of lightning into the blackness splashed with foam, the blackness of the fiery element of the horned monster that, according to tradition, once kidnapped Europa – and damn it, I understand Europa's yielding to this black devil who tramples everything with his hoofs – this is simultaneously the image of both great Spaniards, El Greco and Pablo Picasso.
>
> They also both seem to be, not for life, but for death (the sword – for the bull or the horn – for the matador!), grappling with nature itself; also in the same way the horn or sword penetrate each other; they penetrated each other in a similar great moment of the mutual merging of life and death, bull and man, instinct and craft: animal nature and the art of man![57]

Rape, death and communication are all confounded here: the bullfight as means of sensual thought, as the locus of all the pain, change and potential packed into the mythological tradition of metamorphosis. The matador and the bull meet, pierce each other, transform themselves into a complex package where actor and object, life and death, can no longer be extricated neatly one from the other. The bullfight, 'still alive today in Spain', is a preservation in life of the moment of death, just as the fetus represents the preservation in death of the moment when life begins.

In Dovzhenko's *Earth*, the mad thrashings of the 'naked dame' are contrasted with a female body (this one covered up by its clothing) involved in a very different kind of activity: giving birth. The mother of the martyred young man whose Soviet funeral is being celebrated even as she labors produces a future hero, another child. The problem of the female body as '*foreign* body' is highlighted by the split here between the woman whose mind and body behave appropriately (the clothed mother giving birth), from the figure of which all hint of sexuality is removed and the one whose body, abandoning mental and social controls, becomes the excessive, obscene mote in the film's (or in the spectator's) eye.

In Switzerland Eisenstein was not as interested in the pregnant woman as in the fascinating fetus she could produce; in Hollywood he had worked long and hard on that ill-fated film treatment of *An American Tragedy*, in which it is a pregnant woman who represents the downfall of the American youth's hopes and dreams. But something happens in Mexico and to see what that something is, we need to consider Eisenstein's plans for the 'Soldadera' section of *Que Viva Mexico!*, a section for which the footage was never shot. In this part of Eisenstein's Mexican epic, set in the revolutionary battles of 1910, the shift in Mexico from civil war to national unity was to be embodied in a woman, 'Pancha', who bears a child to a soldier in one faction and then, after the lover's death, moves to another group of soldiers. The 'Soldaderas' (so named because they followed the soldiers' camps) thus become responsible for the knitting together of hostile communities, with their children symbolizing the transcendence of the ruptures of the civil war:

Pancha gets on the engine platform.

The angry voice of the sentinel calls to her.

'What have you there under your shawl?'

And lifting her rebozo, Pancha answers quietly:

'Who knows, senor, it may be a girl or it may be a boy...'[58]

The baby is born on the train and when Pancha's soldier, Juan, is killed in action, the very soldier who suspects her of smuggling becomes her new husband. The circulation from man to man seems perfectly natural, part of the process of Mexico knitting itself back together as the civil war ends, a physical symbol of the 'fraternization between armies' with which the 'Soldadera' chapter of the scenario ends:

The civil war is over.

Revolution has triumphed.

There is no need now of Mexicans fighting Mexicans...

The armies are fraternizing.

One might decipher on the banner – the last word of its device.

Towards Revolution.

Towards a New Life... says the voice of the author.

Towards a New Life!... [59]

This scene (like the 'Soldadera' episode as a whole) marks a series of reconciliations that reach far beyond the temporal and geographical borders of the Mexican revolution. The image of the pregnant woman/new mother traveling on a train packed with soldiers during a revolutionary civil war is borrowed from Isaak Babel's 1923 story about the Russian Civil War, 'Salt'. In Babel's chilling story, told by the gruff, trigger-happy Nikita Balmashev, 'Soldier of the Revolution', in the form of a 'letter to the editor', the venom of the revolutionary targets the Revolution's worst enemy: women. The first line of Balmashev's letter contains the theoretical foundation of his polemic: 'I want to describe to you about the unconsciousness of the women who are doing us no good' (p. 122).[60] Balmashev is incensed by one woman in particular, whose crimes include sneaking onto the military train and wheedling herself safe transport by passing off a bundle of black-market salt as a new baby. He berates her once her ruse has been unveiled:

> But you look at the Cossacks, my good woman, the boys that put you on a pedestal for being a mother that labored for the republic. Look at them two girls crying at present on account of what they went through from us this night. Look at our wives in the wheat plains of the Kuban that are spending their women's strength without their husbands and the husbands, alone too, all through dire necessity violating the girls as come into their lives. And nobody touched you, you wicked woman, though that's what would have served you right... (p. 125)

Having slyly escaped rape (which in Balmashev's universe would have been nothing more than her just deserts), the salt-carrying woman is thrown off the train and shot by an injustice-maddened Balmashev, who sees this summary execution as nothing less than 'wiping something shameful off the face of the laboring earth and Republic'.[61] In Eisenstein's reworking of this situation, the 'props' (train, soldiers, woman with suspicious lump under her wraps) are retained – and then put to very different moral effect. No longer is 'woman' the worst enemy of any revolution; now, in fact, she becomes an honorable participant in Mexico's struggle for liberty and 'fraternization' in the most bodily sense becomes part of that struggle: woman as copula. This reconciliation with the physical body of woman serves as antidote not only to the venom of 'Salt', but also to Dovzhenko's problematic 'naked lady', the too bodily woman whose nakedness got in the way of the viewers' appreciation of *Earth*. Had this episode been filmed, it would have made up a very rare moment in Eisenstein's creative universe, within which positive female figures – positive mothers, in particular – are decidedly uncommon. Perhaps it is fitting, however, that the section of *Que Viva Mexico!* that never even got as far as filming was the one in which contradictions between warring parties were resolved within the figure – and body – of a woman. Before the radiant Pancha could become the catalyst for Mexican fraternity, the conflicts surrounding Eisenstein's Mexican project would tear it from his hands, leaving the world with 35 miles' worth of unedited footage, thousands upon thousands of shots destined never to be joined together by the director who loved these images so.

5. Orpheus Torn Asunder

The original agreement with Upton Sinclair had been for financing to the tune of $25,000; this money disappeared quickly and a financial tug-of-war arose between Eisenstein in Mexico and Sinclair in California, with the filmmaker constantly asking for more money and the Sinclairs feeling more and more pressed and, eventually, deceived.[62] Since part of the agreement was that all footage would be sent directly to California for processing, Sinclair could see thousands upon thousands of feet of film piling up, much of it seemingly wasted in numerous repetitions of the same shot (necessary from Eisenstein's perspective because he did not have access to the developed footage and thus could not afford to wait to correct errors). What Sinclair did not get a clear sense of was the narrative direction of the film; indeed the project seemed to be undergoing a process of inflationary expansion! He urged Eisenstein to focus on some single, gripping story (the 'Maguey' episode, for instance) and he sent his brother-in-law, Hunter Kimbrough, to monitor the progress of the Eisenstein group in Mexico.

Kimbrough was horrified by what he saw as Eisenstein's wild behavior and obscene interests, reporting that: 'E. spent a lot of his time and our film in shooting pictures of animals copulating and of human beings in degrading positions and he used his leisure in making elaborate drawings of pornography.'[63] Sinclair's caustic analysis of the source of the ill feeling between his brother-in-law and Eisenstein laid the blame squarely at the feet of the filmmaker: '[Kimbrough] was told that E was a great artist and expected to honor and help him. I doubt if he had ever heard of such a thing as a homo and he was bewildered to find himself in such company. He discovered that E wanted money, money, money and never had the slightest idea of keeping any promise he made.'[64] Relations between the Sinclairs and Eisenstein eventually reached breaking point and the Sinclairs removed their support from the film, retaining, to Eisenstein's eternal and bitter regret, all the unedited footage.

Eisenstein left Mexico, that marvelous Land of the Dead, hoping his film would follow him. In the end, however, the unthinkable happened and the film was lost to him forever, another Eurydice in Eisenstein's life:

After we [the Sinclairs] had got the film back from Mex we made a precise deal with Amkino in NY. The stuff was to be sealed and shipped to them and they were not to open it but ship it direct to Moscow where E was to cut it and the government would then ship the negative back to us. Two or three weeks later we learned from friends that E was still in NY and running the film for all his friends. We had our lawyer in NY, BML Ernst, recover the film and ship it back to us and of course that was the end of both E and Russ for us. We never had any idea of shipping him a print or anything else after that. We'd as soon have shipped it to the devil.[65]

The fate of the footage Eisenstein shot in Mexico was complex. Upton Sinclair, who compared the unedited miles of film to a 'backyard filled with white elephants',[66] was loath to let his investment come to nothing. He handed over the footage to the producer Sol Lesser and had him put together a picture, *Thunder Over Mexico* (1933), based on Eisenstein's 'Maguey' episode. Braving the criticism of many in the film industry who were distressed to see a prominent filmmaker like Eisenstein stripped of the ability to edit his own film, Sinclair stoutly described *Thunder Over Mexico* as 'one of the most beautiful pictures ever made'. He had Charlie Chaplin and Douglas Fairbanks add their admiring words to his: 'It is lovely, it is revealing and it is powerful,' said Chaplin, while Fairbanks praised the film's combination of 'charm' and 'purpose'.[67] Although the images of *Thunder Over Mexico* are recognizably the work of Eisenstein and Tisse, they are put together with more sentiment – and more flowery titles – than the Soviets surely would have employed: 'To your care, Sebastian Enriquez, I commend my daughter Maria – to become your wife before the setting of the sun...' The cultivation of the maguey (also known as the century plant) is shown in such great detail that the average spectator after seeing the film might have hoped to do a half-decent job of maguey-farming himself and double exposures are used liberally whenever the film's emotional level needs ratcheting up.

Still stranger than this 'bastard child' were all the other films carved out of Eisenstein's treasure trove of Mexican footage. Marie Seton, Eisenstein's admiring biographer, put together in 1939 a version of Eisenstein's film according to her interpretation of his plans and wishes and called it *Time in the Sun*.[68] Undeniably a labor of love, Seton's version suffered from an overemphasis of the religious theme (Anita Brenner's thesis in *Idols Behind Altars*, a book credited in the film's titles, that the Mexicans simply added Christianity to their mystical pagan roots gets central billing in *Time in the Sun*, whereas in Eisenstein's plans for the film that theme is one among several) and from very flatfooted editing that manages to make the scenes set in matriarchal Tehuantepec look like illustrations for an old National Geographic article.[69]

In 1934, Upton Sinclair arranged for another Sol Lesser production, a short entitled *Death Day*, and this film was followed by a series of educational shorts carved from various segments of the Eisenstein footage and given titles like *Land and Freedom*, *Conquering Cross*, *Spaniard and Indian* and *Mexico Marches*.[70] The mining of Eisenstein's passionate, violent and erotic imagery for sober educational narratives led to breathtakingly ironic juxta-positions. In one sequence from *Spaniard and Indian*, for example, the sober narrator informs us that the Spaniards brought to Mexico 'previously unknown' elements like the wheel and the horse. The images chosen to illustrate this point, meanwhile, are the rearing horses of the 'Maguey' episode, their hoofs about to come down (we know) on the skulls of the peon martyrs. The martyrs are invisible here; their horrific story transformed into a cheerful tale of the cultural advantages brought to Mexico by the Spanish. It is downright spooky to see Eisenstein's highly erotic footage of the maguey, the milk of which, like the milk of *General Line*, could play all sorts of roles (tears, blood, semen, milk), turned into a cheerful 'how to' documentary on pulque production, as it is in both *Spaniard and Indian* and, to a lesser extent, in *Thunder Over Mexico*.

After Eisenstein's death, Upton Sinclair eventually donated the Mexican footage to the Museum of Modern Art, New York, where Jay Leyda, editor of *The Film Sense* and *Film Form*, used it to put together a study film and eventually, more than 30 years after Eisenstein had lost his Mexican film, the footage traveled back to Moscow where a now rather elderly but still energetic Grisha Alexandrov undertook the construction of his version of Eisenstein's intentions, yet another incarnation of *Que Viva Mexico*. Despite this film's attempt to stay close to Eisenstein's own intentions, the smoothness of its transitions and the saccharine nature of its score show the heavy hand of Alexandrov, whose career in the 1930s (as we shall see in the next chapter) had been devoted to creating glossy Stalinist musicals more indebted to Busby Berkeley than to Eisenstein.

The multiplicity of fates that awaited Eisenstein's Mexican footage could be seen as, in a sense, the ironic fulfillment of the director's discovery in Mexico of an open, communal approach to art that promised the release from the dark inwardness of individual psychology; the proliferation of versions of Eisenstein's Mexico over the years and the consequential blurring of notions of authorship, could then be taken as merely the most extreme instance of 'outspreading of one's innermost!' The attraction of primitive thinking lay in its invitation to let the community (understood in a trans-historical sense) think for you, in the discovery that ancient patterns of thought were still decipherable under the skin of the most 'advanced' notions of aesthetics. But Eisenstein himself was, alas, not nearly so much a 'savage' as he may have on occasion dreamed of being (or as the Sinclairs probably thought him) and the loss of Mexico was for him very much a personal tragedy.

6. Epilogue: The Land of the Dead in the Home of the New

By using Isaak Babel's 'Salt', a tale of the Soviet Civil War, as a model for the planned 'Soldadera' episode of *Que Viva Mexico!*, Eisenstein transformed Mexico into a place where not only psychological but also political traumas could be resolved on that marvelous two-dimensional screen of Mexican culture and history. Mexico was not just Eisenstein's psyche spread out horizontally, but could also serve as a kind of 'exterior unconscious' for Soviet history as well. In the mid-1930s, Eisenstein would try to apply some of the lessons learned in Mexico to Russian material – with disastrous results. The disaster of *Bezhin Meadow*, which brought Eisenstein closer to political ruin than any other event in his life when it was banned in 1937, served as a kind of delayed coda to his Mexican misadventures and it is in that vein that we will be examining it here. In this coda, a crucial role would be played by the same Isaak Babel' who had provided some stimulus to Eisenstein's narrative imagination in the course of the filmmaker's work on *Que Viva Mexico!*

The careers of Isaak Babel' and Sergei Eisenstein intersected at many points both prior to and following Eisenstein's work in Mexico. They knew each other (both were affiliated with the journal *LEF*) and had worked together before, in the early 1920s. In 1924, Eisenstein wanted to make a film based on Babel's *Red Cavalry*, the collection of stories to which 'Salt' belonged.[71] Although this project was eventually set aside in favor of *The Year 1905* (soon whittled down to *The Battleship Potemkin*), it brought Babel' and Eisenstein together for a period of intense cooperative brainstorming. *Red Cavalry* never developed, however, to the point where the brilliant peculiarities of Babel's prose (its beautiful cruelty!) could be perceived in the scenarios. Even if *Red Cavalry* was not to be, Eisenstein did not give up the idea of working in collaboration with Babel; for a while they moved on to Babel's colorful description of Jewish life in Odessa, 'Benya Krik'.

Eisenstein would later describe those days in 1925 when he was already at work on what would become *Potemkin* but still hoped to do something with Babel, too:

> I worked on the upper floor [of the dacha] with Agadzhanova [official scenarist for *Potemkin*], writing the screenplay for 1905 and on the lower floor with Babel, on the screenplay for *The Career of Benya Krik*... But of course Babel's stories were the most amazing... Who else but Babel would come across a bonfire on his way to the dacha from the station at Nemchinovka? By the fire there was a Jew... A solitary Jew, playing the cello... by an open fire... in a coppice near Nemchinovka station... (BTS 112)

A photograph exists that shows that, although the Babel projects did not get made, Eisenstein did try to insert this image – a cellist by the railroad tracks – into *The Year 1905* (as part of an episode on railway strikes that was cut from the film as it became more and more focused on the Potemkin uprising).[72] As the subtle reference to 'Salt' in *Que Viva Mexico!* also demonstrates, Eisenstein did not leave Babel' behind. In the 1930s, in a period of artistic and political crisis, Eisenstein would call Babel back into his creative life for the reshaping of *Bezhin Meadow*, the ill-fated project in which Eisenstein tried to bring the lessons he had learned in Mexico back to Russia.

Eisenstein's effort to retell the story of Pavlik Morozov, a Young Pioneer hero and martyr who was murdered by his family for having denounced his corrupt father to the authorities, was at first based on a literary scenario by AG Rzheshevskii, who folded ample servings of Ivan Turgenev's nineteenth-century pastoral color ('Bezhin Meadow' is the name of one of the stories in Turgenev's collection, *A Sportsman s Sketches*) into a tale of modern Soviet youth in a countryside in transition. The young hero of the film (here called 'Stepok', though he was meant to be a transparent reference to the heroic young Morozov), loses his mother to abuse by his father. Near the opening of the film, in its first version, Stepok is shown accompanying the body of his mother (angelic and peaceful in her coffin) in an idyllic and beautiful natural realm: a death that seems almost eerily 'Dovzhenkan', a little quote from *Earth*, particularly reminiscent of the moment in the prior film when the hero is taken to burial and the very sunflowers seem to dip down to pay their last respects.

It was difficult in some respects to make the story of Pavlik Morozov fit into the Socialist Realist universe. Eisenstein's research into the story of Pavlik Morozov revealed some pitfalls. For example, one of the items he collected was the typescript of a conversation between Nadezhda Krupskaia and a group of youthful representatives of Morozov's village, an interview not yet quite suitable for *Pravda*! At one point Krupskaia asks young 'Misha', the only one present with the glorious record of having actually lived on a 'collective farm' (even if one with only 14 members!), whether he's seen 'how *kolkhozniki* (collective farm workers) work'. Says Misha, more honest than tactful: 'They work badly; they don't have a tractor.'[73] Krupskaia immediately turns away from this unsatisfactory portrayal of Soviet life: 'Who else has seen work on a collective farm?' – and the discussion soon degenerates into a young girl reciting a canned history of collective farming in the Soviet Union and Krupskaia responding with a longwinded lecture on the necessity for bonds between country and city and the improved status of women in the contemporary Soviet state (ll. 36-40).

Although Rzheshevsky's scenario had been approved by March 1935,[74] as soon as Eisenstein was involved in the project, the criticisms began to mount. Many of these complaints, which would eventually lead to the most serious disgrace of Eisenstein's career (during a perilous political period), seem to have been triggered by the authorities' resentment of what they saw as Eisenstein's arrogance. Already by the fall of 1935 (while Eisenstein himself was recovering from smallpox), the Central Cinema Commission (headed by the hostile Boris Shumiatiskii) was complaining about the way that footage from the film was being kept from them: 'This viewing was insufficiently organized. Comrades Usievich and Zel'dovich and I [Shumiatskii] did not have access to a list of all of the already exposed frames and thus were deprived of the possibility of choosing those that interested us most.'[75] The tussle for control over this project continued until 1937, when *Bezhin Meadow* was proclaimed a hopeless failure and Eisenstein was forced to take the humiliating step of making a 'self-criticism' in print ('The Mistakes of Bezhin Meadow').[76]

Bezhin Meadow was the sinking ship that brought Babel and Eisenstein into their closest cooperation ever, as Babel labored to rework the script of the film. The problem, of course, was that the script was not really the heart of the dispute, whatever criticisms might be made of it. The real trouble with *Bezhin Meadow*, according to Shumiatskii, was Eisenstein's unwillingness to submit himself to tight creative control by Mosfil'm and Shumiatskii's Central Cinema Committee; his tendency to indulge in dubious Biblical parallels and overly metaphorical imagery; and what the authorities considered his utter inability to work with actors. This last complaint (made most dramatically perhaps in a memorandum from GUKF to Mosfil'm's Babitskii, in which the reviewers claimed testily that only the frames with no people in them were any good)[77] stood for all that Eisenstein, hero of the old-fashioned montage-based cinema of the 1920s, was now supposed to outgrow: his affection for crowds over individuals, his suspected ongoing romance with the now derided 'formalism'.

In *Que Viva Mexico!* the infant at the end is a kind of bridge to a new era of reconciliation: the women who circulate from military camp to military camp producing living symbols of fraternization and mixing. The status of Pavlik Morozov/Stepok is interesting in this regard, for the new Soviet child-hero is the child of kulaks, the most demonized 'enemies of the state'. In the Rzheshevskii scenario, this issue of paternity is questioned and sidestepped in an interesting way: '"Who gave birth to you, me or them in the political section?" quietly asked the father. "My mother" – spoke Stepok quietly and calmly...'.[78] Then the father goes into a Biblically inspired rage: 'When the Lord God created the heavens, water and earth and such people as you and I, dear son, he said... Be fruitful and multiply, but if a natural son betrays his own father, "kill him like a dog," it says in the holy writ of Lord God. Kill him right then.'[79] The question of genealogy is particularly problematic given the contemporary political situation, in which children of kulaks were – effectively –branded as such their whole lives long.

If Biblical and metaphorical imagery were problematic, Babel was probably not the right person to bring in as surgeon. In fact, there are aspects of Eisenstein's treatment of the Rzheshevskii scenario that suggest that Babel was already present in Eisenstein's mind well before he turned to him for help in reconstructing the film's scenario. In fact, ironically enough, the most 'Babelian' moment in the first version of *Bezhin Meadow* was also one of the scenes of the first version that upset the authorities enough that Eisenstein was driven to try a much altered second version. (In other words he brought in the writer whose stories were the inspiration for some of the early version's 'sins' as the man who would help him rescue the film from those sins.) The scene in question is the one where the villagers ransack the local church in order to turn it into a clubhouse. They take down the icons and laughingly put the frames around their heads, becoming 'saints' and 'gods' for a moment. This was exactly the sort of religious tinge (even if fervently democratic in intent) that set the nerves of the Soviet authorities on edge; they complained again and again about the overly Biblical elements in the film (the aureole around Stepok's head, etc.).[80] When Babel reworked the scenario, this scene was one that went – although, ironically enough, it was a kind of visual reworking of Babel's own 1923 story, 'Pan Apolek', another tale in the *Red Cavalry* cycle. In 'Pan Apolek', set in a village in Poland during the Polish Campaign of 1920, the story is told of a painter who comes to town and who becomes a populist hero and an alarming object for the authorities by painting the faces of the local populace into the religious icons and frescoes that he creates for churches and homes. (Thus a village whore finds herself recast as the Virgin Mary.)[81]

As in *Que Viva Mexico!* old Biblical roles are reassigned to living, breathing, 'ordinary' human beings. The Soviet reviewers of *Bezhin Meadow* neither appreciated the force of old paradigms, a power that Eisenstein was very eager to tap into for new purposes – nor did they think that the iconoclastic thrust of these scenes outweighed the riskiness of anything smacking of religion in a Soviet film. When the peasants of *Bezhin Meadow* try the gilt icon frames around their own beaming faces, we are experiencing the animation of the picture: the icon, the religious fresco, coming to life. In *Que Viva Mexico!* we have animated tableaux reminiscent of the Pietà, of Sebastian, of the Virgin and Child – and in the Prologue, the explicit comparison between the faces carved into the stones of the pyramids of the Yucatan and the living faces of their descendants. Important here is the move from artwork to the living embodiment thereof.

This particular fascination – with the picture and with the animation of that picture – would remain with Eisenstein all the rest of his career. Just as 'Mexico' existed for Eisenstein as a series of two-dimensional pictures on the Moebian surface of that new kind of museum, the Ministry of Education, so would other pictures be asked to come to life throughout the next 18 years, from *Bezhin Meadow* to the comedy *MMM* to *Ivan the Terrible*. We will begin the exploration of the significance of 'animation' for Eisenstein in the next chapter.

Eisenstein left Mexico and returned to the Soviet Union with the bitter loss of his film and the displeasure of the Soviet authorities hanging over his head and the loss of Mexico – both his film and the country – would remain galling all the rest of his life. But although Eisenstein left and could not return, he not only carried the memory of Mexico within him, but also became a part of the Mexican landscape that meant so much to him: in 1931 Roberto Montenegro painted Eisenstein into a fresco at the Colegio de Pedro y Pablo in Mexico City. The Soviet wanderer who had found in Mexico the sublime surface in which his own psyche and the history of his own country could find themselves 'flattened' and healed left in that surface a two-dimensional reflection of himself: he had joined, at least in effigy, the great artwork.

Figure 20.
Roberto Montenegro,
'Eisenstein', Colegio de Pedro y
Pablo, Mexico City

6. The Skeleton Dance: Animation, Terror and the Musical Comedy

Eisenstein returned to the Soviet Union in 1932, without his Mexican film and under vague shadows of disgrace; on 21 November 1931, Stalin had sent a telegram to Upton Sinclair, the language of which was ominous:

EISENSTEIN LOOSE [sic] HIS COMRADES CONFIDENCE IN SOVIET UNION STOP HE IS THOUGHT TO BE DESERTER WHO BROKE OFF WITH HIS OWN COUNTRY STOP AM AFRAID THE PEOPLE HERE WOULD HAVE NO INTEREST IN HIM SOON STOP AM VERY SORRY BUT ALL ASSERT IT IS THE FACT STOP.[1]

Eisenstein had been gone since 1929, and so he had been abroad for most of the frenzy of collectivization, industrialization and general upheaval that accompanied Stalin's first Five-Year Plan. The year that Eisenstein returned, 1932, that upheaval had spread very dramatically to Soviet cultural organizations. In April, all of the literary groups that had fermented throughout the 1920s were dismantled overnight, to be supplanted by one overarching Union of Writers and all the other arts were soon following suit.[2] The arts were to be reorganized and centralized under the slogan of 'socialist realism', now the official mode of expression of Soviet art in general.[3]

Eisenstein had to find a place for himself in this changed and changing world, and his attempts to do so would be made even more difficult by the growing hostility of Boris Shumiatskii, the new head of GUK, the central agency controlling Soviet cinema. Shumiatskii, who had heard Upton Sinclair's version of Eisenstein's Mexican adventure, was not very favorably disposed to this renegade, and it was Shumiatskii who would be in charge of Eisenstein's chastisement over the Bezhin Meadow affair later in the 1930s.[4] One of

Shumiatskii's early functions in Eisenstein's post-Mexico career was to drive a final wedge between Eisenstein and his long-time collaborator Grigorii Alexandrov.

1. The Carcass of Grisha Alexandrov

Alexandrov had worked with Eisenstein since the days of the Proletkul't theater productions; he had collaborated on every aspect of the film-making process on all of Eisenstein's films of the 1920s, but as the years went by, he began to chafe under the burden of being the eternal apprentice. Before Eisenstein, Alexandrov and Tisse left for the West in 1929, Alexandrov wrote a scenario for a film about the Revolution as seen through its effects on a provincial ballet theater, a film he wished to call *Sleeping Beauty*.[5] When he showed an early version of that scenario to his mentor Eisenstein, he got a very caustic reaction. In some notes from 1929, Eisenstein, who was, after all, part of the Soviet cult(ure) of 'criticism', held nothing back: 'The defects aren't so much formal as ideological.'[6] 'Wozu? Wozu? Wozu? the demeaning demeaning [repetition sic] of the Civil War.'[7] Even, at one point: '*It is shameful to read, as a Bolshevik*. The falsity of the aesthetic aims!!!!'[8] Eisenstein, clearly, could be a harsh critic, something which he himself, as a former student of the famously demanding Meyerhold, would probably have counted a virtue.

Despite Eisenstein's acid critique, *Sleeping Beauty* was destined to be Alexandrov's first stab at separation. Before he left with Eisenstein for Europe and America, Alexandrov presented the scenario to Goskino and received a promising response: the Soviet cinema authorities felt it should be made into a film and they assigned it to the promising newcomers to film-making, S and G Vasiliev, the unrelated 'brothers' who would ascend to immense celebrity a few years later as the directors of the epic *Chapaev*. In his memoirs Alexandrov claimed that when the scenario was assigned to the Vasilievs, a member of the cinema committee took him aside and said, 'You yourself are the "sleeping beauty." When will you begin to film things on your own?' (GA 125)

Alexandrov, the 'Sleeping Beauty', received the long-overdue kiss that would awaken him to an independent and successful film career several years later, if we take Alexandrov's own biographical narrative at face value, from no less a prince than Stalin himself, in the grounds of Maksim Gorky's dacha in August 1932, when Alexandrov had just returned from the United States. 'Our people and the Bolshevik party, have every reason to look with optimism towards the future,' Stalin proclaimed to him then. 'Art, unfortunately, has not kept up with the tempos of economic construction... It's well known that the people love hearty, cheerful art, but you [artists] don't yet take that into account. More than that... in the arts those people who suppress everything amusing have not yet become extinct.' (Ga 181) Whether or not his intention was really shaped by one pivotal encounter in a country house garden with the Soviet Union's supreme leader, Alexandrov could see that 'comedy' was a promising direction for creative exploration. He had always had a good sense of humor himself and had learned a great deal from his time in Hollywood and so when Eisenstein turned down a rather farcical scenario, 'Jolly Fellows', and Boris Shumiatskii offered the film to Alexandrov, he accepted eagerly, thus finalizing a break with Eisenstein that had been brewing over the past few years.

Like most 'sudden awakenings', Alexandrov's blossoming into an independent director had been underway for a while. There had been the making of 'Romance Sentimentale' in Paris, a short film, and an experiment in sound, that Eisenstein found too schlocky to associate himself with.[9] More recently he had spent the early summer of 1932 in New York, staying after Eisenstein's departure to make and present a propaganda film glorifying the Five-Year Plan (since Alexandrov had not, obviously, been 'on location' for most of those Five Years, this film was more an exercise in editing found footage than 'directing' per se). When he returned, he made another film of this kind (*Internatsional*, celebrating 15 years of Soviet achievements) for Boris Shumiatskii, who was impressed enough by his work to offer him his first real feature, *Jolly Fellows* (*Veselye rebiata*, 1934).

This film was to be a musical comedy and as such Alexandrov would be borrowing as much as he could from the lessons he had learned in Hollywood. The Russians had met a great many actors and directors over the course of their travels through Europe and America, but the filmmaker who may have taught both Alexandrov and Eisenstein the most about the integration of sound and image was the great Walt Disney, whose studios had been especially fascinating to the visitors from the Soviet Union. Apart from the charming and debonair Mickey Mouse, Alexandrov had been swept off his feet by the sophisticated synchronization techniques behind Disney's cartoon shorts, the 'Silly Symphonies' and, in particular, 'The Skeleton Dance':

> Walt Disney presents the 'Dance of Death' by Grieg, and in this
> amusing cartoon the comic effect is achieved by means of dancing
> skeletons who have left the cemetery... The Disney method of filming
> held great interest for us. The famous cartoonist began with the
> phonogram. The carefully prepared phonogram would become, as it
> were, the skeleton ['carcass'] of the film. (GA 143–144)

As he worked on his own first feature, Alexandrov himself carefully
transferred the lessons of the 'Skeleton Dance' to his own live-action
comedy. The opening sequence of the film works from a 'phonogram', a recording of the film's theme song, the 'March of the Jolly
Fellows', the first in a long line of hits to be generated by
Alexandrov's musicals and, specifically, by the collaboration
between the composer Isaak Osipovich Dunaevskii and the lyricist
Vasilii Ivanovich Lebedev-Kumach.[10] The hero of the film, as yet a
cheery, pipe-playing shepherd, marches through a beautiful
landscape, all the inhabitants of which, be they girl or sheep,
resonate with the same happy song:

> Legko na serdtse ot pesni vesëloi,
>
> Ona skuchat' ne daët nikogda,
>
> I liubiat pesniu derevni i sëla,
>
> I liubiat pesniu bol'shie goroda.
>
> Nam pesnia zhit' i liubit' pomogaet,
>
> Ona, kak drug, i zovët i vedët,
>
> I tot, kto s pesnei po zhizni shagaet,
>
> Nikogda i nigde ne propadët![11]

> [The heart is made easy by a jolly song,/That doesn't let us ever feel
> blue/Village and hamlet love the song/And big cities love the song,
> too./The song helps us to live and to love,/Like a friend, it calls and
> leads us,/And he who strides through life with a song/Will never and
> nowhere be lost.]

Just like the skeletons in Disney's Silly Symphony, the jolly shepherd
knows how to turn the bars of a fence into a xylophone and how to
dance out tunes on the boards of a little bridge. The film does contain
moments of 'actual' animation: the opening credits are enlivened
by winking heads of famous actors – Charlie Chaplin, Harold Lloyd,
Buster Keaton – and the film's title is written out by a lively cow,

drawn very much in the Disney style; later animated clocks and moons appear to inform us how much time has passed between scenes. What is, however, perhaps most striking is the wholesale transfer of the laws of animation into a live-action universe.

Certain tropes govern animated worlds; these are laws with philosophical as well as practical implications. One of these laws can be described as the exaggeration of cause and effect. Alexandrov's *Jolly Fellows* contains an elaborate slapstick sequence in which animals and their keepers thoroughly disrupt a pretentious dinner party. The animals (outside, at least at first) are literally bound – by rope – to human beings within the mansion, the premise being that the animals will then be unable to run away. The result, of course, is a grand exercise in 'push me, pull you', in which the least move at one end of the rope cause great commotion at the other end, a perfect illustration in the large effects of little causes, a primary component of the animated world.

'Cause and effect' is not the only principle exaggerated in the animated universe. A second rule of thumb emphasizes the animation itself: everything turns out to be more alive than you think. Walt Disney, of course, used this trope extensively, making not only little furry animals, but also trees, plants and various household objects more alive – and more human – than they have any right to be. In Alexandrov's *Jolly Fellows*, the animals have 'professional names' (the goats being called 'Secretary', 'Bureaucrat', and 'Professor') and in the most dramatic illustration of this rule of (excess) animation, a would-be aristocrat attempts to slice into a roast suckling pig which turns out, due to the chaos provoked by the slapstick application of exaggerated cause-and-effect previously, to be a *real live piglet*.

A third and most fundamental, principle of animation is the one vividly demonstrated by the opening credits and may be considered, I suppose, the synthesis of the previous two: the whole 'animated' world is joined together, bound not merely by the ropes of 'cause and effect' but by the 'carcass' upon which it is all constructed, the phonogram. The animated universe sings, with its many voices, a single, very catching, tune. 'The March of the Jolly Fellows', with which Alexandrov's pioneering contribution to Soviet synchronization begins, foregrounds the importance of the very phonogram upon which the film depends: truly here is a song which 'calls to us and leads us'.

These principles, as it happens, are not merely handy rules for the construction of clever animated shorts, as Alexandrov's extensive use of them in a live-action musical comedy demonstrates; they are also the laws of the Soviet utopia, of a truly 'totalitarian' universe, in which cause and effect are tightly bound together (no effect without some cause; no disaster without some traitor), in which every element of the world has a potentially significant political meaning (there is no object so innocent that it remains 'just an object') and in which, finally, all must be brought together to sing, in many voices, even many different languages, the same great song of praise.

The transformation of 'Mickeymousing' into a Soviet mechanism is made most baldly in Alexandrov's first feature, in the sense that it is there that the laws of animation are most plainly translated into this foreign medium (doubly foreign, being both Russian and a different medium, live-action film), but in Alexandrov's remaining three musicals of the 1930s, *Circus* (1936), *Volga-Volga* (1938) and *Bright Path* (which I am counting as a product of the 1930s, although it was released in 1940), the laws and rhythms of the 'Skeleton Dance' still wield their mysterious magic.

When he began his next film, Alexandrov was working with a scenario (*Pod kupolom tsirka*/'Under the Big Top') produced by two of the Soviet Union's most accomplished and beloved humorists, Il'ia Il'f and Evgenii Petrov.[12] 'Under the Big Top' started its life (in December 1934) as a successful play in the very Moscow theater (the *Miuzik-Kholl*) in which much of the musical action of *Jolly Fellows* takes place. In its early versions (as in the play it was based on), the scenario was a cheerful farce set in the world of the circus; the chief stimulus to the action being the need to save hard currency by replacing an American act (an aerial stunt performed by a woman who has come to the Soviet Union to escape US prejudice against her secret biracial baby) with a Soviet equivalent. A running gag about a running taxi meter seemed to have been borrowed lock, stock and barrel from René Clair's 1931 *Le Million*. As the various levels of cinematic oversight tinkered with the scenario, Il'f and Petrov became more and more offended; they had been traveling in the United States during much of the filming and so the changes made in their scenario came as quite a shock upon their return to the Soviet Union in February 1936. Alexandrov, as well as the studio authorities found their emphasis on money distasteful – the Vice Director of Mosfil'm, Elena Sokolovskaia, objected specifically to a gag in which one of a talking dog's three words is *fininspektor*, the equivalent of an IRS agent[13] – and Mosfil'm went so far as to term the first scenario too 'Odessan', a backhanded way of saying it was too Jewish.[14] Eventually, relations between Il'f and Petrov on the one hand and Alexandrov and Mosfil'm and GUK on the other, became bitter enough that the humorists insisted their names be pulled from the credits of the film, now titled *Circus* and Mosfil'm responded with a final blistering critique of their scenario's defects:

> The fundamental idea of the piece – the internationalism of our Soviet people, the absence of racial prejudices in the USSR, motherland of all laborers – has become the central theme of the picture. It is now unblemished by the hard currency problem, which, although it was no longer topical, was given in your scenario an extraordinarily large place, to the point where the Soviet number on the cannon – one of the central motifs of the piece – was really done in the name of economizing hard currency...
>
> We decidedly reject your reproach that the picture's quality has diminished as a result of the corrections made in the scenario and believe that from an objective point of view, freed from that overvaluation of one's own work that sometimes affects authors, as you yourself mention in your letter, it will be impossible not to acknowledge that the picture has benefited in many respects.[15]

As some of the farce and most, though not all, of the discussion of financial matters was eliminated from the scenario,[16] what set the tone for the revisions was Alexandrov's understanding of the laws of animation, as described above, here brought into closer step with their social and political implications than they had been in *Jolly Fellows*. One of the changes from the Il'f and Petrov scenario, for instance, involved the unsuitability of the circus manager's daughter, Raechka, for stardom in the new Soviet spectacle; in the early versions, she was unsuitable because she was a little chubby and her extra weight messes up the aerial act she has been practicing with the Soviet hero Martynov: he is bounced too high (the actual mechanical details of this act and this accident remain somewhat blurry) and falls. But when Alexandrov reworks this episode into *Circus*, Raechka's chubbiness is no longer allowed to remain unmotivated. Now that fatal 'extra half-kilo' becomes, following the law of exaggerated cause and effect, the result of overt sabotage and treachery: the evil Kneischitz, German entrepreneur and racist proto-fascist, seduces the silly girl into eating a whole chocolate cake.

The subplot concerning Marion Dixon's 'black baby' is submitted, too, to the lessons of 'animated Stalinism': the scene where the baby is revealed to the audience and where Kneischitz learns to his horror that in the Soviet Union, racism is dead and gone (this in a scenario, let us recall, labelled 'too Odessan' by the cinema authorities) is inflated in *Circus* to incorporate a powerful illustration of the law of the single song. In one of the most famous sequences from any of Alexandrov's films, the audience catches up the child and passes him from arm to arm as representatives of several Soviet nationalities take part in a serial lullaby. Marion Dixon, American circus star (played by Alexandrov's second wife, Liubov' Orlova, the star of all four of these musicals), learns Russian and political culture through song as well (in the original Il'f and Petrov scenario, the first attempts at her Russian education were devoted to learning the names of salads served in the Restaurant 'Monopol')[17] and the dashing Martynov teaches her the film's big musical hit, Dunaevsky's and Lebedev-Kumach's 'Broad is My Native Land'. By the end of the film, Marion Dixon marches with thousands of others in a May Day celebration and sings this hymn in quite admirable and enthusiastic Russian.

The transition from circus performance to May Day parade is made seamless by the clever use of 'transparencies' permitting the combination of characters filmed in one shot with a separately filmed background, another trick Alexandrov had picked up in Hollywood and had already made use of in *Jolly Fellows*.[18] This technique sometimes involved animation in the literal sense, as when Alexandrov makes the transition from Von Kneischitz spying on Marion Dixon and Martynov from a snowy ledge to the springtime language lessons of the next scene. Von Kneischitz peers in through the window. Martynov stares at him coldly. Animated frost grows over the window, hiding Von Kneischitz from view and drawing that scene to a close. The frost metamorphoses into palm fronds, a blue sky, a different season and we enter, by means of a different window, Marion Dixon's bright and cheerful hotel suite right on Red Square. In keeping with his affection for the 'carcass' that ties a whole scene together, Alexandrov loved not only phonograms, but also seamless transitions, an emphasis on continuity (again a technique with political as well as practical ramifications) that becomes a fetish. Whenever possible he would tie a scene to the next, by means of animated interludes, transparent shifting backdrops, music, or whatever else he could think of. The universe was not only to be joined in a 'single song', but was also to be made as seamlessly unified and continuous as possible from beginning to end.

The 'circus' of *Circus*, then, is resolutely an anti-carnival, in the sense that it reinforces, rather than subverts, the established hierarchy of political ideas. As AV Lunacharskii (former Commissar of Enlightenment) had pointed out in a 1931 article on Il'f and

Petrov: 'Laughter can be extremely serious, because at the same time as it amuses, it destroys: it gives a feeling of confidence to the one who laughs and pours poison, more or less cruelly, on the one being laughed at. Not for nothing the French say that laughter is murder.'[19] Satire, then, must always be directed safely at social enemies, although a much-diluted 'humor' could be used by the proletariat in attempts to educate members of sympathetic but backwards social groups. Eisenstein picked up this martial theme in a manuscript from 1935:

> Laughter is simply a light weapon whose strike is just as deadly and which can be deployed where there is no sense in bringing in the all-crushing tanks of social wrath.
>
> Whereas, in the oppressive atmosphere of nineteenth-century tsarist Russia, or in the twentieth century anywhere except the Russia that is now the USSR, lampoon, satire and laughter have been the skirmishers of social protest, in our country the role of humor remains the conquest of the enemy, just like the infantry that floods the whole line of the enemy's trenches when the heavy artillery has cleared the way for the stab of bayonets.
>
> Serving as the start of the battle there, the conqueror's laughter surges at the approach of victory in our country. (SW1 72)

What we find in *Circus* is that ecstatic political phenomenon of 'the conqueror's laughter', of laughter from above, a laughter that can annihilate all social enemies.[20] This is how Von Kneischitz is defeated: not by force but by gales of laughter, as the circus audience responds wholeheartedly to the circus director's explanation that in the Soviet Union babies of all colors, even light blue, are perfectly welcome. Von Kneischitz looks around wildly, unable to understand this joke of which he finds himself the butt and then he simply vanishes from the film as it moves into the sublime solidarity of the lullaby, Soviet circus act and May Day.

Alexandrov was by no means the only or the first portrayer of this peculiar form of annihilation. A prototype can be found already in Dovzhenko's 1930 *Earth*, where the kulak, attempting to confess his vile murder of the young hero of collectivization, is annihilated by the crowd's complete unconcern: they listen instead to the funeral oration, with its leap into the sublimities of the Soviet future and the kulak is destroyed by his own inconsequence. True, this is not laughter, *per se*, at work, but the episode does hinge on that same collective ecstasy underlying laughter-from-above. In Eisenstein's *Bezhin Meadow*, there was to have been a scene in which annihilating laughter explicitly replaced physical destruction as a way to do away with enemies of the Soviet Union. When the kulak prisoners are being led to prison along the main highway, the riled peasants at first can hardly hold themselves back from lynching them, but young Stepok turns the scene into a joke (by wondering in mock-seriousness what would happen if the kulaks could really return the Tsar to power) and soon the whole mob lifts its head to the sky and laughs in annihilating joy: 'Something unbelievable happened to the people there... People writhed, sobbed, cried with laughter.'[21] (Perhaps this scene is a Soviet, atheistic descendant of Pierre's famous epiphanic hilarity in *War and Peace;* the French may be able to hold him prisoner in a shed, but how can they hope to imprison his immortal soul?)

In *Volga-Volga*, Alexandrov's musical production from 1938, the scope of the map within which 'continuity' is asked to play its key role is broadened: this story of country musicians competing for the honor of a trip from the periphery to Moscow finds a source of motivation, in the style of *Jolly Fellows*, in the conflict between classical and popular music.[22] The laws of animated Stalinism provide for a resolution of the difficulty that maximizes continuity: the difference between styles of music is immaterial, compared to the thrill of singing the same song together, and the periphery turns out to be not so far from Moscow after all, bound to the capital by waterways and canals as surely as man was attached to cow in the more boisterous *Jolly Fellows*. Orlova this time plays the young woman (a letter-carrier with the nickname 'Strelka', or 'arrow') who produces the song that everyone will sing; a storm literally rips the music out of her hands and distributes it all over Moscow so that by the time she arrives in the capital, her song is already on all lips, a heartening allegory for the instantaneous broadcasting of ideology (in this case really the 'words of the people') that underlay the 'continuity' dreams of the Soviet state.

In the final of the four musicals of the thirties, the goal once again is Moscow, the starting point once again the periphery somewhere, but where in *Volga-Volga* the lesson provided by the laws of animation was the tie forged by means of 'continuity' – in specific, canals – between country and capital, in *Bright Path* (1940) the moral is taken to more ecstatic lengths. Now it turns out that Moscow was always already everywhere, and Orlova, portraying this time a young country maidservant who evolves into a Stakhanovite textile worker, must discover that in the Soviet Union, 'fairytales really do come true', as the title song repeats again and again. Even deep in the countryside, where an ignorant girl like

Tania can find herself playing nursemaid to the offspring of lingering bourgeois elements, signs of Moscow are everywhere around, needing only to be recognized: loudspeakers broadcast Moscow's voice and keep Moscow time, the golden onion domes of the Kremlin appear on a box of matches and are even reflected in the domes of the town church, which picturesquely appears in the window at every possible moment, a visible reconciliation of two times and places (two 'chronotopes'): the fairy tale time of long long ago and the Moscow of today, when fairy tales of a new sort are being played out everyday.

The fairytale was not a new device for Alexandrov, who had made his first move away from Eisenstein's tutelage under the star of 'Sleeping Beauty'. Here the fairy tale he was working with was 'Cinderella': anybody, no matter how lowly, can aspire to the heights of Soviet achievement and to the geographical center, Moscow. The fairy godmother was in this version of the old story represented by a stern and determined female political worker, Pronina, who takes young, smudge-faced Tania under her ideologically unyielding wing. The authorities guiding Alexandrov's production were made somewhat uneasy by this woman's role as the representative of Moscow, of the central authority. A transcript of a discussion of Alexandrov's project reveals these tensions: a number of people suggest she be softened down somewhat, or at least given a husband, maybe a child:

> In the scenario Pronina turned out extremely dry and dull... True, she's brought in here as a good fairy, but in a realistic work even a fairy should have some connection to life. For example, I think that Pronina should have a family. That doesn't mean that it's necessary to show a husband and children in her room, but somewhere something should be said about that. Maybe she has an excellent daughter somewhere whom she thinks about'.[23]

Comrade Cherniavskii, head of the Scenario Section of GUK, agreed that Pronina needed to become more of a real person: 'The heart of the matter here is that it is undesirable to revive in any form the figure of that kind of Party raisonneur, the 'Party-Auntie', about whom so much has been written.'[24] Although it is not said explicitly, the demands for the addition, somehow, of a husband and/or child also suggest that the utter absence of an interest in men made the character somehow suspect: even though the moral of the film was to be that a woman (Tania) could triumph in life by means of hard work, a female character who lacked the softening charms of foolishness and youth could find herself condemned as 'unwomanly'.

Eisenstein had run into similar difficulties a few years previously with the role of the Praskov'ia Osipova, wife of the director of the collective farm, in *Bezhin Meadow*. In May of 1936 Babitskii, head of the Mosfil'm Studio, called for a different actress to be brought in for the role, 'to give this figure more weight – the leader of the collective farm as a strong-willed, stubborn woman of strong character, a Soviet aktivistka'.[25] On the other hand, the same Babitskii complained at a discussion of the film (according to Eisenstein's scribbled notes, date uncertain): 'The wife of the leader of the collective farm is less pleasant than the director,' to which Eisenstein responds in his notes, 'Take this into consideration and soften up.'[26] Eventually, for Eisenstein's second version of the film, the character would be scrapped.

In *The Bright Path*, Alexandrov allowed his passion for 'continuity' to surpass all reasonable bounds: if a cut between scenes can in any way be made less of a cut and more like a seamless transition, by means of framing, cuts 'in and out' (allowing a shift in background while the central figure remains constant), little snippets of animation, or any other device the director could devise, then it would be. Examples abound: by means of transparent backgrounds, a musing Tania segues directly from the little hotel where she works into an adult school classroom; from the classroom, a little figure of a dinosaur is matched by means of a dissolve (and with the help of some off-screen bellowing) with the figure of Tania's arrogant employer trying in vain to keep her own baby quiet (Tania having been off getting an education); an elaborate dream sequence, against a backdrop of a fairytale Kremlin, segues seamlessly into the equally fabulous world of the textile factory where Tania is about to get her first real job; the cotton fluff she sweeps up there flies into the sky, where it looks a little like snow and then, against cottony clouds, turns into rain, which segues into the water of the communal showers where the women workers squeal with pleasure; and so on and so on and so on, the more contrived the better. As a result, the whole film seems drenched in a kind of temporal syrup, in which every segment clings stickily to the segments before and after. There is little difference here between animation and live action – all are equal in the animated utopia of the fairytale (in the spirit of everything more alive than you think). Little bits of animation are tossed into the film as yet another way to make all transitions as continuous as possible: when Tania bends her head over a manual for weavers, the illustrations come to life before our eyes, starting a cascade of transitions that will in short order transform her into the Stakhanovite worker old Pronina, the 'fairy godmother', always knew she could be.

Tania herself, after all, is a fairytale illustration come to life, as she discovers at the very end of the film, when she and her heroic engineer true love meet each other again beneath the carved friezes of the great agricultural-technical exposition in Moscow. Tania and her engineer (Aleksei Nikolaevich) are the living embodiment, the animation, of those heroic statuary workers. Perhaps Alexandrov was remembering here his work with Eisenstein in Mexico, when for the Prologue of *Que Viva Mexico* they so assiduously posed living Indians against a backdrop of stone profiles, carved by and representing their ancestors.[27] In Mexico, too, pictures had a way of coming to life. In *Bright Path* it is the artwork, the *skazka*, that exists first and the living citizens of flesh and blood struggle and work to become that artwork's animated embodiment.

As Grigorii Alexandrov moved into his independent career as a maker of musical comedies, he took the lessons he had learned from Walt Disney – about the importance of a solid musical 'carcass', about the laws governing the well-designed animated universe – and applied them with ever-increasing zeal and subtlety to the live-action, ideologically animated world of Stalinist cinema. Eisenstein, too, had been deeply impressed – even moved – by Disney's achievements and in the 1930s, a decade that was laced with creative and political disasters for him until the saving grace of *Alexander Nevsky* (1938), Eisenstein experimented both practically and philosophically with the lessons of animation. His and Alexandrov's experiments would echo each other in certain respects, both being inspired by the same American Mouse, but where Alexandrov imported techniques he found remarkably congenial to the ideological and practical demands of the Soviet cinema of the 1930s, Eisenstein managed to discover yet another area of philosophical inquiry where the terrain became murkier – and thus more fascinating to him – the farther he progressed. This is not to say that he did not, like Alexandrov, begin with the lessons of the 'Skeleton Dance'. That was the common starting point for both directors: eventually, from that shared beginning, they would find themselves traveling exceedingly different paths.

Eisenstein, like Alexandrov, was determined to try his hand at 'comedy' on his return to the Soviet Union. In 1933 his plans were approved for a comedy entitled *MMM*, the three M's standing for the initials of the project's sad-sack main character, Maksim Maksimovich Maksimov, a man with lingering petty bourgeois aspirations. The premise of the film (what would today be called a 'situation comedy') was to be the return to modern Moscow – under the guise of tourism – of a set of Boyars from long, long ago. The means by which these strange tourists would arrive in town was a device very much in line both with Eisenstein's renewed interest in animation and with some of the most striking aspects of Mexican culture. In short, an old church comes to life, all its pictures beginning to move, starting with an old fresco portraying the infant John the Baptist, who 'began to play in her womb' – the fresco animates itself and 'the infant begins to play a violin'.[28] Next a Patriarch 'slips from the wall' where he has been contained in a fresco (1. 7). Even the little stone birds decorating the capitals 'fly down' (1. 7). The first of the tourist boyars emerges from a crypt and soon is surrounded by a whole company of his ilk, some women included. They converse in Old Church Slavic about their desire to visit MMM (whose drunkenness may be the source of all this excessive animation; in accordance with that law of the animated world, the exaggeration of cause and effect, Maksim Maksimovich's drunken calling out to Old Rus' in the church seems to be the trigger for all the magic chaos that ensues) and form a procession to leave the church.

As stunning as this scene would surely have been visually, some pitfalls are already clear from the scenario. The 'church' in this scene becomes another museum in the mode of the Hermitage, not Mexico's Ministry of Education. It harbors old, outgrown, retrograde mementoes of a pre-Soviet past that bear within them the potential for coming to life: once again, 'everything more alive than you might think' – but here in an ideologically treacherous vein, since the thing that comes unexpectedly to life is the past. In Mexico the constant ebb and flow of animated pictures had been possible without the present inevitably suffering from the poison of the past: in that great 'picture', all had been equally present at all times and the flow between artwork and 'real life' had been steady, a source of strength and beauty rather than paranoia. It was extremely difficult, probably impossible, to translate the great potential of two-dimensional history into the Russian context, however, since in Moscow there must always be a sense of contamination and peril as one era penetrated another. As in Disney's 'Skeleton Dance', here the dead came to life and the scene was to be constructed around the skeletal framework of music, as in the Silly Symphonies or *Jolly Fellows*: Eisenstein called for the 'animating frescoes' to be coordinated to appropriate music: the singing of the stone birds, the violin of the Infant and so forth. They would all be singing the same song ('law' number three) but in this case, the wrong one.

MMM did not survive the spring of 1933; its obsession with animated frescoes had to be set aside (until that obsession could be revived in *Bezhin Meadow*'s ransacked church, in *Ivan the Terrible*'s rich and eloquent interiors), but that did not mean that Eisenstein had left his interest in animation behind and indeed the project that restored Eisenstein's reputation and salvaged his career, *Alexander Nevsky* (1938), was his closest approach ever to the goals of the 'Skeleton Dance' and the laws of Stalinist animation. In fact, we can think of *Alexander Nevsky* as Eisenstein's attempt to do something 'Alexandrovian': an epic, yes, but also a musical comedy.

2. The Bones of *Alexander Nevsky*

> Through the descending bands of wire we carefully lower ourselves.
>
> What shines whitely there at the foot of the wire spiderweb?
>
> Not concrete posts,
>
> not metaphors.
>
> Bones... (IP1 297)

Walt Disney's 'Skeleton Dance' – which Eisenstein called 'a masterpiece of the moving equivalent of music'[29] – was at least as much an inspiration for Eisenstein as for Alexandrov, but Eisenstein appreciated this Silly Symphony not just for its technical innovations, but for its thematic content, its skeletons. For Eisenstein had always liked bones: 'a kind of illness', he called this affection, but as diseases go, it was a very productive one (BTS 408–409). In his description of scrambling through the barbed wire fences of an old Civil War battlefield near Dvinsk to look at the gleaming white bones left there, he places 'bones' within a particular kind of series: not concrete posts, not metaphors. This is itself a metaphorical use of 'bones', of course: Eisenstein was still searching for objects that (like the dying ox in *Strike*) would make art real. In this vein he returned to skeletons for help with the opening scene of *Alexander Nevsky*:

> Having conceived of the prologue to *Alexander Nevsky* as a panorama of fields, strewn with the 'mortal remains' of those who died fighting the Tatars for Russian land, I was bound to remember the battlefield outside Dvinsk.

> I ordered a consignment of skeletons, human and horse and carefully arranged their component parts on the grass: a fresco of a battle, frozen... Hell, none of it worked!
>
> It was revoltingly 'stagy' to look at and not at all convincing on screen.
>
> On screen, the skeletons looked like white monkeys, parodies of real people.
>
> I scrapped them. (BTS 408)

This was the challenge for Eisenstein as he worked on *Alexander Nevsky*: to create something that would transcend staginess; to find an approach to skeletons, metaphorical and otherwise, that would serve to reconnect him to the Soviet audience.

Where the 1930s had brought Grisha Alexandrov independence and success, they led Eisenstein to the very brink of disaster. In the years following his return to the Soviet Union in 1932, his arrival shadowed by the loss of his Mexican film and the intensifying hostility of the Soviet cinema authorities, Eisenstein had encountered one setback after another: after his attempt at comedy (*MMM*) had failed to get off the ground in 1933, an epic treatment of Moscow's history never got beyond the planning stages (*Moskva*, 1934). Then, in January 1935, he had found himself transformed into the whipping boy of the All-Union Conference of Workers in Soviet Cinematography: nobody there had wanted to listen to Eisenstein's ideas about the value to cinema of the laws of primitive thinking, about the link between Soviet actors and the Bororo Indians who considered themselves to be both men and red parrots. All that interested Eisenstein's colleagues in the film industry was whether he was ever going to start making films again. Eisenstein's slide into disgrace was capped by the failure of *Bezhin Meadow* to satisfy the cinema authorities (Boris Shumiatskii in particular); when that film was banned, on 17 March 1937, Eisenstein's career had reached its lowest point. In April, he was fired from his teaching job at VGIK (the Higher State Institute of Cinematography) and in desperation Eisenstein wrote a letter to Stalin in which he begged to have his talents employed productively.[30]

The project that Mosfil'm sent his way was the heroic history of Alexander Nevsky (a subject Eisenstein preferred to the story of the struggle of Minin and Pozharskii against the Poles, his other option)[31] and he worked very hard on this project through the fall of 1937, even though it was not yet clear to what degree GUK was willing to consider him rehabilitated.[32] In the end, it took another man's tragedy to bring Eisenstein back into the clear: at the end of 1937 Eisenstein's long-time opponent, Boris Shumiatskii, was removed as head of GUK and arrested; early in the next year he would be convicted of 'wrecking' and eventually shot. Since one of the objects Shumiatskii had 'wrecked' was determined to be Eisenstein's career, as the 'negative of a negative', Eisenstein now became, for a time, something like a 'positive'. (It would take about eight years for the higher authorities to realize that two negatives, although dialectically interesting, did not necessarily a positive make.)

At an early screening and discussion of *Alexander Nevsky*, late in 1938, the comments made reflected Eisenstein's new identity as 'victim of Shumiatskii'. The director Annenskii hailed Eisenstein's return to the limelight:

> This picture is exceptionally meaningful because one of the greatest masters of cinematography has returned again and has demonstrated all his strength and power – a master whom the former sabotaging administration oppressed in every way and to whom that administration did not give a chance to develop all his brilliance, his talent – in this picture is unveiled one of our strongest masters – a master of enormous emotional force and culture.[33]

Such words must have seemed very sweet to the long-beleaguered Eisenstein – if he could keep himself from a more sober reflection on the twists and turns of political fate.

Eisenstein had the great good fortune to enlist the aid of Sergei Prokofiev in his project; like Eisenstein, Prokofiev also needed to polish up his reputation since he had only recently (1936) moved to the Soviet Union from a long exile abroad. He threw himself into the project after his return in early 1938 from a tour of the USA. As it happened, Prokofiev, like Eisenstein and Alexandrov, had worked with Walt Disney and had been suitably impressed by the American's mastery of synchronized sound effects; Prokofiev, too, knew how to appreciate a good skeleton. Prokofiev and Eisenstein worked together to bring the glories of sound synchronization to this epic project: one of the evil German knights sinks into the icy water and a deep orchestral burp accompanies the bubbles; a horse whinnies in fear and an instrument screams in its place.[34] The very exactness of such moments of synchronization recalls not only their cartoon origin, but also the live action synchronization practiced by Grisha Alexandrov in his musicals.

The whole notion of the skeleton expanded significantly, however, in the process of making *Alexander Nevsky*. The film was not constructed solely on the principle of the pre-existing 'phonogram'.

Instead, Eisenstein and Prokofiev worked so closely together that sometimes it seemed that Eisenstein's shots or his montage of shots could serve as 'skeleton' for Prokofiev's music and sometimes, as Eisenstein reminisced later, it could be difficult to say who was providing the skeleton for whom:

> It should be said that in *Alexander Nevsky* literally every possible permutation of these methods is to be found. There are scenes in which the pictures were edited in accordance with music pre-recorded on the soundtrack. There are scenes where the music was entirely written to fit a fully completed visual montage; and there are scenes in which every available intermediate method was used. Finally, there are also some cases that have become almost legendary, such as, for instance, the scene with the pipes and tabors played by the Russian troops: I was totally unable to explain in detail to Sergei Prokofiev exactly what I wanted to 'see' in sound for that scene. Finally, losing my temper, I ordered up a selection of the appropriate property instruments (i.e. soundless ones) and made the actors visually 'play' on them what I wanted; I filmed them doing this, showed it to Prokofiev and... almost instantly he produced for me an exact 'musical equivalent' of the visual image of those pipers and drummers which I had shown him.[35]

It was not only a musical score that could serve as skeleton, but also an image or images; whether Eisenstein or Prokofiev was to be the one providing this fundamental underpinning for audiovisual montage, the nature of that basic structure upon which the rest of the film would be constructed was essentially rhythmic:

> As a rule, Prokofiev and I bargain long and earnestly over 'which is to be the first': whether he should write music for unedited pieces of representation which would then be edited accordingly, or I should complete the montage of a scene first and have music afterwards.
>
> This is because the first has a more difficult task to solve: he must determine *the rhythmic course of the scene*.
>
> The second has a 'much easier' time.
>
> He must erect an adequate 'building' with the 'building materials' of his own art.[36]

In Grisha Alexandrov's cinematic universe a single 'jolly song' carried images and characters along; Eisenstein's refinement on that principle was the discovery that the song providing a film with its audio-visual structure need not be a 'song' at all. The trick was to find the rhythm, the pulse, governing both images and music: 'the music also must be governed not only according to those same images and themes but also by the same basic laws and principles that govern the thing as a whole.'[37] This need to seek out 'basic laws and principles' was by no means limited specifically to the construction of audiovisual montage: it was also the process underlying thinking.

Let us take another look at the moment of 'picture-thinking' at the heart of *Alexander Nevsky*. Nevsky discovers in the earthy Ignat's pornographic joke about the hare who traps a fox between two birches and rapes her from behind the solution to his most important tactical quandary: how to defeat the Teuton forces. Not only does bawdiness reveal itself to be a place where serious thinking can take place, but this episode became for Eisenstein the quintessential example of genius in action:

> I was all for presenting Alexander as a genius. When we speak of genius we always think (and quite correctly!) about something like the apple of Newton or the bobbing lid of Faraday's kettle.
>
> This is quite correct, because the ability to discover in a particular phenomenon a general law and bend this law to the service of man in different spheres of life is certainly a trait to be found in the intricate mental apparatus we call genius.
>
> In everyday life, in practical experience, we define genius simply as an ability to apply deductions drawn from minor chance instances to unexpected major phenomena...
>
> And Prince Alexander appears with the halo of genius surrounding his head.
>
> The film offered him only one opportunity of displaying his genius – through the strategic plan of the Battle on the Ice.[38]

'Genius' was required at several levels, for not only Nevsky, but also Eisenstein on Nevsky's behalf had to discover a way to derive the 'general law' from the flotsam of everyday life. As Eisenstein describes the process, he and Piotr Pavlenko (with whom he was writing the screenplay) had a terrible time finding just the right image for this scene ('The edge of the ice-covered lake and... a cat treading on it. The ice was thin at the edge. The ice... broke... under the weight of the cat. The stupidity of our reasoning was unbearable'),[39] until, just by chance, a sleepless Eisenstein reaches for a book and finds his hand on the collection of scandalous folktales containing 'The Vixen and the Hare'. Here was truly a 'trouvaille' in the Surrealist sense: a found object that one finds not just by 'chance' but by design, a design that turns out to be much larger and much more profound than any single object it encompasses.[40] This design is what the genius knows how to find; it is the 'skeleton' underlying thought itself. As Eisenstein summed up the moral of the 'Vixen and the Hare' story (the story of that story!):

> We could achieve nothing while we sought to substitute plastic prototypes, such as the cat, billets, etc., for the plastic image of battle.
>
> Then came a suggestion from material of another plane – a tale, a story.
>
> There must be some law or other for this. The suggestion must come from the dynamic scheme underlying facts or objects, not from details themselves.
>
> And if the facts or objects belong to a different plane, say, to the plane of sound and not plastics, the sensation produced by the dynamic scheme becomes more poignant, the mind capable of transplanting it into another plane must be sharp and the effect becomes many times stronger.[41]

In Eisenstein's hands the same 'laws' that governed animation (and Alexandrov's live-action animated world) became the products of all of world culture and the cornerstone of a philosophical view of man's place in the world. The trope of 'everyone singing the same song' was milled as he worked on *Alexander Nevsky* – and as he pondered the film afterwards – into something grander: 'vertical montage', montage now expanded by 'synaesthesia' into an all-encompassing interlocking of image, sound, landscape and the man inhabiting that landscape:

> [O]n what psychological phenomenon is based the possibility of an equal combination of audiovisual elements – elements of audiovisual polyphony?
>
> Of course, everything is based on that same *synaesthetics* – that is, on the ability to gather *into one all the variety of feeling brought from different areas by different organs of sensation.*[42]

Within the synaesthetic juncture elements that seemed to belong to different worlds could be brought together on the basis of an underlying unity (or shared pulse). Eisenstein had a true genius for perceiving correspondences between objects and phenomena; one of the most notorious instances of his synaesthetic imagination running wild comes in Eisenstein's description (in 'Vertical Montage') of his intentions as he assembled the scene where the opposing forces assembled on the lake. Taking the score in one hand and frames representing each shot in the sequence in the other,

Eisenstein discovers isomorphic correspondences between music and image: '*the movement of the music and the movement of the eye over the lines of the graphic composition coincide*. In other words, *the same gesture, common to both, is the basis of both the musical and the graphic structures*.'[43] Eisenstein reads the landscape as if it were a musical score; he reads the score as if it were a landscape. He discovers in this peculiarly synaesthetic landscape its essential 'gesture', its bones, the way music and landscape animate and inhabit each other. Although the gesture here is grander, Eisenstein's musical landscape here echoes Alexandrov's earlier and cruder version of 'visual music', when in *Jolly Fellows* the film's music is literally spelled out by the birds sitting on a staff made of telegraph wires.

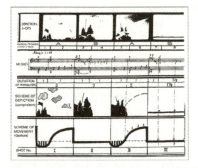 

Figure 21.
'Vertical Montage'
(*Nevsky*)

Figure 22.
Another musical landscape
(*Jolly Fellows*)

The last image of the series examined in 'Vertical Montage' is particularly intriguing.

Figure 23.
Horizon
(*Alexander Nevsky*)

Here we have one of the quintessential landscapes of socialist realism, a landscape one finds not just in *Alexander Nevsky*, but in many other places as well (including Dovzhenko's *Earth*): the low horizon line that calls us into the Big Sky. The tension of the sequence is created by a long wait as Russians (and the film's audience) squint at that line, seeking confirmation that that horizon is actually composed of many people, of Teutons: their 'line' will disintegrate as they fight with the Russians and their landscape will collapse underneath them (in the form of some very fake icebergs), even as the Russian side is transformed, by means of 'vertical montage', into the very landscape they love and defend.

The relation of man to horizons such as these was a major concern of a larger theoretical project that occupied Eisenstein from the 1930s on, the series of essays that would eventually become 'Nonindifferent Nature'. The very title of this work reflects one of those basic laws of animation: everything more alive than it looks. In Disney's 'Silly Symphonies' that meant that any object could be brought to life, could be made to resonate with the musical 'skeleton'. As Eisenstein pondered the possibilities of animation (in its broadest, most philosophical senses), it became less clear what that central skeleton should be: nature was not 'indifferent', it was more like man than one might have thought, but at the same time man was more like a landscape.

Like *Nevsky*'s Russian soldiers peering at a horizon that might at any moment swallow them up, the spectator gazed at art and when the common pulse between viewer and artwork was attained, so would be the juncture. This juncture was neither purely natural (not just a product of 'chance'), nor entirely unnatural (since it was produced by the resonance of laws operating also in nature). Art, at its most 'interesting', was a phenomenon both 'organic' and 'artificial', with the two aspects blending into each other in unexpected ways:

> The perceiver feels organically tied, merged and united with a work of this type, just as he feels himself one with and merged with the organic environment and nature surrounding him.

> To a greater or lesser degree this feeling is inevitable in each of us and the secret consists of the fact that in each case both *us and the work* are governed by *one and the same canon of law*.[44]

Man and artwork merged into the larger landscape formed by the intersection of natural and cultural laws. That intersection was itself marked by a formula equally central to both realms: the mathematics of the Golden Section, the abstract skeleton behind both Greek architecture and the whorls of a seashell.[45] In one of *Nonindifferent*

Nature's more exuberantly synaesthetic passages, Eisenstein brought sunflower seeds, logarithmic spirals, the use of *caesura* in poetry, the art and science of Leonardo da Vinci and *The Battleship Potemkin* under the overarching canopy of the *sectio aurea*, the Golden Section (*Nonindifferent Nature*, pp. 16-23). Every 'part' in a world governed by the law of the Golden Section corresponds to and replicates the 'whole' from which it stems.

Man stood with his conscious, creating, observing mind at a pivotal point: he could be thought of as a mere 'part' of the broader world, but at the same time he was a 'whole' who could create other 'wholes'. Grasping this relationship between 'part' and 'whole' required a special kind of leap, the sublime and dialectical leap that allowed one to be, simultaneously, both 'whole' and 'part' – the same leap the Soviet hero was asked to take when he faced death with heroism and nonchalance, both nothing and something at the same time. The term Eisenstein used for this leap into a new quality, a leap which brought an individual into the greater whole of not just art, but also history (the two not being for the post-Mexico Eisenstein so very different), was pathos: 'This experience of a moment of history is imbued with the greatest pathos and sense of unity with this process. A sense of being in step with it. The sense of collective participation in it. Such is pathos in life.' (*Nonindifferent Nature*, p. 36) This was what was achieved when the laws of nature and art came together: the sublime horizon of socialist realism. Defined this way, pathos was what *Alexander Nevsky* brought Eisenstein – a chance once again to be part of the greater Soviet collective, a chance to sing its praises and to have his own praises sung back to him.

Thus the horizon line marking the intersection between the individual and history – the individual and the collective – was also the line of pathos, by means of which man and landscape intersected each other, nature becoming more animate (less indifferent) and man becoming less different from, say, a rock, a tree, or... a vast frozen lake. The Big Sky beckoning to the viewer is an invitation into the collective and into death.

The experience of 'pathos' was synchronization on the grand scale: what happened when a spectator and a film, a man and a landscape, an image and a melody, found the pulse that tied them together. Naturally there were some pitfalls involved. If the synchronization was too precise, one ran the risk of slipping from the exalted state of pathos into plain comedy:

> The too-frequent coincidence of inner accents of music and picture
> inevitably gives the feeling of a marching type of people's behavior,

especially if the musical accent also coincides with their *movements*. This produces a rather comic effect and therefore it often is used in comedies, in this case as if laughing at the very principle of the correspondence of music and picture. The baring of the actual principle translates it from the area of the *organic* into the area of the *mechanical* and it inevitably seems funny in its application to the conduct of living beings. (The *bared* application of the principle of 'repetition' is just as funny.)[46]

The difference between the 'organic' and 'mechanical', the comic and the epic, is narrow indeed. *Alexander Nevsky* is a film very much perched on this thin edge between comedy and pathos; when the peasants pop up from holes in the ground to the thrilling strains of 'Arise, O Russian People', there is a literalness to their 'arising' that is only a hair's breadth away from comedy.[47] (This phenomenon is separate from the film's use of 'comic relief' and homespun folksy characters as a foil to Alexander Nevsky's heroic brilliance.)[48] Also posing a threat to *Alexander Nevsky*'s epic sense of pathos is the film's tendency towards kitsch, another effect closely tied to excessive synchronization. Over the battlefield littered with the dead and dying wafts a plaintive melody, a song about soldiers thinking longingly of their womenfolk; right on the musical cue, we hear and see men groaning out the names of particular women: Mari-i-i-i-i-a!

Pathos and comedy, opposite sides of a very thin coin, shared a common mechanism: the ecstatic leap. 'Ecstasy', by means of which the unity of opposites could be achieved, came in many forms. There was, on the one hand, the Eastern fondness for trying 'to bring opposites together by *dissolving them into each other*' (*Nonindifferent Nature*, p. 151), what one might call, thinking of Alexandrov's obsession with smooth transitions, an 'excess of continuity'; on the other hand – and labeled 'Western' by Eisenstein – one found the 'explosiveness of 'active' ecstasy' (*Nonindifferent Nature*, p. 151), the forcing of opposites to '*penetrate each other*' (*Nonindifferent Nature*, p. 152). Eisenstein found both of these routes to ecstasy compelling: synaesthesia, Chinese painting and 'vertical montage', all more or less phenomena where dissolution into a common landscape created the potential for ecstasy, being just as fascinating for him as, say, the bullfight, that quintessential example of 'interpenetration' (see *Nonindifferent Nature*, p. 362).

Some opposites, however, one did not want to find unified. There is a certain ambiguous 'reversibility' to *Alexander Nevsky* that goes beyond the question of epic and comedy. Eisenstein meant the film to be an allegory for the present tensions in Europe, as evil Germans came spreading mayhem among the stalwart early Russians. A version of the scenario dating from the end of 1937 went so far as to start the film with a lengthy quote from Hitler: 'HITLER SAYS:... "Having decided to carve out for ourselves new territories in Europe, we will be able to gain them by and large at the expense of Russia. In this case we should... travel by the same road, along which once went the knights of our orders." – A Hitler, *Mein Kampf*.'[49] Eisenstein's film would thus be presenting itself as a response to *Mein Kampf*, as *Mein Kampf* turned into 'Our Battle'. Even as a satire of Hitler's hopes and intentions, however, making the German leader so central to the genesis of *Alexander Nevsky*'s central idea (that Russia will surely also 'travel by the same road' as its early heroes) comes treacherously close to positioning Hitler's Germany and Stalin's Russia as mere reflections of each other; opposites, yes, but opposites separated only by the glass of a mirror. (Eisenstein eventually thought better of this start, which would have put Hitler's words in the position held in almost all of his previous films by quotations from Lenin.)[50]

Giving oneself over to the kind of thinking that was based on pathos meant becoming frighteningly permeable. To choose 'nonindifference' was to throw oneself into the greater artwork of history, a choice that came with a certain price (thence its pathos), as the rhetorical flourish at the end of *Nonindifferent Nature*, in its attempt to leap stylistically into high Soviet bombast, demonstrates:

> For – damn it! – 'nonindifferent nature' is above all within ourselves: It is not the nature around us that is particularly nonindifferent, but our own nature – the nature of man who approaches the world that he recreates, not with indifference, but with passion, actively and creatively.
>
> And the temperamental recreation of nature in a work is, as it were, an image of that mighty recreation of the world in which our great generation participates.
>
> For around us is not a world 'seen through a temperament', but a world created and recreated according to the commands of that creative revolutionary temperament of our inimitable country and epoch.
>
> And the nonindifference of our own human nature, participating in the great historical act of the best part of humanity – is the invincible guarantee of the undying essence of the great arts, glorifying with every means available to it the greatness of Man – the maker and the creator. (*Nonindifferent Nature*, p. 396)

These paragraphs are the essayistic equivalent of Alexandrov's dissolve into the scene of a glorious May Day parade at the end of

Circus: every anomalous individual subsumed into the uniform whole, the whole universe echoing to the strains of one great patriotic hymn.

'Pathos in life,' Eisenstein had said, was the sense of 'collective participation.' In the real world, however, it was extraordinarily difficult to sustain any perfective collectives – something Eisenstein had experienced at first hand. As Lenin himself had admitted in a set of posthumously published 'notes on the dialectic' (which appeared in the journal *Bol shevik* in 1925 and was one of Eisenstein's favorite essays), although parts and wholes enjoyed a dialectical relationship that connected even opposites, 'particulars' could never be perfectly integrated into the 'general':

> [O]pposites (the particular opposing the general) are really one and the same: the particular does not exist otherwise than in that bond that leads to the general. The general exists only in the particular... Every instance of the general only approximately comprehends all separate articles. Every instance of the particular incompletely enters into the general and etc. and etc.[51]

What this meant for the individual was that his political synchronization would always be 'incomplete'. The shadow side of pathos, in the Soviet Union of the 1930s, was terror.

A taste of this terror comes in the essay 'Montage 1938', when Eisenstein discusses yet another variation on the theme of pathos: how an actor identifies with the character he plays.

> The fear aroused by an awareness of criminal liability induces a feverish evocation of mental pictures of the consequences. And the sum total of such pictures will play on the emotions and heighten them even more, bringing the embezzler to the utmost degree of horror and despair.

> On stage in the theater, the actor, by an absolutely identical process, will start to bring himself to the same state of mind. The only difference is that he is consciously forcing his imagination to picture the same consequences that in real life the imagination would evoke of its own accord...

> As an example, let us select from that multitude the first two situations that come to mind. Without analyzing them, we will try and write them down exactly as they now pass before my mind's eye: 'I am a criminal in the eyes of my erstwhile friends and acquaintances. People shun me. I have been ostracized by them,' and so on. In order to feel all this emotionally, I will, as has been said, picture to myself specific situations, real-life scenes of what awaits me...

Here I shall record the first thoughts that came into my mind when I set *myself* this particular exercise.

The courtroom. My case is being heard. I am in the dock. The public gallery is full of people who know me. I catch sight of my neighbor, who is watching me. We have lived next door to each other for thirty years. He notices that I have caught his eye. With feigned vagueness, his glance slides away from me; pretending to be bored, he looks out of the window... Over there is another member of the public: the woman who lives on the floor above mine. Meeting my gaze, she looks nervously down, while still continuing to watch me out of the corner of her eye. My usual partner at billiards turns his back on me with a deliberate movement... And over there the fat proprietor of the billiard-hall and his wife are staring insolently at me, glassy-eyed... I fidget uncomfortably and look down at my feet. Now I cannot see anyone, but all around me I hear the hiss of voices, whispering censure... The words of the verdict of guilty fall on me, blow by blow...

That is approximately how an honest transcription of the ideas swarming and flashing through my mind might look when, as director or actor, I would attempt to achieve an emotional grasp of the proposed situation.

Having mentally put myself in the first situation... I gradually arrive at an authentic perception of what awaits me and from there I achieve a feeling of the hopelessness and tragedy of the situation I am now in.[52]

The negative of pathos was isolation, disgrace and condemnation. In 1938 Eisenstein was just emerging (thanks to the removal of Shumiatskii from head of GUK) from the period of his creative life when he was at greatest risk of finding himself in a 'hopeless and tragic situation' like the one he fantasizes here. The vividness of this exercise suggests that Eisenstein may have gone over this territory mentally on more than one occasion; on the other hand, perhaps it was elation at being relatively out of the woods that made it possible for him to incorporate a scenario like this one, with all too many possible ties to 'real life', into his essay (which was not published until after *Nevsky*'s triumphant opening in any case).[53]

Thinking as 'skeleton dance': this model can be immensely attractive. It promises the thrill of connection – with object, landscape, audience, community – that Eisenstein knew as 'pathos'. But pathos is also intrinsically unsustainable; the 'thrill' runs the risk of being too cheap, especially if one substitutes an ecstatic leap for critical thinking, or a rhythmic pulse for a more studied connection. What's more, sometimes the leap simply cannot be made on cue. The prospect of failure hangs over communication based on pathos. The 'part' may find itself once again exiled from the 'whole'; the bones one brings in by the truckload to add an aura of authenticity to the beginning of one's epic film may stubbornly refuse to coalesce into something moving, genuine, powerful: 'The failure can of course be attributed partly to the fact that these carefully separated bones came from a museum of anatomy,' said Eisenstein regretfully about the beginning of his own *Alexander Nevsky* BTS 409). But this failure could be understood metaphorically as well: ideas brought into proximity might remain, despite everything, inert, unsynchronized by pathos. 'But... on these pages there are all the bones you could want and they absolutely won't come together into a frightening combination!' as Eisenstein wryly concluded. The failure of things to connect was the truly frightening prospect: then one would have no 'skeleton dance' at all, but merely a pile of bones.

Gradually Eisenstein made a shift in his approach to the philosophy and practice of audiovisual film, moving from an almost Alexandrovian appreciation of the 'skeleton' – the 'carcass' – that could serve as the basis of the musical film, to a fascination with another feature borrowed from animation: the contour of the protoplasmically shifting figure. This interest would be very much with him as he once again turned to Disney while working on the great epic of the 1940s: *Ivan the Terrible*. Eisenstein's love of bones, metaphorical and otherwise, ensured that the 'Skeleton Dance' would never be entirely left behind. But the fascination with skeletons was countered by another interest, one already emerging, as we have seen, in the Mexican period of Eisenstein's development: an interest in the human being before it is ruled by a fixed immutable skeleton and in the shifting contours of the fetus, a little exemplar of which, floating in a jar, Eisenstein kept affectionately on a shelf in his study.

7. Beyond Pleasure: *Ivan* and the 'Juncture of Beginning and End'

Quotations! Quotations! Quotations!

Even Prince Kurbsky, that elegant author of a treatise on punctuation, though otherwise a traitor to his country, reproached Tsar Ivan the Terrible for his quotations.

I quote: 'How many holy words have you taken and those with great anger and ferocity, not by the line or verse, as is the custom of skilled experts (if one happens to write of something then it is done using short words which evidence great reason) – but excessively, with a superfluity of detail and hostility – whole books, tracts, epistles!'

But quotations differ...

I see quotations as outrunners on either side of a galloping shafthorse. Sometimes they go too far, but they help one's imagination to bowl along two distinct paths, supported by the parallel race.

But don't let go of the reins![1]

SM Eisenstein, Beyond the Stars

When the editors of Eisenstein's collected works in Russian describe the vast intellectual spadework that went into Eisenstein's preparations for *Ivan the Terrible*, they quite naturally emphasize the weightier aspects of his research: 'In the course of work on the scenario,' they say, 'Eisenstein studied an enormous quantity of material – chronicles and eyewitness accounts of Ivan the Terrible's contemporaries [Prince Kurbsky, for instance], folklore and iconography, the works of historians and the work of his predecessors on his theme.' (IP6 548) Not mentioned in this impressive list is another source of inspiration

– a real 'outrunner', to follow Eisenstein's equine analogy – one encountered by the director a little more than a month before he accepted the *Ivan* project in January 1941.[2]

In a notebook entry dated 21 November 1940, Eisenstein recalls three scenes from stories he encountered in childhood. He remembers an Arab caught between an angry camel and a precipice who forgets everything as he reaches for a few red berries; another story of angels who dispense a few drops of comfort in hell; Esmeralda giving a suffering Quasimodo something to drink on the scaffold:

> While watching Disney's *Snow White*, I recall these three scenes.

> But not because Snow White kisses the funny and ugly gnomes one by one on their bald heads; not because a flock of no less elegant deer and wild goats follows behind her; and not because she is surrounded by fairy tale terrors and horrors.

> But because Disney's works themselves strike me as the same kind of drop of comfort, an instant of relief, a fleeting touch of lips in the hell of social burdens, injustices and torments, in which the circle of his American viewers is forever trapped.[3]

A reader familiar with the rules and paradigms of Soviet criticism fully expects the next point to be a pious condemnation of Disney's lack of political commitment and irrelevance to the class struggle, but here Eisenstein surprises us.[4] While admitting that, to be sure, 'the triumphant proletariat of the future will erect no monument to Disney as a fighter either in their hearts, or on street squares' (EOD 8), Eisenstein does not fault Disney, whom he had met and liked in Hollywood in 1930, for what might usually (in the Soviet context) appear to be the mortal sin of social irrelevance: instead he makes the extraordinary declaration that 'Disney is simply "beyond good and evil"' (EOD 9), putting a Nietzschean twist on what amounts to an even more scandalous assertion, that the art of Walt Disney is somehow to be located beyond the class struggle.[5] Described by Eisenstein in positive terms that, strangely enough, come within a hair's breadth of the notoriously negative 'opiate of the masses', Disney's medicine chest of animated anodynes evidently contains potions that Eisenstein finds appealing. He speaks of the drug-like effect of Disney's works not with a communist's moral outrage but with real affection:

> And Disney, like all of them, through the magic of his works and more intensely, perhaps, than anyone else, bestows precisely this upon his viewer, precisely *obliviousness* (*zabvenie*), an instant of complete and total

release from everything connected with the suffering caused by the social conditions of the social order of the largest capitalist government. (EOD 8, my emphasis)

It is astonishing how eloquently Eisenstein, famous for earlier attempts to create a cinema based on shocking its viewers with dialectical truths (the 'montage of attractions'), here defends the virtues of 'obliviousness', a state generally associated, he admits a page later, with 'evil' (EOD 9). But in the special case of Disney, obliviousness is a gift to the masses rather than their downfall. After all:

Even the string of a bow can't be strained forever.

The same for the nerves.

And instants of this 'releasing' [...] are just as prophylactically necessary as the daily dose of carefree laughter in the well-known American saying: 'A laugh a day, keeps the doctor away.' (EOD 8; the saying is in English in the original)

Lurking very near the surface here is the even better-known American saying concerning apples and doctors, a proverb Disney's Evil Queen takes a wicked delight in perverting as she peddles a beautiful, healthy-looking apple drenched in the potion known as the 'Sleeping Death'. Could there be a connection between the benevolent 'obliviousness' Disney grants his viewers and the 'Sleeping Death' presented by the witch to Snow White? Certainly if Disney in general – and *Snow White* in particular – can be said to have taken the role of the (possibly poisoned) apple for Eisenstein, it was an apple the Soviet director could not or did not wish to resist. Over the next few years, as Eisenstein worked on his *Ivan* project, *Snow White* was clearly often on his mind and sometimes, we might even venture to say, on the tip of his tongue.[6]

What was it about Disney's work that made it, as Eisenstein reiterates over the years, so 'attractive' (EOD 21), even (as he writes in late 1941, shortly after being evacuated with the major film studios to Alma-Ata) 'the most appealing I've ever met' (EOD 41)?[7] This was a question Eisenstein returned to again and again. The key to the charm of Disney's animation lies for him in the mysteries of a contour that has learned to exceed itself; the name he gives this phenomenon is 'plasmaticness':

[H]ere we have a being represented in drawing, a being of a definite form, a being which has attained a definite appearance and which behaves like the primal protoplasm, not yet possessing a 'stable' form, but capable of assuming any form and which, skipping along the rungs of the evolutionary ladder, attaches itself to any and all forms of animal existence.

Why is the sight of this so attractive? ...

[T]his picture is inescapably attractive through its trait of all-possible diversity of forms. (EOD 21)

Disney's animated characters allow the viewer to venture vicariously 'back down the evolutionary ladder' (EOD 21, slightly corrected) to those primordial times when existence is all possibility, identity a future potential rather than a present constraint. In Alma-Ata a year later, Eisenstein delighted himself by discovering the link between 'plasmaticness' and 'ecstasy':

In terms of their material, Disney's pictures are pure ecstasy – all the traits of ecstasy (the immersion of *self* in nature and animals, etc.)

Their comicality lies in the fact that the *process* of ecstasy is represented as an *object*: literalized, formalized.

That is, Disney is an example (within the general formula of the comical) of a case of *formal ecstasy*!!! (Great!) [...] Ecstasy is a sensing and experiencing of the primal 'omnipotence' – the element of 'coming into being' – the 'plasmaticness' of existence, from which *everything* can arise. (EOD 42; 46)

What Eisenstein loved about Disney's characters was the way their contours could work constant 'plasmatic' miracles of meta-morphosis (he was particularly fond of remarking on the stretchiness of the characters' necks).[8] Disney's creatures were free to romp through an infinite number of identities and morphologies, in what Eisenstein referred to at one point as a 'unique protest against the metaphysical immobility of the once-and-forever given' (EOD 33). The natural element that Eisenstein (at great length!) compares in the notes of 1940 to the plasmaticness of Disney is fire. Eisenstein runs through a kaleidoscopic series of references to the meaning and images of fire: ranging from Disney's 'The Moth and the Flame' through German analyses of the sexual nature of the crime of arson, to Wagner, Nero, Gorky and Zola (EOD 24–32). This part of his argument also nods to the Disney film he had been watching most recently: 'The ghostly mask which prophesies to the witch in *Snow White*, appears in... fire. And what, if not fire, is capable of most fully conveying the dream of a flowing diversity of forms?!' (EOD 24)[9]

With *Snow White* and *Ivan the Terrible* in mind, we might perhaps take that last remark as a *real* rather than *rhetorical* question, for strangely missing from the long discussion of fire that follows (as well as almost entirely absent from the discussion of plasmaticness in general) is another highly plasmatic phenomenon which Eisenstein was to make the object of very serious experimentation as he worked with the *Ivan* material: that phenomenon is shadow.[10] In our everyday lives, shadow (even more than – but not entirely disassociated from – fire) is the place where ordinary existence meets the miraculous plasmaticness of constant metamorphosis: all people living in a place with a light source and a wall will soon rediscover the potential for dogs and rabbits latent in their own ordinary hands.[11]

When Eisenstein did mention the use of shadow in Disney, it was disapprovingly ('I have always liked Disney and his heroes, from Mickey Mouse to Willie the Whale. Because of their moving figures – again animals and again linear. The best examples had neither shading nor depth' BTS 42), but what he really seems to be objecting to here is not the shadow *per se*, but the use of shadow to make the animated figure more 'real', more three-dimensional and thus less linear. What's striking about the use of shadow in *Snow White* is how the shadows occasionally emancipate themselves from their own figures and thus recuperate the power of the linear contour for themselves. When the dwarfs are marching home along a cliff and their huge giant shadows march in one direction while their little dwarf 'bodies' march in another, the shadow as such is beginning to discover its own 'plasmaticness'. The shadows in *Snow White* are not merely fuzzy puddles testifying to the animators' clever understanding of light, they are contour in the process of rediscovering its own strengths: in one gag, as the dwarfs search the house for the monstrous invader who has swept the floor and removed the cobwebs', Doc's shadow turns and whispers to the shadow following it, a textbook example of how a 'contour' may, as Eisenstein claims, 'begin to take on an independent life' (EOD 59).

One of the most persistent formal themes in *Ivan the Terrible* (especially in Part I) is likewise the motif of the gradually emancipated shadow and although this play with shadow obviously owes a great deal to the German Expressionist tradition,[12] Expressionism is here mediated by Disney. *Ivan*'s armed warriors, like *Snow White*'s dwarfs, gradually acquire the ability to march more or less independently across the walls; early in *Ivan the Terrible* the shadows are blurry and indistinct (with some notable emblematic exceptions, like the double-headed eagle on *Ivan*'s cheek during the coronation scene and the great shadow cast by a candlestick on the wall), but as the film gathers momentum, the shadows grow clearer and clearer, their contours ever more distinct. At several points Eisenstein demonstrates the amazing ability of huge shadows to shrink themselves to the size of tiny dwarf-sized doorways.

Figure 24.
Plasmaticness
(*Ivan the Terrible*, Part One)

This motif echoes Snow White's stooping entrance into the dwarfs' cottage: as in the terrifying, claustro- and agoraphobic incommensurability of the architectural spaces of *Ivan* with the figures, always too small or too large, who inhabit them, Snow White is also the wrong size for the miniature-but-huge home of the dwarfs.[13] In both cases, the figure must always be remolding its contours to fit its impossible environment.[14]

The climax of the shadow motif comes in the scene in which Ivan discusses policy with Nepeya, his Ambassador to England. On the wall is projected a huge shadow of Ivan in profile, looming over another one of those little doorways and at other times over the equally dramatic shadow of the globe. But the shadow that achieves the greatest degree of 'emancipation' is the Ivan profile, which in its vastest incarnation is evidently no longer attached to any real figure anymore, but seems rather to have been cast with the help of a large paper cut-out.

Figure 25.
Inanimation
(*Ivan the Terrible*, Part One)

Here the tables are really turned; the demands of the shadow have the figure in thrall: the actor Cherkasov must freeze, must imitate the actions of his own 'shadow'. Meanwhile the shadow's emancipation is marked by its awkward attempts to move despite the separation from the figure of Ivan.[15] The shadow's lower jaw is made to move as Ivan speaks – as if the shadow were still subservient, but now that he's emancipated, the movements are jerky, a pallid shadow of live beings' movements. As it emancipates itself, the shadow discovers that the price of independence is, strangely enough, inanimation.

Before we decide that the cut-out's awkwardly jerking jaw is a sign of failed emancipation, or that its fall into 'inanimation' marks a defeat, (just another robot failing to make the leap into genuine humanness), we should note that 'inanimation' is in fact precisely the fate of the human figure in *Ivan the Terrible*. The trembling jaw of the huge shadow echoes the slight shake human limbs are prone to in *Ivan*, as the actors attempt to force their own contours into extraordinary poses at impossibly slow speeds: in short, to inanimate themselves. Thus the huge shadow, just when it finds itself emancipated but *de*humanized, is actually closer to being a 'real human being' than it probably realizes. Hidden in *Ivan* is a parable of the complicated and jealous relationship between 'real' and 'animated' figures.

Stalin himself reportedly admired the actor Nikolai Cherkasov's incredible ability to shape and reshape himself on demand.[17] We find ourselves again in the realm of 'plasmaticness'. Where does Ivan's hugely overextended neck come from, after all? According to Eisenstein at least partly (with all due respect to its other eminent parents, the great Meyerhold among them) from a not particularly aristocratic ancestor:

> Mickey starts to sing, his hands folded together. The hands echo the music as only the movements of Disney's characters are capable of

echoing a melody. And then reaching for a high note, the arms shoot up far beyond the limits of their normal representation. In tone to the music, they stretch far beyond the length allotted them. The necks of his surprised horses stretch the same way, or their legs become extended when running. (EOD 10)

In *Ivan* the contours of the human figure are tortured in order to create a grotesque imitation of a cartoon figure's plasmatic lines. In Disney this plasmaticness of contour leads to comedy, to 'formal ecstasy'; in *Ivan* the effect is grotesque, contorted, forever reminding us of the *pain* involved when a figure trapped within a three-dimensional universe where the rules of physics apply is asked to behave as if he were fundamentally linear. This strain is part of the essential sensibility of *Ivan*.[17]

Even in animation, however, certain characters are by necessity more plasmatic than others (not all contours are created equal). In the production of *Snow White and the Seven Dwarfs*, the dwarfs could be relatively plasmatic and grotesque, with no harm done, but Snow White was another thing entirely. She should not be particularly comic or, certainly, grotesque! The solution hit on by Disney was to bring in a real girl (Marge Belcher, later destined for fame as Marge Champion) as a model for his animated princess. By studying Marge's movements as she danced and twirled, the animators could avoid letting any of Snow White's contours get too plasmatic for their own good. Snow White needs a dose of 'inanimation' (provided by the 'real girl') to keep her from becoming too grotesque.

But this is not the last twist of the spiral in the animation/inanimation story of *Snow White*: the presence of a flesh-and-blood model as a guarantee of realism, as a concrete tie to the real world, is no failsafe antidote for 'excessive plasmaticness'. The very models who were to serve as the animated characters' anchor in realism were themselves selected for their almost inhuman elasticity, their ability (to echo Stalin's praise of Cherkasov) to reshape themselves: in short, for their ability to imitate the plasmatic moves of animated characters. Thus the dwarfs (relatively 'plasmatic' characters) had their 'real life' models, too and one of those was none other than the very Marge Belcher brought in to save Snow White from her potentially too-mobile contours (to keep her, one might say, from looking like a dwarf). Indeed, in one of the film's most plasmatic moments, Belcher obligingly served as model (wrapped in a baggy overcoat) for two dwarfs at once, when for the 'Silly Song' dance, Dopey gets on Sneezy's shoulders to dance with the (also modeled by Belcher) lovely and non-grotesque Snow White.

Not only are these figures in multiple layers of disguise, they are also what one might properly term 'in drag', where the boundaries between male and female, real person and animated character, are shown to be contingent and malleable.[18] Many layers of drag are functioning here: a girl who becomes two dwarfs who become a man; a 'real' girl in drag as a 'cartoon' girl; animated characters dressing up in the form of 'real people'. As a special kind of play with one's form in which the contours of an identity are exaggerated, the concept of drag reflects and emends Eisenstein's more abstract idea of 'plasmaticness'. A plasmatic figure is one that revels in its ability to change form, but adding 'drag' to the equation allows us to think of contour as a kind of costume, one that can be made to take on a series of exaggerated, momentarily frozen forms. The costume of contour can be shifted at will – with the caveat that such costume-changing can be very difficult or even painful. For the heart of the practice of 'drag' lies in the ephemeral fixing of identity, the exaggerated fixing rather than fluid mobility of contour. (Although the costume or identity can be changed, it is no longer in constant, protoplasmic flux.)[19]

The *Ivan* films add another of layer of costume and shifting identities to the equation. Let us consider a scene that seems at least partly modeled, strangely enough, on the dwarfs' dance with Snow White: the famous 'Dance of the Oprichniki' from *Ivan, Part II*.[20] Here again we see a band of merry men singing and dancing, with a pale 'princess' in the midst of them. The female figure, with its 'crown' and stiff, white mask, leaps about in the dance and conceals the flexible form of Fyodor: in drag, we might claim, as a monstrous and totemic variation on Snow White (Snow White as potentially murderous puppet). Fyodor's jolly face, which peeps out from behind this mask as he sings his own set of *chastushki*, could not be in greater contrast to the frozen features of the mask,[21] but the words he sings are threatening. In this case the 'Silly Song' of the *oprichniki* is one that despite the sound and look of nonsense contains a very non-nonsensical message, one that anyone should be able to read (but one that evidently escapes the simpleton Vladimir). Indeed, the doomed Vladimir plays out with his all-powerful cousin Ivan a tragic and grotesque version of his cartoon prototype, Dopey's unrequited infatuation with Snow White. Tsar Ivan exploits most adeptly his 'role' as poor 'orphan', chased by an Evil Queen (Efrosinia, of course), in his seduction of Vladimir: 'An orphan I am and abandoned, with nobody to love me or pity me' (Eizenshtein VI, p. 347); needless to say, the theme of the orphan is

Figure 26.
Mask
(*Ivan the Terrible*, Part Two)

central to *Snow White*; not only is the title character herself an
orphan, but it's the thought that 'perhaps they HAVE no mother!'
that endears to her the 'untidy little children' she originally imagines
the dwarfs to be.

Tsar Ivan is not merely the equivalent of that other royal orphan,
Snow White: his identities, his contours and indeed his very relation
to 'animation' make such equations distinctly more complex. The
very transformation of Ivan that occurs over the course of the two
completed parts of the project echoes neatly a transformation central
to *Snow White*. There, the Evil Queen is a beautiful, if severe,
creature who stands straight and tall. To carry out her plan to poison
the princess, she chooses to try a disguising potion, one that will
turn her into an ugly hag (or rather, the moral seems to be, to turn
her into the ugly witch she truly is inside already). As her fingers
claw up and her shoulders hunch over and she adopts the dark
hooded garment of any witch or peddler, she grows closer and closer
in appearance to the old Tsar Ivan, whose contours (as we have
mentioned above) are made to shift as he 'ages'. The two figures
(the witch as witch and the Old Ivan as witch) are remarkably similar
in appearance; Ivan too (though his transformation takes place over
a considerably longer amount of time) develops a stoop and wizened
features and puts on a black hood.

Ivan – as 'witch' here, rather than 'orphaned princess' – offers
Vladimir an 'apple' he cannot refuse: the Tsar's seduction succeeds
when he has persuaded Vladimir to don the Tsar's robes for that
fateful procession into the cathedral; Vladimir, in short, is also 'in
drag' – this time as tsar (though one should also point out the
unremitting exaggeration of the feminine side of Vladimir's features
throughout *Ivan*; his face, indeed, seems painted as almost a
caricature of a woman's face; so in a sense he has been in some
kind of drag all along): and his manipulation of his contours into

the drag of Tsardom turns out to be his undoing, of course, as the assassin intending to kill Ivan makes do with the mere caricature of Ivan. Like the frozen mask of the white lady that is the highlight of Fyodor Basmanov's costume (the loyal Fyodor also being dressed for the occasion in 'drag'), the tsar's robes weigh on Vladimir: he walks stiffly as he heads toward what even he senses (as the famous 'blue blush' reminds us, a blush that Eisenstein himself compares to that of the skunk in *Bambi*)[22] are the perilous depths of the cathedral. In fact, Vladimir must learn the fatal lesson that some identities, some contours, lend themselves above all to inanimation. This moment, too, has a predecessor in *Snow White*, in the scene in which a reluctant, quavery Dopey is sent upstairs to face the possible monster Snow White turns out not to be.[23]

Figure 27. Dopey with candle (*Snow White*) ©1937, The Walt Disney Company; Vladimir with candle (*Ivan the Terrible*, Part Two)

The importance of 'drag' in these wild and deadly celebrations reveals to us, as Eisenstein explains in some unpublished notes from the late 1940s, the hidden nature of the rituals with which Part II of *Ivan* closes: the 'Dance of the Oprichniki' is not just an example of the 'carnival tradition',[24] and certainly not merely a dance, but at heart nothing less than a wedding. The ill-fated 'fool' Vladimir, having put on the Tsar's raiment, enters into an ancient exchange whose origins Eisenstein traces to the old marriage custom of bride and groom trading clothes: 'The exchange of clothes (and of "places") between *king* and *slave* is not only a phenomenon of a piece with the exchange of male and female clothing – but the direct *derivative* of that exchange. A man and a woman exchange clothing, entering into marriage.'[25] In the case of Ivan and Vladimir, this 'wedding' will find its consummation only in death, as Vladimir is pierced by the knife intended for the Tsar.

The transvestitism of the wedding is itself a kind of substitute for more primitive exchanges: 'The exchange of clothing... is the exchange of M and F essences – *the crudest form* (English in original) of the materialization of these 'essences' is the different sexual organs. Such that the exchange of clothing is the exchange of organs... – the exchange of essences.'[26] The 'wedding' takes its place in a chain of repetitions of the ancient drive towards what Eisenstein refers to as 'bi-sex', the combination of female and male 'essences' (and their symbolic representations) within one arena. That 'arena' can certainly be the literal one of the circus or theater. When Eisenstein returned, as he pondered the multiple layers of meaning in *Ivan*, to the fundamental issue of 'bi-sex', he took up a thread he had explored more than a decade earlier, in 1933–1934, a period when he had been particularly intrigued by the archaic imagery at work in the (practically and etymologically 'circular') circus: 'In a less "content-oriented" art we should find, more cleanly, a full picture of pre-logic and maximum conservatism: the circus! [1] costumed animals; [2] the bisex of costumed clowns...'[27] (Eisenstein's theoretical notes on the circus came at a time – 1933 – when he was thinking of staging a politically-oriented circus spectacle of his own, 'The Hand of Moscow'.)[28] His own most circus-like production, the staging of Ostrovsky's *Enough Simplicity in Every Wise Man* (1923) had come to a ribald conclusion around a plot device of a wedding impeded at every hand; this was the dramatic moment where Eisenstein's first short film intervened to illustrate not only a chase up and down towers, but also the series of metamorphoses imposed on the luckless Glumov, the culmination of which was a 'wedding' of clowns, in which the female participant was dressed in men's clothing and which ends, not with a kiss, but with rude gestures (a 'fig') directed first between characters and then, in close-up, towards the film audience itself.[29]

Weddings are places where identities get very tangled throughout Eisenstein's life and career. Recall the knots in operation during the wedding of Fomka the bull and his bovine bride: the cow representing both the underdeveloped Soviet countryside and 'Europa', the West from which Soviet Russia wishes to claim its independence; Fomka standing in for the 'industrial' stimulus so needed in rural Russia, a stimulus whose bloodlines go back to that Westerner, Henry Ford – and also representing Stalin, progenitor of the future. But Eisenstein's interest in the complex interplay of identities that weddings suggest significantly predates his film-making career. One of the earliest childhood memories described by Eisenstein in his autobiography is a wedding game he used to play with his friends:

> Another friend, who was French and whose name and surname I have forgotten, was the son of the owner of the pen factory...
>
> There was a trio of plays we performed on Sundays, with him, Alyosha Bertels and myself.
>
> The happy ending of one of these plays.
>
> Alyosha *en travesti*.
>
> The French boy was dressed as an English 'bobby.' And I, for some reason, was dressed as a fantastic... rabbi (!) who married them.[30]

In this early game, identities, whether sexual, national, or religious, are the product of costuming (and one wonders which irony it is in the young Sergei's disguise as a 'rabbi' that inspires his middle-aged self to append the exclamation point.)

It was during the *Ivan* years, during the forced period of convalescence following the heart attack of early February, 1946, that Eisenstein wrote his memoirs and in fact the film *Ivan the Terrible* shows a turn towards the autobiographical mode. In it are repeated not only those broad cultural patterns, like the role of 'bisex' in marriage rites, that underpin so much of humanity's art and ritual, but also key moments of Eisenstein's own artistic past.

One figure who resurfaces, perhaps unexpectedly, in Eisenstein's notes of the 1940s is his one-time collaborator and student, the director Grigorii Alexandrov. In late 1947, while pondering the ubiquitous (and co-existing) imagery of 'womb' and 'phallus', Eisenstein thinks back to none other than that Proletkult production of 1923, early experiment in bringing the 'shocks' of the circus into the arenas of theater and film, *Enough Simplicity in Every Wise Man*, in which the actress Ianukogo, with whom both he and Alexandrov were at that time in love ('and more!' Eisenstein scribbles in a margin),[31] sheds a circular (womblike) skirt and scrambles up a (phallic) pole with a moon-sign at the top. 'Reminiscences of *Wise Man*' of course lie at the foundation of [Alexandrov's] most successful production, *Circus*,' Eisenstein claims – and considering Liubov' Orlova's sensational 'flight to the Moon' in that film, the claim seems thoroughly reasonable.[32]

In notes from November 1947, Eisenstein reveals another '*Wise Man* reminiscence': none other than *Ivan the Terrible*. 'Kurbsky is curious: a double (by design) of Ivan the Terrible – Ivan as a blond!

– made similar by typage to the blond aspect of Golutvin [character from *Wise Man*] – and to the actor: Gr Alexandrov!'[33] Then, switching into English, Eisenstein appends a crucial and fascinating comment: 'The conflict of Ivan and Kurbsky had to incorporate my conflict with Gr Alexandroff. Quite consciously. And this conflict helped me to "feel" the Grozny-Kurbsky drama. The psychology of the f[r]iend Kurbsky and the sufferings of John [Ivan] when he has left him.'[34] There is a lovely classical Freudian slip here, because Eisenstein leaves the 'r' out of 'friend': Kurbsky/Alexandrov, the 'friend' and 'fiend'. So Alexandrov's musical comedy *Circus* and Eisenstein's operatic epic *Ivan the Terrible* can be seen as another set of oddly matched twins, a charming idea that once again puts a different spin on the carnivalesque atmosphere of the 'Dance of the Oprichniki'.

In *Ivan*, as in *Wise Man*, Eisenstein muses, a man 'liquidates' his rival in a womb-like setting: the cathedral in *Ivan*, the circular arena in the 1923 play.[35] Thus Eisenstein's latest creation reaches back into the director's past and brings back motifs from his creative origins. This thought fascinates Eisenstein – and leads him, on this day less than three months removed from his own death, to a meta-autobiographical and somewhat melancholy pondering of the relation of beginnings and endings: 'This is quite striking – to what degree *geschichtlich* for my work is the juncture of Beginning and End. Is *Ivan* the end of my biography as a director?'[36]

With its repetition of moments from Eisenstein's personal and cultural history and its mysterious conflation of womb and tomb, *Ivan the Terrible* plays through the paradigms provided by another strange work (well known to Eisenstein) obsessed with the 'juncture of Beginning and End': Freud's *Beyond the Pleasure Principle* (1920).[37] This was the essay in which Freud explored those psychic phenomena that seemed somehow to ignore – or predate? – the general rule that 'the course taken by mental events is automatically regulated by the pleasure principle'.[38] At the heart of the mysteries Freud wrestles with in *Beyond the Pleasure Principle* is the 'compulsion to repeat'.[39] This compulsion is also central to *Ivan*: not only in its recycling of themes from Eisenstein's past and not only in its formal repetitions of motifs (the shadow, the candle, the eye), but even in its narrative, within which the flashbacks to Ivan's childhood, a kind of psychoanalysis of Ivan the Terrible's motivations, establish patterns that Ivan relives. Our glimpse, within these flashbacks, of the dying woman in white who so eerily resembles his later bride, Anastasia, in appearance and fate, would thus seem to be a version of the childhood game of 'Fort/Da' that is Freud's entree into the world of repetition. In that game the little boy flings a spool out of his crib (Fort!) and then winds the spool back in by means of the thread attached to it (Da!). Freud deduces a causal link between this game and the child's abandonment by his mother for some hours at a time:

> Throwing away the object so that it was 'gone' might satisfy an impulse of the child's, which was suppressed in his actual life, to revenge himself on his mother for going away from him. In that case it would have a defiant meaning: 'All right, then, go away! I don't need you. I'm sending you away myself.'[40]

Ivan, abandoned early by his murdered mother ('Fort!'), replaces her with the equally white-clad Anastasia ('Da!'), only to be the unwitting poisoner of his replacement; Ephrosinia adulterates the drink, but Ivan hands his wife the cup (and 'Fort!' again).

Freud is led by his discovery of a 'repetition compulsion' to acknowledge that there may be some kind of instinct 'inherent in organic life to restore an earlier state of things' (p. 43) and that, more dramatically, this drive back towards one's origins is also, since 'inanimate things existed before living ones' (p. 46), a way of taking 'circuitous paths to death' (p. 46). Viewed most severely, this would permit one to say that 'the aim of all life is death' (p. 46). This mysterious bond between 'womb' and 'tomb' was, as we have already begun to see, very much on Eisenstein's mind in the 1940s. The death of Vladimir in the 'womb' of the cathedral[41] was far from the only illustration of this fundamental and fatal correspondence. Eisenstein found echoes of this profound pattern in many, many places, as his notes of the late 1940s suggest. In the last days of his life, he undertook a protracted analysis of Gogol's terrifying story 'Vii', in which a schoolboy, Khoma Brut, is seduced by a witch-girl and, despite his attempt to protect himself from demonic forces by tracing a magic circle around himself, is murdered in an old church by the piercing gaze of the eponymous monster. Everywhere in this story, Eisenstein saw reiteration of the most archaic themes of death and sexuality: the name 'Khoma' could be seen as a feminized version of 'Homo', or 'man', thus placing Khoma 'in the series of Gogolian b S [bisexual] characters'.[42] Khoma Brut was also another 'Doubting Thomas', putting his finger in the wound, 'towards the reading of "wound" as "vulva",'[43] and he perishes within a double womb – magic circle; church – when those are pierced and betrayed by Khoma's doubts and Vii's gaze.[44] On 25 January 1948, Eisenstein scribbled among his notes, 'Despite my sick condition, I am terribly proud of my decoding of "Khoma Brut".'[45]

Gogol was far from the only source of imagery combining the 'bisex' mysteries of womb and tomb. One of his more surprising finds was a 1 September 1947 advertisement in *Life* magazine for 'Sinclair Opaline Motor Oil'.[46]

Figure 28.
'One could write a whole book about this little page of advertising'.

The ad shows Danny Kaye floating through a hoop held by Virginia Mayo ('stars of Samuel Goldwyn's "The Secret Life of Walter Mitty". In Technicolor'): 'Like Magic, Premium Sinclair Oil gives your car more power. Your car's power goes up like the magic of levitation when you use *premium* Sinclair Motor Oil'. On 16 October 1947, Eisenstein gushed happily: 'One could write a whole book about this little page of advertising.'[47]

> It's difficult to imagine a clearer image... in which the theme of unity – through substitution (sinking back into the womb and the drive towards the womb *ersatz* – 'the girl of my dreams') would be presented so literally (and at the same time allegorically *umschrieben*)... The passage through the circle – into the interior – *into to girl* [English in the original], part of whom is that circle – she holds it – and with that the condition of 'levitation', that is, the *Schwebe-Zustand* [floating condition] within the *Mutterleib* [womb] – the psychological condition of levitation and its like attributed to 'saints' is a reminiscence of the state freed from the force of gravity – the 'gyroscopic' state in the womb.[48]

With the return to the imagery of the womb comes an interest in the relatively 'plasmatic' characteristics of primordial matter (as exhibited by floating fetuses, amoebas and Mickey Mouse). This fascination, too, reflects the logical paths set forth in Freud's *Beyond the Pleasure Principle*, in which the 'compulsion to repeat' (and the drive to return to prior states that repetition implies) leads to a consideration of life's protoplasmic beginnings:

> Let us picture a living organism in its most simplified possible form as an undifferentiated vesicle of a substance that is susceptible to stimulation... Indeed embryology, in its capacity as a recapitulation of developmental history, actually shows us that the central nervous system originates from the ectoderm...' (Freud, pp. 28–29).

The embedded story in *Beyond the Pleasure Principle* of the trials and tribulations of protoplasm at the very dawn of the human drives towards death and sex was one that had caught Eisenstein's eye long before, in 1933, at the very same time as he had been pondering the 'regressive' and 'bisexual' attributes of the circus. On a sheet of notes about the theme of regression in Hegel, Eisenstein added then, 'Could also refer to Freud: the libido theory (the most obscurantist [*mrakobesnoe*]) is the reproduction of the protoplasmic stage.'[49]

In the 1940s, as we have seen, Eisenstein's interest in protoplasm, a fascination that bridged the theme of the return to the womb (and to death) and the 'omni-appealing' nature of the animated character, was especially focused on the problem of the contour. Here, again, we are returned to part of Freud's protoplasmic story:

> [A]s a result of the ceaseless impact of external stimuli on the surface of the vesicle, its substance to a certain depth may have become permanently modified, so that excitatory processes run a different course in it from what they run in the deeper layers. A crust would thus be formed which would at last have been so thoroughly 'baked through' by stimulation that it would present the most favorable possible conditions for the reception of stimuli and become incapable of any further modification. (Freud, p. 29)

This 'crust' becomes the necessary precondition for consciousness, according to Freud. It also represents a fixing of protoplasmic contours: once again we find ourselves within the realm of inanimation.

In the universe of *Ivan the Terrible*, the relationship of a character to his/her shifting contours is tortured. That certainly does not mean that 'ecstasy' is excluded, but rather that the kind of ecstasy achieved through the imposition of a kind of slow plasmatic deformation on the inherently non-plasmatic human form is different (perhaps more perverse) than the thrill of possibility conveyed by Disney's animated

contours. Here we find ourselves moving from the play of shapes in
the flames Eisenstein found so attractive, to the effect of those flames
on a human being, an effect which Eisenstein also found profoundly
'appealing' from childhood on. In his memoirs, Eisenstein described
the dangerous thrill of illicit glances into the works of Mirbeau and
Masoch and then relates a sort of 'primal scene' from his own
childhood (a primal scene experienced, appropriately enough, at
the cinema):[50]

> I came in contact with the alarming vein of cruelty much earlier through
> a living impression, a living impression from the cinema screen.
>
> It was one of the earliest films I ever saw, no doubt produced by Pathé.
> The story took place during the Napoleonic Wars. In the house of a
> blacksmith was a military billet. The young wife of the blacksmith
> commits adultery with a young Empire sergeant. The husband finds
> out, catches and binds the sergeant. Throws him in the hayloft. He tears
> off the soldier's uniform, baring his shoulders and brands him with a
> red-hot iron.
>
> I remember vividly the naked shoulder, a great iron bar in the muscular
> hands of the blacksmith, the black smoke and white steam rising from
> the charred flesh.
>
> ... [T]he scene of branding remains ineradicably in my memory to this
> very day.
>
> In childhood it tortured me with nightmares. I imagined it at night. I
> saw myself either as the sergeant or the blacksmith. I caught hold of
> the bare shoulders. Sometimes they seemed to be mine, sometimes
> someone else's. It was never clear who was branding whom. For many
> years, fair hair (the sergeant was blond) or black barrels and Napoleonic
> uniforms inevitably recalled that scene to my memory. Indeed, I
> developed a partiality for the Empire style.
>
> No ocean of cruelty, such as permeates my own films, has yet drowned
> – like that sea of fire that swallowed the brand of the convict – the
> early impressions of that ill-starred film...[51]

Endless fiery shape-changing may be a perfect example of 'formal
ecstasy', but the cruel limit set on identity by the brand has its own
erotic attraction for Eisenstein, an erotic effect which branding
shares in Eisenstein's aesthetic universe with many forms of piercing,
with bullfights, with the rape of Europa...[52] If the free flow of
identity is 'inescapably attractive' (EOD 21), so too is the moment
when identity is suddenly, inescapably fixed by the brand.[53]

All of Eisenstein's later works are affected by his encounter with
Disney's animated art. The synchronized sound (and its more

aristocratic theoretical cousin, 'vertical montage') of *Alexander Nevsky* (1938) testify to the lessons learned by both Eisenstein and Prokofiev from the creator of Mickey Mouse and the *Silly Symphonies*.[54] Where *Alexander Nevsky* emphasizes animation as synchronized motion, *Ivan the Terrible* forces us (and motion) to stop in our tracks, to take the process of metamorphosis frame by frame. Run as a series of frames rather than as a fluid fast-flowing illusion, plasmaticness reveals its darker nature.

Figure 29.
Ouch! (*Snow White*)
©1937, The Walt Disney
Company

It is something about the intense erotic painfulness of *Ivan the Terrible*, Parts I and II, that brings them close to – and yet not quite within – the definition of 'camp', as Susan Sontag describes that elusive category: 'the essence of Camp is its love of the unnatural: of artifice and exaggeration' (p. 275); 'Camp is a vision of the world in terms of style – but a particular kind of style. It is the love of the exaggerated, the "off", of things-being-what-they-are-not' (p. 279).[55] Sontag says of the *Ivan* films that

> A work can come close to Camp, but not make it, because it succeeds. Eisenstein's films are seldom Camp because, despite all exaggeration, they do succeed (dramatically) without surplus. If they were a little more 'off', they could be great Camp – particularly *Ivan the Terrible I & II*. (p. 284)

Ivan the Terrible is just slightly too 'serious', too 'tragic', to make it as 'camp' (in which, she insists, 'there is never, never tragedy' [p. 287]); *Snow White* would presumably be just off the edge at the other extreme ('without passion, one gets pseudo-Camp – what is merely decorative, safe, in a word, chic' [p. 284]); taken together, these two films mark the boundaries of some unstable, fluctuating realm. They certainly share the fundamental preoccupation with contour that Sontag describes as essential to camp:

> Camp sees everything in quotation marks. It's not a lamp, but a 'lamp';
> not a woman, but a 'woman'. To perceive Camp in objects and persons
> is to understand Being-as-Playing-a-Role. It is the farthest extension,
> in sensibility, of the metaphor of life as theater. (p. 280)

If this fundamental sensibility ends up, via plasmaticness, giving
Snow White its magic power to convey sweet 'oblivion', *Ivan the
Terrible* puts the same interest in identity and transformation to very
different use. In *Ivan* 'being' may well be 'playing a role', but playing
a role hurts. Here we may want to question Sontag's claim that since
'to emphasize style is to slight content', 'it goes without saying that
the Camp sensibility is disengaged, depoliticized – or at least
apolitical' (p. 277). Indeed, it seems to me that Eisenstein uses *Snow
White* as a kind of costume trunk for *Ivan*'s sadistic – and political –
theater: instead of the 'free play of signifiers', we have in *Ivan*'s
multivalent appropriation of *Snow White*'s forms and figures a move
towards the un-free play of identities, allowing practice in many
formal variations on an essential theme: that is, 'Ways to be – or be
with – a sadistic beloved'. Just as in the young Eisenstein's dreams
'it was never clear who was branding whom', *Ivan* allows a formal
rehearsal of the many painful versions of what Russians refer to
succinctly as *kto-kogo*: '*who* is doing what to *whom*?'

'Identity' is not absolute in *Ivan* and neither is 'good' or 'evil'. In
fact, it is in its dark reshaping and reinterpretation of the contours it
takes wholesale from its Disney predecessor that *Ivan* really devastates
Snow White; everywhere 'good' and 'evil' are clearly marked in the
American cartoon, Eisenstein adds layer upon layer of contradiction
and ambiguity. If even Ivan (in his relationship with the Dopey-like
Vladimir) can play the role of 'Snow White', then Dopey may be
right to run from the monstrous flapping bed-sheet upstairs as if his
life depended on it! The very identification of 'white' with 'innocence'
or 'virtue' is a theme *Ivan the Terrible* makes mincemeat of (following
here in the tracks laid in a lot of very artificial snow by the white-
clad evil German invaders of *Alexander Nevsky*). As Efrosinia mutters
when the evil but white-draped Pimen suggests that the sacrifice of
Filipp will do their cause more good than his rescue: 'White is the
raiment, but black the soul' (Eizenshtein VI, 340). In the film Efrosinia
punctuates this statement by revealing the white headdress beneath
her own black shawl.

In the case of Efrosinia, we are not surprised to find a black soul
lurking beneath whatever white garment she may feel like putting
on; however, a subtle lesson running under the surface of *Ivan the
Terrible* is that there can be no 'Snow White' without a touch of

blackness somewhere. The prime example of this rule is the unremittingly white figure of Anastasia, who is shown 'adoring' her Tsar and husband, who is murdered by the 'Evil Queen' (Efrosinia) by means of a poisoned goblet (that looks like the twin of the cup from which the Evil Queen in *Snow White* sips the potion that turns her into a witch), who lies dead but as if asleep on a bier surrounded by candles and mourning men and so on... But Anastasia is an ambivalent character as well, as Eisenstein uses his polyphonic editing to let us know. Should she really be exclaiming 'akh!' and falling back on her sickbed at the mere sound of Kurbskii's name? Anastasia's relentless association with the color white does not save her from the character's moral ambiguities.[56]

The faithful low-born Maliuta, the Tsar's watchdog and eye, would probably agree with Grumpy (to whom, it must be said, he bears something of a physical resemblance), who says about the sleeping Snow White in particular and all women in general, in response to Bashful's 'She's beautiful! Just like a angel!': 'Angel! Heh! She's a female! And all females is pizen! They're full of wicked wiles!'

It is tempting to approach *Ivan* armed with that simple and appealing formula, 'Ivan = X', where the 'X' may be Stalin, or Meyerhold, or Eisenstein, or Eisenstein's papa, but what *Snow White*'s presence in Eisenstein's film reminds us is that there are many more variables than 'x' involved.[57] ('Snow White' can be played by Anastasiia, by Fyodor, by Vladimir, by Ivan; both Efrosiniia and Ivan can try out the role of the 'evil queen', and so on.) The real calculus comes in the relations between these characters, as they are branded and re-branded with new identities. Here, as in so many of its aspects, *Ivan the Terrible* demonstrates its disdain for streamlined, efficient forms of creative endeavor; this is a film that prefers, at every juncture, excess to safety.

In her analysis of the 'excess' at work within (and counter to) the formal structures of *Ivan the Terrible*, Kristin Thompson shows how even the repeated motifs so central to *Ivan*'s aesthetic can also work to derail, rather than reinforce, the film's narrative unity. These 'floating motifs' can confound the critic who wants to fit them into any kind of tidy formal structure:

> [A] single motivation may serve to justify a device that is then *repeated and varied many times*. By this repetition, the device may far outweigh its original motivation and take on an importance greater than its narrative or compositional function would seem to warrant. This kind of excess is extremely common in *Ivan*. The introduction of the bird motif, for example, is realistically motivated: a couple of the objects in the

coronation ceremony have historically authentic bird emblems on them (the scepter, the little rug on the dais). But later the birds become less integral to the action at hand. They have associations, but, as we have seen, these associations are relatively arbitrary. We cannot say that these birds are unmotivated, for they all relate to each other and hence form a unified structure. But they do draw attention to themselves far beyond their importance in the functioning of the narrative. Indeed, by the time the last bird appears in the film – the white 'Holy Ghost' icon on the ceiling of the feast hall – I am hard put to assign it any function at all.[58]

The key here would seem to be not the object repeated, but the film's insistence on repetition, *per se*. In 1940, Eisenstein had suggested that 'repetition' in its 'purest form' took shape as 'ornament'.[59] At that time he recalled – and sketched – a kind of 'repetition machine' that had charmed him in his childhood, by means of which one could trace an image (Eisenstein sketches the contour of a head) and have it reproduced precisely, though perhaps in a different size, by the mechanism's second pencil: 'I remember in childhood I had just such an apparatus!'[60] Certainly all those polysemous yet excessive motifs dominating *Ivan the Terrible* serve, among many others, an ornamental function. The 'compulsion to repeat' that the ornament indulges and reflects is part and parcel of *Ivan*'s ascent/descent into the dark allure of the womb.

Eisenstein's last years and months were marked by the resurgence of the autobiographical impulse, the desire to bring together the ideas and discoveries of a lifetime into some kind of greater unity. At the end of 1947, he proposed to himself a form that had captured his imagination 15 years earlier: the spherical book.

> In 1932 I was preparing to organize my theoretical materials into a book (fifteen years I have continued to collect these materials) – somewhere I wrote, 'I dream of creating a *book in the shape of a sphere* – for everything I do touches everything else and everything crosses into everything else: the only form capable of satisfying this condition is a sphere: from any meridian transition is possible to any other meridian. Even now I yearn for this form of a book – and now perhaps more than at any other time.[61]

Such a book would allow the kind of connection and repetition which other, more linear forms tended to deny; perhaps *Ivan*, too, was a film longing to become more 'spherical'. The fantasy of the 'spherical book' can also be seen as another incarnation of the 'return to the womb' that was such a dominant motif in Eisenstein's last years. Like the 'plasmatic' animated character – or the fetus – much of the allure of the 'spherical book' stemmed from the infinite flexibility of its connections: thought itself, within the form of the sphere, would find its contours liberated and newly plasmatic. The sphere is also, however, as Eisenstein remarked, the very shape things take when freed from outside stimuli, as when they are suspended in the liquid environment of... the womb.[62] Eisenstein's 'spherical book' would thus be the record not only of his highest intellectual achievement, but also the embodiment of his mind's ultimate regression. A remarkably abstract form, the spherical book could not, in the end, be compatible with the messiness of life: its perfect shape, like that of all originary and final 'protoplasms', could only be achieved at the very beginning or very end of all things.

In his last days, Eisenstein took some time away from his other studies to ponder the ultimate mystery of that other state, the ultimate 'unity' that is possible only on the far side the thresholds of birth and death. On 7 February 1948, only two days before his death, he copied out a few paragraphs from a French translation of the oldest of Hindu sacred texts, the *Rigveda*, on this state out of which the world long ago emerged and to which we all eventually return. 'Here is everything,' he mused at the bottom of the page. 'The *status quo* of the situation of Unity, which is neither being nor not-being. And the originary indivisibility of things. And the method of attaining that state through immersion.'[63] As his own life neared the end of what Freud, in *Beyond the Pleasure Principle*, speculated was merely a kind of detour, an individual's 'circuitous path to death' (Freud, p. 46), Eisenstein found in the reconciliation of womb and tomb, in the 'juncture of Beginning and End', a meaningfulness that neither being nor non-being could exhaust.

Many long years before these final days, as he pondered the significance of the image-driven philosophy of *October* in 1928, Eisenstein had turned to Hegel as he described the yearning for each other of 'abstract idea' and that idea's 'materialization'.[64] This longing, it turned out, was part of yet another story, endlessly repeated over the ages: 'This "yearning for each other" of two separate or separated elements, dialectically necessarily monistic, is the most "lawful" of tendencies. From the Platonic myth of single creatures separated into two and seeking reunification...'[65] This very myth, from the *Symposium*, is the story upon which Freud closes *Beyond the Pleasure Principle*, as he contemplates the mysteries of the origins of sexuality:

> Shall we follow the hint given us by the poet-philosopher and venture upon the hypothesis that living substance at the time of its coming to

life was torn apart into small particles, which have ever since endeavored to reunite through the sexual instincts?' (Freud, pp. 69–70)

Eisenstein's entire creative life had revolved around bringing things together, often in scandalous combinations and especially in combinations of abstract ideas and concrete, sometimes bawdy, materializations. Such combinations were most often explosive, hazardous, dialectical: they would not, in fact, lend themselves well to the smooth abstract curves of the 'spherical book'. In his final ruminations, Eisenstein seemed headed for other understandings of the desire of things to come together: here we move, with him, beyond the reach of the 'light of the image' (Breton) and on into that darker realm where beginnings and endings, finally, enter their ultimate embrace.

Conclusion:
The Shape of Thinking

Eisenstein dreamed, as we have seen, of creating 'a book in the shape of a sphere', but there were many good reasons why this dream could never be fulfilled. The abstraction of the sphere is incompatible with the untidy riches of a living mind, and Eisenstein himself associated spheres with prenatal experience and with death. In those realms there is no place for the conscious and creative mind: they are properly the territory of whatever it is that follows or precedes thought, not of thinking itself.

Image-based thinking does have a shape proper to it, however, and in his quest for that form Eisenstein (in what was supposed to be the final chapter of his book on the practical mechanics of directing) turned to Lenin for philosophical support: 'Human cognition is not (nor does it travel along) a straight line, but rather a curved line, endlessly approaching a series of circles, a spiral.'[1] With this citation from Lenin, Eisenstein brings to a close a long excursus on the history and meaning of the spiral, a digression that itself traces a spiral path (from seashells and yin/yang symbols through Hogarth and Fibonacci to Leonardo and Lenin) with respect to the chapter's starting topic, the 'problem of the figurativeness of the mise-en-scène' (IP 667). The main point of this digression turns out to be that digression itself is a fundamental characteristic of thinking-in-images:

> Here we arrive at the last twist of the spiral of our digression. At first glance it might seem to be spirally diverging. In fact, however, it turns out that we took up one random and tangential point and ended up at the very centermost point. (IP 667)

An image leads necessarily to other images; any image would then seem to be a digression or detour from the idea at hand. But what may seem like a 'digression', Eisenstein says here, may in fact turn out to be the path leading to 'the centermost point'. In other words, when traveling the spiral of image-based thinking, it is difficult to know whether one is outbound or inbound, digressing or honing in on the essential.

Thinking is a kind of movement, like dancing or shaking a fist.[2] Like any physical movement, thinking, too, depends for any forward motion on the dialectical incorporation of 'recoil' (*otkaz*).[3] Eisenstein buttressed this argument with another quote from Lenin: 'The movement of cognition towards an object may always proceed only dialectically: withdraw, so as better to arrive – recoil, so as better to leap (to know?).'[4]

Figurative philosophy is also built upon recoil: the image lures the mind onto the curving path of digression and detour. This distracting and derailing function of the image may make it seem like a trap (the detour could become interminable), but one may also discover, as Eisenstein claims in *Rezhissura*, that the trap of the image, by preventing us from charging forward along the straight line of our reasoning, permits a kind of mental deepening that otherwise might be missed: 'figurative meaning... is much deeper and more seriously grounded than it might seem at first glance' (IP 668).

Figure 30.
Saul Steinberg doodle. ©2001
The Saul Steinberg Foundation/
Artists Rights Society (ARS),
New York

As an example of this process at work, let us take a simple image by Saul Steinberg. Eisenstein discusses this cartoon at some length in *Nonindifferent Nature*; like the ad in *Life* magazine (discussed in Chapter 7), this is a deceptively 'low' image with almost unlimited philosophical potential. 'For the uninitiated,' says Eisenstein, 'this is the point of stopping dead in place.'[5] Like any image, this figure arrests its viewer. This cartoon, however, thematizes its own ability to arrest. The naive spectator ('uninitiated') presumably finds himself completely unable to decide which direction 'really' leads to the exit, here doubly deferred and displaced. Ambushed by paradox, he can only conclude that in fact there is no exit available to him at all.

Here the imagined naive spectator has made a grave mistake. The exit, of course, is neither off somewhere to the right nor a little bit to the left: it is right here, in the very arrest itself. Like Kant's seeming dead-ends that provoke leaps into the sublime (as in Chapter 5), this little drawing supplies the somewhat less naive (the 'initiated') spectator with an opportunity for ecstasy:

> For the initiated – this is the formula of that double path by which a truly effective work is constructed – equally descending by its roots into the subsoil depths of the accumulation of the past experience of humanity and by its crown, growing into infinity of heavenly perspectives of the future social and spiritual progress of humanity.[6]

The sign's misleading arrows restrict the spectator to the horizontal axis, but Eisenstein shifts our attention splendidly to the vertical (represented in the drawing by the post holding the sign). He also reveals a great organic image – a figurative tree, with roots in humanity's most distant past and its topmost leaves stretching into the future – lurking behind the artificial and manmade construction of the signboard. Within even an image as simple as Steinberg's 'Exit', the alert spectator can find an entire world of correspondences ready to explode, like the hollow/not so hollow images of *October*, into action.

In this way, an image is a double trap for the mind: not only does it arrest the viewer's attention, but it then sends the spectator from association to association (that spiral path that may eventually turn out to be carrying us towards 'the very centermost point'). These associations (as we saw in the case of *The General Line*) have a remarkable tendency to accumulate and the image's accumulated associations do not always observe the rules of decorum. Steinberg's 'Exit' follows this pattern as well. In our present context (as we move towards this book's exit), the image offers us, among other things, another figure of 'bi-sex', as the vertical post pierces the closed circuit described by the signboard's edges: we travel again back to the acrobatic exploits of *Enough Simplicity for Every Wise Man* (1923), back also to the unfunny circus arena of *Ivan the Terrible*, when the foolish Vladimir enters the church to meet his death. There, 'womb' and 'tomb' came together, as they do again here, in the signpost's paradoxical conflation of 'exit' and 'no exit'.

Let us follow Steinberg's dialectical arrows, then, as they lead us back to the end of the second part of *Ivan the Terrible*. An image there responds: the walls are covered with frescoes; across them march the hooded shadows of Ivan's guards, the 'oprichniki'; before this spectacle stands our naive spectator, Vladimir, looking up at the walls with a candle in his hand. He looks, but he is looking away from where the true 'danger' lies; nevertheless he sees something, he understands something and then the dagger sinks into him and he dies (or rather, as Freud and Eisenstein would have us say, his 'detour' comes to a close). Like the Steinberg cartoon, the richly layered shots of this sequence both arrest and transport the spectator; like the cartoon, this moment from *Ivan* is very much a self-referential commentary on the pleasures and hazards of thinking in images.

Figure 31.
'Here we arrive at the last twist
of the spiral...'.
(*Ivan the Terrible*, Part Two)

Each representational layer invites the spectator to move farther along the spiral of connections and associations that images inaugurate. The frescoes on the walls repeat tragic Biblical stories; the picture facing Vladimir portrays a staring, bearded God seated in judgment: the damned are thrown into the gaping maw of Hell on the wall's lower right. The painted walls provide a backdrop of myth that reminds us of the deep patterns of 'primitive thinking' (*pensée sauvage*) that so moved Eisenstein in Mexico, where he learned what it might mean to have all of history spread in paintings across an architectural surface. In *MMM*, Eisenstein had planned to play with the conceit of such images – also in a church – coming to life; in *Bezhin Meadow*, he attempted with disastrous consequences to have his film embody Biblical archetypes. In *Ivan the Terrible*, the link between fresco and person is made more ambiguous and indirect (an indirection that is punctuated by certain exact correspondences: when the young Ivan's feet, for instance, dangle exactly the same way as the painted feet behind him). The walls tell their own stories, remind us that old tales underlie new ones and all the while (since in *Ivan* the walls have not just ears, but eyes) they stare at us in the most disconcerting way.

A second cascade of associations is inspired by the shadows that march across these frescoed walls. Here the second part of *Ivan* nods to the film's first section, in which highly stylized shadows, more than frescoes, dominated the walls. The shadows remind us of Eisenstein's debt to Disney, but they also invite us to move towards the basic problems of perception as outlined so long ago by Plato: in that proto-cinematic cave, it was shadows cast on the wall that the prisoners mistook for truth. Here the shadows are of men cloaked in hoods, a touch which not only adds to the sense of threat but also compounds the effect of disguise and misdirection (nothing is seen clearly; nothing is what it seems to be). In front of fresco and shadow, Vladimir finds himself gazing at a contrapuntal representation of two precursors of the cinema: the painting and the shadow play (the latter adding the element of movement to visual representation).

Vladimir himself belongs to yet a third layer, the properly cinematic, and he also seems to play the role here of spectator: despite the indirection of his gaze, despite the fact that the images he gazes at are a kind of lure away from the truth (they lead him deeper into the cave), he manages nevertheless to see and understand something. That 'something' is, I think, the same message as is inscribed on Steinberg's helpful signpost: 'exit (no exit).' (Or perhaps: 'This way to the womb/tomb.') Then the cave drives the point home.

If we read this sequence in this way, as a kind of meta-cinematic allegory, we may find ourselves wondering whether ecstatic leaps can mean anything to Vladimir, whose position here is so patently un-free. Is only the 'initiated' spectator able to see in the images of cinema something more than a dead-end, a 'point of stopping dead in place'? What shape of thinking is produced by a stab in the back?

André Bazin's famous complaint about montage-based cinema was indeed that it was fundamentally coercive: '[M]ontage by its very nature rules out ambiguity of expression.'[7] It is hard to imagine a more tyrannical scene than this one, in which Vladimir holds his candle up to the scene of Judgment Day and then is cut down as a traitor. Even here, however, I think we find as much ambiguity as despotism. The excessive richness of the images presented to us – indeed, their sheer quantity – has the qualitative effect of forcing the mind onto the curving path of cognition and association. The paths leading outward from the death of Vladimir travel, as we have seen, in many different directions: towards the circus arena and its echoes not only in Eisenstein's first major artistic production (*Enough Simplicity for Every Wise Man*), but also in Alexandrov (*Circus*), Gogol ('Vii') and that advertisement for Sinclair Opaline Motor Oil;

towards the frescoes of Mexico and Eisenstein's abortive comedy project, *MMM* (1933); towards the ecstatic piercing that joins bull and matador and the bi-sex costume-play of weddings; towards Freud's thoughts on death and the origins of life in *Beyond the Pleasure Principle* and towards that linear descendent of the contour-shifting amoeba, Dopey with his wavering candle in *Snow White and the Seven Dwarfs*. By scenes such as that of Vladimir's death we are not only arrested, but also moved and once set in motion the mind can travel not only the paths (of which *Ivan* proposes a dizzying array) indicated variously by the filmmaker, but also move in entirely unexpected directions. In these ways montage, however tyrannical, also incorporates within itself, by its very nature, the relative freedoms of digression and detour: not solely a 'montage of attractions', then, but also a 'montage of distractions'.

This book has followed the pull of Eisenstein's films along both of these axes: not just that of attraction, but of distraction, too. The astounding heterogeneity of the materials held in Eisenstein's enormous archive serves as a constant reminder that Eisenstein's approach to art and thought was aggressively and unrepentantly omnivorous. In his view, the most important aesthetic and philosophical ideas did not languish in some splendidly high-minded isolation; to the contrary, they were waiting to be discovered in the most unexpected places, even in the 'low' humor of a cartoon or a dirty joke. Perhaps the essential distinguishing feature of that 'initiated viewer' who Eisenstein says can find ecstasy in Steinberg's blocked 'Exit' is a sort of peripheral vision, an openness to the potential for insight present in what might otherwise seem like the mere debris of representation.

To think in images is to travel the spiral of cognition in both directions at once, to be always both outbound and inbound. Eisenstein's experimentation in image-based thinking has been the centripetal core of this book, but as I have traced the evolution of these experiments, I have also tried at all times to respect the more centrifugal aspects of Eisenstein's work. The image, the figure, makes possible philosophy's movement towards apprehension of life's central truths and at the same time it undercuts attempts to settle upon any single general line. In Eisenstein's fertile, contradictory and image-soaked world, abstract thought finds itself in perpetual collision with the particular instance. From this savage juncture between general line and specific image, between philosophy and figure, derives Eisenstein's particular mode of thinking about the world: the doubly winding path of a figurative philosophy.

Notes

Introduction

1. *Za bol shoe kinoiskusstvo. Vsesoiuznoe tvorcheskoe soveshchanie rabotnikov sovetskoi kinematografii*, 8–13 January 1935 (Moscow: Kinofotoizdat, 1935), pp. 33; 40. Translations are mine unless otherwise indicated.
2. *Eisenstein: Three Films*, ed. Jay Leyda, trans. Diana Matias (New York: Harper & Row, 1974), p. 121.
3. See BTS 878.
4. Viktor Shklovskii, 'Iskusstvo kak priem', in *O teorii prozy* (Moscow: Federatsiia, 1929), 7–23: 7.
5. Theodor W Adorno, 'Die Aktualität der Philosophie' (1931), in Theodor W Adorno, *Gesammelte Schriften*, ed. Rolf Tiedemann, with Gretel Adorno, Susan Buck-Morss and Klaus Schultz, Volume I, *Philosophische Frühschriften* (Frankfurt am Main: Suhrkamp, 1973): pp. 325–344. This quote p. 332.
6. See Maxim Gorky, 'The Lumière Cinematograph (Extracts)' in Richard Taylor and Ian Christie (eds), *The Film Factory* (Cambridge, Massachusetts: Harvard University Press, 1988), pp. 25–26.
7. Fond 1923, op. 1, e/kh 82, l. 1. RGALI.
8. 'The Montage of Attractions (On the production of AN Ostrovsky's *Enough Simplicity for Every Wise Man* at the Moscow Proletkult Theatre)' (1923), in SW1 33–38: 35.
9. L Vygotsky, *Thought and Language* (Cambridge, Mass: MIT Press, 1962), p. 149.
10. Boris Ejxenbaum, 'Cinema Stylistics', trans. Herbert Eagle, in *Formalist Film Theory*, Michigan Slavic Materials 19 (Ann Arbor: University of Michigan Press, 1981): 55–80, pp. 79–80.
11. Viktor Shklovskii, 'O kinoiazyke' (1926), in *Za 60 let. Raboty o kino* (Moscow: Iskusstvo, 1985), pp. 32–35, this quote p. 34.
12. The promise of the hieroglyph for contemporary (and Western) culture was also being explored at this time by Walter Benjamin, who described in 1928 the potential role of 'picture writing' in a new age: 'But it is quite beyond doubt that the development of writing will not indefinitely be bound by the claims to power of a chaotic academic and commercial activity; rather, quantity is approaching the moment of a qualitative leap when writing, advancing ever more deeply into the graphic regions of its new eccentric

figurativeness, will take sudden possession of an adequate factual content. In this picture writing, poets, who will now as in earliest times be first and foremost experts in writing, will be able to participate only by mastering the fields in which (quite unobtrusively) it is being constructed: the statistical and technical diagram. With the foundation of an international moving script they will renew their authority in the life of peoples and find a role awaiting them in comparison to which all the innovative aspirations of rhetoric will reveal themselves as antiquated daydreams'. Walter Benjamin, 'One-Way Street' (1928), in *Reflections*, ed. Peter Demetz, trans. Edmund Jephcott (New York: Schocken, 1978), 61–94, p. 78.

13. 'The Montage of Attractions', SW1 34.

14. 'It is then possible to envisage in both theory and practice a construction, with no linking plot logic, which provokes a chain of the necessary unconditioned reflexes that are, at the editor's will, associated with (compared with) pre-determined phenomena and by this means to create the chain of new conditioned reflexes that these phenomena constitute,' for example. See 'The Montage of Film Attractions' (1924), SW1 39–58: 49.

15. 'An Unexpected Juncture' (1928), SW1 115–122: 119.

16. Theodor W Adorno, 'Charakteristik Walter Benjamins' (1950), in *Prismen*, in Theodor W Adorno, *Gesammelte Schriften*, ed. Rolf Tiedemann, with Gretel Adorno, Susan Buck-Morss and Klaus Schultz, Volume 10.1, *Kulturkritik und Gesellschaft I* (Frankfurt am Main: Suhrkamp, 1973): pp. 238–253. This quote p. 250.

17. See Benjamin's 'Surrealism: The Last Snapshot of the European Intelligentsia', *Reflections*, p. 179.

18. '[Montazh]' (1937, 1945), IP2 239–484: 386.

19. Eisenstein cites here the 14th element of the dialectic as described by Lenin in his conspectus of Hegel's *Science of Logic* ('Konspekt Lenina k 'Nauke logiki' Gegelia,' *Leninskii sbornik IX*, [Moscow, 1929], p. 277).

20. André Breton, 'Manifesto of Surrealism' (1924), in *Manifestoes of Surrealism*, trans. Richard Seaver and Helen R Lane (Ann Arbor, Michigan: The University of Michigan Press, 1969), p. 37.

21. 'The Principles of the New Russian Cinema', SW1 195–202: 201–2.

22. See Eisenstein's essay of 1929, 'An Unexpected Juncture' (SW1 115–122), which describes the relationship between Soviet cinema and Japanese Kabuki theater in the same terms that Eisenstein would use in France with reference to Surrealism.

23. Not only was this play the inspiration for Eisenstein's most famous early theoretical article, 'The Montage of Attractions' (originally in the journal *LEF* no. 3, June/July 1923, pp. 70–71, 74–5), but that phrase appeared on the play's publicity poster (also featured as backdrop in the film sequence as the various characters and finally Eisenstein himself, take their bows).

24. 'The school for the montageur is cinema and, principally, music-hall and circus because (from the point of view of form) putting on a good show means constructing a strong music-hall/circus programme that derives from the situations found in the play that is taken as a basis.' 'The Montage of Attractions', SW1 35.

25. André Breton, *L Amour fou* (Paris: Gallimard, 1937), p. 36.

26. 'Let us take, for example, an extremely popular artistic device such as the so-

called *pars pro toto*. Everyone is familiar with the force of its effectiveness. The doctor's pince-nez in *The Battleship Potemkin* are etched on the memory of everyone who saw it. This device consists of replacing the whole (the doctor) with a part (his pince-nez) which plays him; at the same time it turns out that it plays that role with a much greater emotional intensity than the whole (the doctor) could have done, had he merely been shown a second time. And it turns out that this device is a very typical example of the cognitive forms from the arsenal of early thinking.' SM Eisenstein, 'Speeches to the All-Union Creative Conference of Soviet Filmworkers' (1935), SW3 16–46: 30.

27. Breton ends his discussion of the wooden spoon (and the other 'find' of that excursion with Giacometti – a mysterious metal half-mask) with reference to *Beyond the Pleasure Principle* (Breton, 46); Eisenstein turned to the enigma of the protoplasmic ties to love and death as he considered the ties between fetus and Disney cartoon in the 1930s and 1940s (see the last chapter of this book).

28. Viacheslav Ivanov, *Ocherki po istorii semiotiki v SSSR* (Moscow: Khudo-zhestvennaia literatura, 1976), p. 2.

29. David Bordwell, *The Cinema of Eisenstein* (Cambridge, Massachusetts: Harvard University Press, 1993).

30. When Mikhail Iampolsky describes Eisenstein as enthralled by the general pattern, the 'third text' as Iampolsky calls it, he makes him out to be more reductive than he was in practice. Like his fellow 'collector' Walter Benjamin, Eisenstein was charmed first and foremost by the variety of instances in which some general rule could be discerned. See Iampol'skii, *Pamiat Tiresiia* (Moscow: RIK 'Kul'tura', 1993).

31. See Kristin Thompson's *Eisenstein s Ivan the Terrible: A Neoformalist Analysis* (Princeton: Princeton University Press, 1981).

32. *Za bol shoe kinoiskusstvo*, p. 40.

33. *Za bol shoe kinoiskusstvo*, p. 72.

34. *Za bol shoe kinoiskusstvo*, p. 113.

35. Marie Seton, *Sergei M Eisenstein* (London: Dennis Dobson, 1978); Yon Barna, *Eisenstein: The Growth of a Cinematic Genius*, trans. Lise Hunter (Boston: Little, Brown and Co., 1973); Barthélémy Amengual, *Que viva Eisenstein!* (Lausanne: L'Age d'Homme, 1980); David Bordwell, *The Cinema of Eisenstein* (Cambridge, Massachusetts: Harvard University Press, 1993); Oksana Bulgakowa, *Sergej Eisenstein – drei Utopien. Archi-tekturentwürfe zur Filmtheorie* (Berlin: PotemkinPress, 1996) and *Sergei Eisenstein: A Biography* (Berlin & San Francisco: PotemkinPress, 2001).

36. SM Eisenstein, 'An Unexpected Juncture', [1928], SW1 115.

37. 'K voprosu o materialisticheskom podkhode k forme' in *Kinozhurnal ARK*, 1925, no. 4/5 (April/May), pp. 5–8; and in IP1 109–116: 113.

Chapter 1

1. Dziga Vertov, 'The Cine-Eyes. A Revolution' [1923], in *The Film Factory*, eds Richard Taylor and Ian Christie, trans. Richard Taylor (London: Routledge and Kegan Paul, 1988), p. 90.

2. IP6 34.

3. Review (signed 'Gagen') in the newspaper *Vecherniaia Moskva* (No. 57, 10 March 1925), p. 4.

4. 'The Montage of Attractions', SW1 33–38.

5. A Fevral'skii, *Krasnaia Zvezda* (15 March 1925).

6. Review in *Kommunar*, otherwise unidentified, clipping held in Fond 1923, op. 1, e/kh 24, l. 99.

7. Review signed 'Khris. Khersonskii', a clipping, source unidentified, in Fond 1923, op. 1, e/kh 24, l. 20.

8. See Sheila Fitzpatrick's overview of the ideological dilemmas dogging the Proletkult in *The Cultural Front: Power and Culture in Revolutionary Russia* (Ithaca; London: Cornell University Press, 1992), pp. 19–23. See also Lynn Mally, Culture of the Future: *The Proletkult Movement in Revolutionary Russia* (Berkeley: University of California Press, 1990).

9. Eisenstein had a hand in a number of Proletkult plays, most memorably *The Mexican* (adapted from Jack London by Boris Arvatov and produced by Valerii S Smyshliaev, 1921; Eisenstein was responsible for the costumes and the decor); *Enough Simplicity for Every Wise Man* (Sergei Tretiakov's reworking of Aleksandr Ostrovskii's nineteenth-century original, 1923); *Do You Hear, Moscow?* (by Sergei Tretiakov, 1923) and *Gas Masks* (by Tretiakov, 1924).

10. Clipping from *Kino-nedelia*, Fond 1923, op. 1, e/kh 24.

11. Fond 1923, op. 1, e/kh 24.

12. *Rabochii zritel'*, 7 October 1924, No. 22, p. 18. According to this account: 'the whole theatrical collective of the Proletkult without exception has taken part in the production of *Strike* under the leadership of the director Eisenstein.' Most intriguing, however, is the claim that 'During filming at the Kolomenskii factory – which took about two weeks – up to 7000 workers participated. Taking part in this shoot was LD Trotsky, playing himself.' Hard to imagine what 'Trotsky playing himself' might have meant in this instance! In any case there is no evidence that his participation was anything beyond a rumor.

13. Fond 1923, op. 1, e/kh 17, l. 1; typescript dated 14 March 1924.

14. Fond 1923, op. 1, e/kh 17, l. 1.

15. Review (signed 'Gagen') in the newspaper *Vecherniaia Moskva* (No. 57, 10 March 1925), p. 4. This reviewer objected in the same terms to the slaughterhouse sequence.

16. Lev Kuleshov, 'Volia. Uporstvo. Glaz' [1926], *Sobranie sochinenii v trekh tomakh*, Vol. I, *Teoriia Kritika Pedagogika* (Moscow: Iskusstvo, 1987): pp. 111–113. This quote p. 112.

17. In *Eisenstein, Cinema and History* (Urbana and Chicago: University of Illinois Press, 1993), James Goodwin associates the 'aura' created by the crowd scenes in *Strike* with 'Cubo-Futurist studies in motion and light radiation': 'in crowd scenes an aura is particularly strong because the rushing figures leave blurred, bright traces on the screen.' (43–44). I would say that the emphasis on the lines of the human contour is particularly important.

18. John Bowlt comments in *Russian Art of the Avant-Garde* (New York: Thames and Hudson, 1988) that 'the upsurge of interest in photography and cinematography in Russia at this time provided an undoubted stimulus to Larionov's concern with light and dynamics' (92).

19. Mikhail Larionov, 'Rayonist Painting', 1913, in *Russian Art of the Avant-Garde*, translated by John Bowlt, p. 92.

20. 'Tak budet vsiudu, esli pobedit Kolchak', *Voronezhskaia bednota. Ezhednevnaia raboche-krest ianskaia gazeta*, No. 89. Voronezh, 26 April 1919, p. 3. Emphasis is in the original.

21. See Anne Nesbet, 'Babel's Face', *Russian Literature*, Vol. 42, No. 1 (1997), pp. 65–83.

22. Kazimir Malevich, 'From Cubism and Futurism to Suprematism: The New Painterly Realism' (1915), in John Bowlt (ed.), 116–135, p. 125.

23. Alexander Belenson, *Cinema To-day* (Moscow 1925), p. 59, cited in Seton, p. 69.

24. Thus perhaps marking the first of a series of 'actions triggered by bad food', if we compare this proposed beginning with the wormy meat that triggers revolt in *Battleship Potemkin*.

25. See Tom Gunning's discussion of the retinal image, or 'optogramme', in 'Tracing the Individual Body: Photography, Detectives and Early Cinema', in Leo Charney and Vanessa R. Schwartz (eds), *Cinema and the Invention of Modern Life* (Berkeley: University of California Press, 1995), pp. 15–45. Gunning mentions the contribution of cattle to this dubious science on p. 38. Also see Eisenstein's memoirs: 'Any line of any picture or person stands out as if branded on one's visual memory. I can believe that absurd popular myth that the murderer's image can be fixed on the victim's retina as clearly as on photographic film. This ridiculous notion is the basis of the substantive proof of the black murderer's guilt in *The Clansman*, which described the Ku-Klux-Klan phenomenon and inspired Griffith's *The Birth of a Nation*.' (BTS 9).

26. See Dziga Vertov, *Kinogazeta*, No. 1 (89), 24 March 1925.

27. In Shklovsky's 'Art As Device', seeing things 'anew' is also shown to be, at least in part, a matter of 'child's play'. Tolstoy, Shklovskii's primary source for quotations, 'defamiliarizes' descriptions by adopting the point of view of innocence (this point of view could be that of a child, a peasant, or a horse): 'The device of defamiliarization in LN Tolstoy consists in his not calling something by its name, but rather describing it as if it were being seen for the first time, or an event as if it were taking place for the first time; and in the course of this he doesn't use, in his description of the thing, the usual names for its parts, but rather uses the terms one might use for corresponding parts of other things.' *O teorii prozy*, p.14.

28. LN Tolstoi, *Povesti i rasskazy v dvukh tomakh*, Vol. 2 (Moscow: Khudo-zhestvennaia literatura, 1978), pp. 39–73. This quote pp. 71–72.

29. Another sacrifice belonging to this tradition can be found in Andrei Bely's novel *Petersburg* (1916; 1922), one of the primary emphases of which turns out to be the tension between abstraction and bodily fluids (between polygons and entrails). This tension, Bely makes clear to us, is the twentieth century's replay, in tones at once speaking of 'tragedy' and 'farce,' of the Nietzschean dichotomy between Apollo and Dionysus, surface beauty and underlying chaos. Thus, while under political or domestic stress, the novel's hopelessly dry statesman, Apollon Apollo-novich Ableukhov, '[a]t times, for hours on end... would lapse into an unthinking contemplation of pyramids, triangles, parallelepipeds, cubes and trapezoids' (p. 11), whereas his son is overtaken by more fleshly visions: 'The reason why Nikolai Apollonovich interrupted Semyonych and flew up the staircase was that he had a clear picture of a scoundrel committing an act. He pictured the scoundrel, the snip-snip of gleaming scissors in the scoundrel's fingers as he clumsily flung himself on a little old man to clip through an artery. The little old man had a neck with a throbbing pulse – it was crayfishlike, somehow. And the scoundrel went snip-snip with the scissors through the artery. And stinking, sticky blood poured

over his scissors. And the little old man – beardless, wrinkled, bald – broke into sobs and stared him straight in the eyes, squatting on his haunches, trying to squeeze shut the opening in his neck, from which blood was spurting in a barely audible whistle...' And one of the leitmotifs of the novel is that of the carving of a suckling pig, a gastronomic image returned to its slaughterhouse roots during the description of the murder of Lippanchenko: 'A jet of boiling liquid slashed along his bare back from his shoulder blades to his buttocks. As he fell he understood: his back had been slit open (this is how the hairless skin of a cold suckling pig with horseradish sauce is sliced). No sooner had he understood this than he felt a jet of boiling liquid beneath his navel.

And from there came a hissing. And some part of him thought that it was gases (his stomach had been ripped open). Bending his head over his heaving stomach, he sank down, fingering the flowing stickiness on his stomach and on the sheet.

This was his last conscious impression of ordinary reality. His consciousness expanded. The monstrous periphery of consciousness sucked the planets into itself and sensed them as organs detached one from the other...' Andrei Bely, *Petersburg*, trans. Robert A Maguire and John E Mamstad (Bloomington: Indiana University Press, 1978), p. 263.

As was also the case for Kholstomer, this murder performed as if it were a methodical slaughtering of animals leads not only to death but to a dramatic 'expansion of consciousness.'

30. Boris Pilnyak, 'Mother Earth' (1924), in *Mother Earth and Other Stories*, trans. and ed. Vera T. Reck and Michael Green (New York: Doubleday, 1968), p. 57.

31. In a 1922 review of a book he seems not to have liked (Vladimir Zazubrin's description of the Civil War, *Dva mira*), Pil'niak had brought in the slaughterhouse as a telling point of comparison. 'On the first 50 pages I counted 27 battles and 141 deaths. Deaths of all sorts: shootings and hangings and rapes and burnings on bonfires and burnings in ovens and dismemberment with swords and rapiers... all sorts of deaths; I haven't listed all of them here. Several times I have been at a slaughterhouse where livestock is killed for meat; my throat was constricted by a shudder and I felt ill: exactly the same feeling was produced in me by this novel.' Boris Pil'niak, 'Vladimir Zazubrin. *Dvamira*. Novel in 2 parts [review]', *Pechat i Revoliutsiia*, 1922, 1 (4), January-March (Moscow: Gosizdat, 1922): pp. 294–296. It is tempting to think that Pil'niak's fieldtrip to the slaughterhouse mentioned here may have been taken as part of his background preparation for 'Mother Earth'. No matter how efficient and modern the work of the slaughterhouse, the intellectual's throat contracts in response to it.

32. John R Commons, 'Labor Conditions in Slaughtering and Meat Packing', in *Trade Unionism and Labor Problems*, ed. John R Commons (Boston, 1905), p. 224. As cited in Upton Sinclair, *The Jungle* (orig. 1906), with an Introduction and Notes by James R Barrett (Urbana and Chicago: University of Illinois Press, 1988).

33. On Sinclair exporting a film version of *The Jungle* to the Soviet Union in 1923, see Kevin Brownlow, *Behind the Mask of Innocence* (New York: Alfred A Knopf, 1990), p. 477; the letter from Upton Sinclair to Sergei Eisenstein, dated 16 February 1927, is mentioned in *Bronenosets Potemkin*, ed. RN Iurenev (Moscow: Nauka, 1965), p. 282.

34. *The Jungle*, pp. 35–36. The processing of cattle is just as regimented: 'It was all highly specialized labor, each man having his task to do; generally this would consist of only two or three specific cuts and he would pass down the line of fifteen or twenty carcasses, making these cuts upon each. First there came the "butcher", to bleed them; this meant one swift stroke, so swift that you could not see it – only the flash of the knife; and before you could realize it, the man had darted on to the next line and a stream of bright red was pouring out upon the floor. This floor was half an inch deep with blood, in spite of the best efforts of men who kept shovelling it through holes' (39).

35. Two years later, Iurii Olesha would return in a more farcical vein to the joint themes of factory and slaughterhouse in his *Envy* (1927). When the 'completely new man', Volodia Makarov, writes a letter to his mentor, sausage-maker extraordinaire Andrei Babichev, the progression from (slaughtered) calf to 'man-machine' becomes a sort of fantastic – and loopy – assembly-line process in its own right: 'I am a man-machine. You won't know me. I've turned into a machine. Or if I haven't yet turned into one, I want to. The machines here are animals – thoroughbred animals! Wonderfully indifferent, proud machines. Not like those things in your sausage factories. You're doing things on the level of cottage industry. All you do is slaughter calves. I want to be a machine. I want to get your advice. I want to be proud of my work – proud of the fact that I'm working. You know, to be indifferent to everything but work. I've begun to envy machines – that's what it is!' Yuri Olesha, *Envy*, trans. Clarence Brown, in *The Portable Twentieth-Century Russian Reader*, ed. Clarence Brown (London: Penguin, 1985), pp. 230–362; this quote p. 285.

36. See *The Film Factory*, p. 92. See also Pascal Bonitzer's discussion of the way *Strike* organizes *vertical* spaces (workers on the surface, bosses above, the 'underworld' literally underground) in 'Système de *La Grève*', *Cahiers du cinéma*, No. 226–227, January-February 1971.

37. See Yuri Tsivian, 'Some Historical Footnotes to the Kuleshov Experiment', in *Early Cinema: Space/Frame/Narrative*, ed. Thomas Elsaesser (London: British Film Institute, 1990), pp. 247–255.

38. Lev Kuleshov, 'Znamia kinematografii' (1920), *Sobranie sochinenii v trekh tomakh*, Vol. 1: 63–85, p. 69.

39. The chopping up of the actor into component 'axes' was a project with a theatrical past; Meierkhol'd and other avant-garde directors (including Eisenstein in his Proletkul't Theater days) were committed to disciplining the bodies of their actors, a discipline which included the control over each distinct part of the body.

40. Commons, as cited in *The Jungle*, p. 224.

41. In *Kinogazeta* No. 1 (89) 24–March–25. Much of what Vertov saw in *Strike* he did not like, however, including all the 'acted' scenes.

42. SM Eisenstein, 'The Problem of the Materialist Approach to Form' (1925), SW1 59–64.

43. Fond 1923, op. 2, e/kh 231, l. 31, dated 5 January 1934. The source for *Foto-Auge*: 1929, Franz Roth, Akad. Verlag Stuttgart. Note that the very name of the journal ('photo-eye') belongs in the 'cine-eye' series.

44. Fond 1923, op. 2, e/kh 232, l. 45, dated 27 October 1937.

45. This term, from the French for 'eye of an ox', refers to a kind of circular window. Like so many of Eisenstein's allusions, the connection to a foreign

phrase like 'oeil-de-boeuf' was, needless to say, well beyond the capabilities of most of his film's spectators.

Chapter 2

1. As cited by Naum Kleiman in 'Vzrevevshii lev,' *Kinovedcheskie zapiski* 1, 1988: 91–110, p. 99.
2. 'Constanţa (Whither 'The Battleship Potemkin')' (1926), SW1 67–70: 70.
3. 'The Method of Making a Workers' Film' (1925), SW1 65–66: 65, translation slightly modified for accuracy.
4. As cited in Lars Kleberg, 'The Audience as Myth and Reality: Soviet Theatrical Ideology and Audience Research in the 1920s', *Russian History/ Histoire Russe*, 1982, p. 232. Kleberg provides an excellent discussion of the attempt to determine audience reaction in the 1920s.
5. Fond 1923, op. 1, e/kh 82. Stenogramma diskussii, otzyvy zritelei i otchet o nabliudenii za reaktsiei zritel'nogo zala po fil'mu SME'a 'Bronenosets Potemkin,' sobrannye Assotsiatsiei revoliutsionnoi kinematografii, 25–30 January 1926, l. 13.
6. VI Lenin, 'Ukazaniia o rabote agitatsionno-instruktorskikh poezdov i parokhodov', in VI Lenin. *Polnoe sobranie sochinenii.* Vol. 40. (Moscow: Izdatel'stvo politicheskoi literatury, 1981), pp. 72–73.
7. VM Bekhterev, *Kollektivnaia refleksologiia* (Petrograd: 'Kolos', 1921). Two chapters of this book ('O kollektivnykh refleksakh voobshche,' pp. 138–143 and 'Razvitie kollektivnykh dvizhenii po tipu sochetatel'nykh refleksov,' pp. 144–158), chapters that analyze the relationship of collective reflexes to various aspects of revolutionary activity, contain a number of prototypes for some of *Battleship Potemkin*'s most dramatic episodes: 'Imagine a crowd being subdued by a military contingent – the crowd taking off in panicked flight under the influence of gunfire – this is an ordinary collective reflex' (144); likewise, 'it's the business of agitators to know when and where to deliver incendiary speeches before the crowd, so as to achieve the necessary effect by appropriate means' (141).
8. M Zagorskii, 'Kak reagiruet zritel'?', in *LEF*, No. 2(6), 1924, pp. 141–151. This quote p. 141.
9. VI Lenin. *What Is To Be Done? Burning Questions of Our Movement*, in *the Collected Works of VI Lenin. Volume IV: The Iskra Period, 1900–1902. Book II* (New York: International Publishers, 1929), pp. 89–258: 114–115.
10. These remarks come from the discussion of *Battleship Potemkin* at one of the Association for Revolutionary Cinema's Thursday discussions, 14 January 1926. (Fond 1923, op. 1, e/kh 82, l. 1).
11. Andrei Belyi, 'Sinematograf', *Arabeski* (Moscow, 1911), p. 349.
12. Lenin, *What is to be Done?*, p. 158.
13. In 'The Fourth Dimension of Cinema', Eisenstein struggles to demonstrate that in fact, though 'the usual formal cinematic criteria' may on occasion fail, there is nevertheless no meaning that would lie outside the reach of scientific explanation, that is to say, beyond the reach of scientific metaphor. The dominant analogy of this essay (music) is chosen because of its ability to mediate between 'art' and 'science.' Eisenstein carves up the equation into montage elements: the famous series of 'metric', 'rhythmic', 'tonal' and 'overtonal', whose sum is, again, the effect on the viewer. SW1 181–194.

14. During his engineering student days, Eisenstein collected, for example, back issues of *Apollon*, a journal in which the relationship of French cubism to 'fourth dimensional' thought was debated; see Sergei Makovskii, '"Novoe" iskusstvo i "chetvertoe izmerenie"', in *Apollon*, St. Petersburg, no. 7 (September 1913). A partial window into Eisenstein's early collecting habits is provided by a catalog he kept of books purchased in the second half of 1917, where several issues of *Apollon* (from 1911 to 1916) are listed; see Fond 1923, op. 1, e/kh 881, 'Katalog knig, kuplennykh SM Eizenshteinom, s iiunia po dekabr' 1917, ll. 5–6.

15. Linda Dalyrymple Henderson, *The Fourth Dimension and Non-Euclidean Geometry in Modern Art* (Princeton: Princeton University Press, 1988). My discussion of the dissemination of 'fourth dimensional' ideas in the visual arts (the non-cinematic visual arts) in Russia is greatly indebted to her. Henderson's analysis of the influence of new trends in physics on avant-garde artists in Europe and America does not consider the political (or 'class') ramifications of references to the fourth dimension and also, with one exception, does not consider the case of the cinema. The single exception is a short passage from Eisenstein's article on 'The Fourth Dimension' – which she cites only as an example of how by the end of the 1920s the standard reference had already become Einstein (whom Eisenstein mentions).

16. Uspenskii's books have enjoyed considerable popularity in the USA, the author's name usually being spelled 'Ouspensky'.

17. As cited in Henderson, p. 373.

18. SM Eisenstein, 'Laocoön' (late 1930s), SW2 109–202: 119.

19. HG Wells, *The Time Machine* (1898), (New York: Dover, 1995), pp. 3–5.

20. Nikolai Alekseevich Umov, 'Kharakternye cherty i zadachi sovremennoi estestvenno-nauchnoi mysli' (Rech', proiznesennaia na obshchem sobranii chlenov II Mendeleevskogo S"ezda 21 dek. 1911 goda)', in *Sobranie Sochinenii*, Vol. 3 (Moscow: Imp. Moskovskoe obshchestro ispy tatelei prirody, 1916), pp. 390–417. This quote p. 410.

21. 'The Fourth Dimension of Cinema', SW1 185.

22. By the time Malevich starts putting the 'fourth dimension' in the actual titles of his paintings, he has discovered exactly this potential of the second dimension. Thus the flat rectangles of works like 'Painterly Realism. Boy with Knapsack – Color masses in the Fourth Dimension', 1915; 'Suprematism: Painterly Realism of a Football Player. Color Masses in the Fourth Dimension', 1915.

23. Edwin A Abbott, *Flatland, A Romance of Many Dimensions* (New York: HarperCollins, 1983), pp. 93–94.

24. See the biographical information contained in Thomas F Banchoff, 'From Flatland to Hypergraphics: Interacting with Higher Dimensions', in *Interdisciplinary Science Reviews*, Vol. 15, No. 4 (1990): 364–372.

25. Upton Sinclair, *The Jungle* [orig. 1906], with an Introduction and Notes by James R Barrett (Urbana and Chicago: University of Illinois Press, 1988), p. 304.

26. Uspenskii attempted to describe the fate of man living life cinematically in a terrible novel named *Kinemodrama*, in which a Nietzschean sense of the 'eternal return' is pasted onto the cinema-inspired notion that one might choose to 'rerun' the film of one's life – only to find, rather drearily, that nothing at all can be changed. Petr Dem'ianovich Uspenskii, *Kinemodrama*

[*Ne dlia kinematografa*], *Okkul tnaia povest iz tsikla idei 'Vechnogo voz-vrashcheniia* (Petrograd: Brianchaninov [Novoe zveno], 1917.

27. Among those who identify Eisenstein's techniques in *Battleship Potemkin* as 'Cubist' is David Mayer, in his introduction to *Sergei M Eisenstein s Potemkin: A Shot-by-shot Presentation by David Mayer* (New York: Da Capo Press, 1972), pp. 13–14. Mayer pays particular attention to the sequence of the breaking plate.

28. 'Dikkens, Griffit i my', IP5 129–: 178.

29. 'A Dialectic Approach to Film Form', trans. Jay Leyda, in *Film Form*, (New York: Harcourt Brace Jovanovich, 1949), pp. 45–63.

30. As corrected by Richard Taylor in his new translation 'The Dramaturgy of Film Form (The Dialectical Approach to Film Form)', SW1 161–180: 172–4. This essay was originally published by Eisenstein not in Russian but in German; see the publication history in SW1 317–318. The German version can be found in H-J Schlegel (ed.), *Sergei M. Eisenstein, Schriften*, Volume 3 (Munich, 1975), pp. 200–205.

31. In his *Petersburg* [1922] Andrei Bely included a disquisition on the way *vdrug* ('suddenly') can function something like a bomb liable to go off at any moment – a description Eisenstein may well have had in mind: '"Suddenlys" are familiar to you. Why, then, do you bury your head like an ostrich at the approach of the inexorable "suddenly"? "It" sneaks up behind your back. Sometimes it even precedes your appearance in a room. You feel horribly uneasy. In your back grows the sensation that a gang of thugs invisible has shoved its way in through your back, as through a door. You turn, you ask your hostess: "Madam, would you mind if I close the door? I have a peculiar kind of nervous sensation: I can't bear to sit with my back to the door." They laugh. You also laugh: as if there were no "suddenly". "It" feeds on cerebral play. It gladly devours all vileness of thought. And it swells up, while you melt like a candle. "Suddenly", like a fattened yet unseen dog, begins to precede you, producing in an observer the impression that you are screened from view by an invisible cloud. This is what your "suddenly" is.' Andrei Bely, *Petersburg*, trans. Robert A Maguire and John E Malmstad (Bloomington: Indiana University Press, 1978), pp. 23–24. For more on the Bely-Eisenstein connection (with a focus not on *Potemkin*, but on *October*), see Iu G Tsivian, *Istoricheskaia retseptsiia kino* (Riga: Zinatne, 1991), pp. 344–347.

32. 'Constanţa (Whither "The Battleship Potemkin")', SW1 67–70: 68.

33. See BTS 523–524: 'An "explosion" in art and particularly a "pathetic" emotional outburst, is constructed according to the very same formulae as a detonation of explosives. I once learned about this in the ensigns' school for engineers in the classes on mines. There, as here, you need first a build-up of electrical charge... Oddly, this effect does not take place if you do not interlay, between the build-up and the actual picture of matter flying in all directions, that indispensable "accentuated" piece which clearly "signals" the explosion. In a real explosion, this is the role of the detonator cap, just as essential in the rear part of a rifle cartridge as it is in the packets of gun-wadding strapped to the girder of a railway bridge. Such pieces are to be found throughout *Potemkin*. At the start of the "Steps" scene there is a large caption: the word "SUDDENLY!" Then this is followed by the aggressively edited shot of the nodding head, in three different sizes, composed from three short montage-cell pieces. (This, incidentally, is a close-up of Olga Ivanovna,

Grisha Alexandrov's first wife!) Here, this also gives the impression of a salvo of rifles "shattering" the silence.'

34. Naum Kleiman, 'Vzrevevshii lev', *Kinovedcheskie zapiski* 1, 1988, p. 91–110. See p. 99.

35. 'Constanta (Whither "The Battleship Potemkin")' (1926), SW1 70.

36. Neil Hertz, 'Medusa's Head: Male Hysteria under Political Pressure' in *The End of the Line. Essays on Psychoanalysis and the Sublime* (New York: Columbia University Press, 1985), pp. 161–193.

37. See Freud, 'Medusa's Head', trans. James Strachey, in *Sexuality and the Psychology of Love* (New York: Collier, 1963), pp. 212–213.

38. My thanks to Harsha Ram, who brought this poem to my attention.

39. Valerii Iakovlevich Briusov, from the section 'Sovremennost'' of the collection *Stefanos* (dedicated to Viacheslav Ivanov), in *Izbrannoe* (Moscow: Pravda, 1982).

40. Louis Fischer, 'Mass Movies', *The Nation* (New York), 9 November 1927, as cited in Jay Leyda, *Kino* (Princeton, New Jersey: Princeton University Press, 1983), p. 241.

41. Leyda, 241.

42. Eisenstein was interested in stereoscopy and assumed that, like color, it would eventually be a widely available technique for the cinema. See, for one example of many, 'The Dramaturgy of Film Form' (1929), SW1 164.

43. In Uspenskii's retelling of Hinton, for example, 'The development of the ability to picture objects to oneself from all sides at once will mean the destruction of the *personal element* (the destruction of oneself) in imagination. The destruction of the personal element in representation should, according to Hinton, lead to the destruction of the personal element in perception. In this way, the development of the ability to picture to oneself objects from all sides at once will be the first step towards the development of the ability to see objects as they really are in a geometric sense, that is, towards the development of that which Hinton calls *higher* [and impersonal] *consciousness* – properly termed a higher psychic level'. PD Uspenskii, *Chetvertoe izmerenie. Obzor glavneishikh teorii i popytok issledovaniia oblasti neizmerimogo*, fourth edition (Berlin, 1931), p. 18.

Chapter 3

1. 'Oshibki i izobreteniia', *Novyi Lef* 1927, no. 11/12 (November-December), pp. 29–33 (as cited in *Film Factory*, p. 183).

2. BTS 363, translation slightly modified.

3. My translation here borrows from that of Herbert Marshall. See Sergei Eisenstein, *Immoral Memories: An Autobiography* (Boston: Houghton Mifflin, 1983), p. 51.

4. Victor Shklovskii, 'Art as Technique', in *Russian Formalist Criticism: Four Essays*, trans. Lee T Lemon and Marion J Reis (Lincoln; London: University of Nebraska Press, 1965): pp. 3–24; p. 12.

5. Neil Hertz points out that Medusan iconography had, in several instances, a state function (to represent its invulnerability to enemies, apparently): 'The *politically* apotropaic effects of the Medusa's head derive from its reappearance on Minerva's shield and from the use of representations of that shield as symbols of the State's power to defend itself against its enemies.' Neil Hertz, 'Medusa's Head: Male Hysteria under Political Pressure', *The End of the Line:*

Essays on Psychoanalysis and the Sublime (New York: Columbia University Press, 1985), pp. 161–193. This quote p. 250 n. 9.

6.   GA 104. A word of warning is in order about Alexandrov's memoirs: his anecdotes are colorful bits of historical narrative, but their truth value is not always unimpeachable; Alexandrov, like all involved with the making of *October*, preferred a good story (History) to historical fact (history).

7.   So obscure was Nikandrov that Alexandrov, from edition to edition of his memoirs, changes his version of where the actor came from originally: 'In the first edition of my book I wrote that the actor playing the role of VI Lenin, VN Nikandrov, had been found in Novorossiisk. That's what SM Eisenstein wrote in the newspaper *Smena*. However, as has now come to light, Nikandrov came from the Urals, from the town Lys'va' (GA, p. 101, footnote).

8.   VV Maiakovskii, comment made at a discussion of Sovkino's future, 15 October 1927, as cited in R Iurenev, *Sergei Eizenshtein. Zamysly. Fil my. Metod. Chast pervaia, 1898–1929* (Moscow: Iskusstvo, 1985), p. 209.

9.   'Bezobrazie' might then be translated literally as 'without-image-ness': 'in poor form'.

10.   V Kirshon, *Kinofront*, 1927, No. 11–12, p. 11, cited in Iurenev, Vol. 1, p. 211.

11.   VV Maiakovskii in *Kino* (No. 45), 7 November 1927, as cited in Iurenev, Vol. 1, p. 209.

12.   Lenin arrives at Finland Station, gives a couple of speeches, takes part in a couple of meetings and comes back from the Underground in disguise in time for the October Revolution – not much scope for 'psychology' or 'everyday life'.

13.   Eventually those actors who played Lenin and then Stalin would find themselves lionized for their mere resemblance to their great models; thus in the 1980s one wall in the Lenfilm studios was devoted to a shrine-like display of all the actors who had ever played Lenin – as a kind of cinematic substitute for a shrine to Lenin himself.

14.   See the account in Isaac Deutscher, *The Prophet Unarmed: Trotsky: 1921–1929* (Oxford: Oxford University Press, 1959), pp. 372–373. The kind of 'sabotage' was very similar, too: the Trotskyites apparently unfurled banners with inappropriate slogans; in this case 'Strike against the kulak, the NEP man and the bureaucrat!' and 'Carry out Lenin's testament!'

15.   Thus goes Alexandrov's story and general legend, but we do not know for certain all the details of what was 'cut' and what 'rearranged' as the film went through the final editing process.

16.   See Sergei Eisenstein, 'Notes for a Film of *Capital*', trans. Maciej Sliwowski, Jay Leyda and Annette Michelson, in *October* 2, Summer 1976: 3–26. Also Annette Michelson, 'Reading Eisenstein Reading *Capital*', an analysis appearing in *October* 2, pp. 27–38 and continued in *October* 3, Spring 1977: 82–89.

17.   In 'The GTK Teaching and Research Workshop' [1928], SW1 127–130: 129.

18.   'Perspectives' [1929], SW1 151–160: 158.

19.   Léon Moussinac, *Sergei Michailovitch Eisenstein*, Cinéma d'aujourd'hui 23 (Paris: Editions Seghers, 1964), pp. 38–39. My translation.

20.   Moussinac, p. 40.

21.   Kerensky gets to the top so that the movie can continue, but this is a compromise with the logic of the moment, which transforms teleology into meaningless repetition and therefore should, in principle, never be 'gotten beyond'.

22. Although we do not know when Eisenstein first encountered Hegel, he refers to Hegel in connection with *October* in notes from 1928 (as we shall see in a moment) and in the lecture mentioned previously (from the early 1930s), he refers specifically to the argument of that chapter of the *Phenomenology* which will be our primary concern here.

23. An interesting analysis of Hegel's images is made by Donald Phillip Verene, in *Hegel s Recollection: A Study of Images in the Phenomenology of Spirit* (Albany: State University of New York Press, 1985).

24. GWF Hegel, *Phenomenology of Spirit*, trans. by AV Miller (Oxford: Oxford University Press, 1977), pp. 30–31.

25. IP2 45–59: 59. The 'Gods' sequence is not to be intellectual montage itself, but a prototype: 'But this, of course, is not yet the intellectual cinema that we have been announcing for some years now. Intellectual cinema will be the cinema that resolves the conflicting combination of physiological overtones and intellectual overtones, creating an unheard-of form of cinema which inculcates the Revolution into the general history of culture, creating a synthesis of science, art and militant class consciousness.' 'The Fourth Dimension in Cinema' (1929)], in SW1 181–194: 193–194.

26. Noël Carroll, 'For God and Country', *Artforum*, Volume XI, no. 5, January 1973, pp. 56–60; p. 57.

27. *Immortal Memories*, p.205.

28. Hegel, p. 210.

29. Freud, *Sexuality and the Psychology of Love*, p. 213.

30. See for example, *Les Totems d André Breton: Surréalisme et primitivisme littéraire.* by Jean-Claude Blachère (Paris: L'Harmattan, 1996).

31. The statues are already hollow in as much as they are examples of kitsch.

32. See Iu G Tsivian, *Istoricheskaia retseptsiia kino: Kinematograf v Rossii 1896– 1930* (Riga: Zinātne, 1991), esp. pp. 344–356.

33. A few years later Walter Benjamin would provide another description of cinema's potential to work mayhem in the museum: mechanical reproduction has, as one of its effects, the ability 'to pry an object from its shell', and thus 'to destroy its aura'. See 'The Work of Art in the Age of Mechanical Reproduction' (1935), in *Reflections*, ed. Hannah Arendt, trans. Harry Zohn (New York: Schocken, 1968), p. 223. *October* reminds us that the aura is a most flexible and durable commodity It can haunt even thoroughly 'shelled' and 'framed' objects long after their taming through reproduction.

34. See 'The Dramaturgy of Film Form (The Dialectical Approach to Film Form)' (1929), SW1 161–180: 'To illustrate General Kornilov's attempted monarchist *putsch* it occurred to me that his militarist *tendency* could be shown in the cutting (montage), but creating the montage material itself out of religious details... To this end a Baroque Christ with beams streaming (exploding) from its halo was briefly intercut with a self-contained egg shape Uzume mask. The temporal conflict between the self-contained egg shape and the graphic star produced the effect of a simultaneous explosion (a bomb, a shot).' (174) Also see Tsivian, 344–356.

35. These concerns resonate with one of Walter Benjamin's 'Theses on the Philosophy of History' (1940): 'Whoever has emerged victorious participates, to this day, in the triumphal procession in which the present rulers step over those who are lying prostrate. According to traditional practice, the spoils

are carried along in the procession. They are called cultural treasures and a historical materialist views them with cautious detachment. For without exception the cultural treasures he surveys have an origin which he cannot contemplate without horror'. In Walter Benjamin, *Illuminations*, ed. Hannah Arendt, trans. Harry Zohn (New York: Schocken Books, 1968), p. 256.

36. Fond 1923, op. 1, e/kh 207, l. 16.
37. And how different this map is from its predecessor in *Strike*: where that was all blobs, the mere 'impression' of a map, this map insists on its exactness and precision – one can read all the street names and see where the new Palace bridge was being constructed.
38. 'Perspectives' (1929), SW1 154.
39. Fond 1923, op. 2, e/kh 228, l. 27; dated 9 August 1928.
40. Fond 1923, op. 2, e/kh 228, l. 27.
41. 'The Dramaturgy of Film Form (The Dialectical Approach to Film Form)', SW1 180.

Chapter 4

1. 'Beyond the Shot', in SW1 138–150: 139. Orig. 'Za kadrom', written as postscript to N Kaufman, *Iaponskoe kino*, Moscow 1929, pp. 72–92.
2. 'The Dramaturgy of Film Form (The Dialectical Approach to Film Form)' (1929), SW1 164. Eisenstein's explanation here is scientifically incorrect, by the way; 'retained impressions' are not the true source of cinema's illusion of movement (the 'phi effect'), which in fact probably owes more to the brain than the retina. See Jacques Aumont's discussion of the problem in *The Image*, trans. Claire Pajackowska (London: British Film Institute, 1997) pp. 30–32.
3. 'The Dramaturgy of Film Form' (The Dialectical Approach to Film Form)', SW1 161.
4. 'Beyond the Shot', SW1 145.
5. According to Grigorii Alexandrov, the film-making team was invited to address the topic by the Central Committee, mediated by Kirill Ivanovich Shutko: 'Already during work on *Battleship Potemkin*, Eisenstein's 'method of production' underwent essential changes under the wholesome influence of Shutko, who always subjected all Eisensteinian innovations to a strict and objective Marxist analysis. So one day Shutko invited us to the Central Committee and said: 'Since you make pictures based on important, socially active themes, we propose to you today's most important theme: the collectivization of agriculture.' GA 88.
6. As a review in the journal *Molochnoe khoziaistvo* put it: 'In *Maklochane* there's no hint of fantasy and fabrication. Here before us is living reality, reinforced by concrete materials in the form of a series of tables of cows' milk-yields, of the growth of the farms of the members of the dairy artel and the accounts of selected members of the artel'. *Molochnoe khoziaistvo*, No. 14 (37), 25 July 1926, pp. 6–7, held in Fond 1923, op. 1, e/kh 155 with other materials collected by Eisenstein and Alexandrov as they worked on the film. The reviewer emphasized the positive role art could play in what was one of the major themes of the 14th Party Congress, the socialist reconstruction of the countryside: 'When we have more such books as the little book of Com. Davydov, more such villages as the village Maklochno and more such workers as the inhabitants of Maklochno turn out to be – then we will come

significantly closer to the fulfillment of the testament of VI Lenin with regard to the creation of a 'system of civilized cooperatives', then in earnest we will be approaching socialist construction in the countryside', p. 8.

7. Fond 1923, op. 1, e/kh 135. The scenario, which is all in Alexandrov's handwriting, is dated 22 June 1926 and a copy was filed the next week in what Alexandrov was already referring to as Eisenstein's 'archive' with the following note appended: 'This scenario I deposit with gratitude and respect in your archive for it could come to fruition only thanks to you! And with your help and with your *School*! Once again with love and respect, your pupil GV Alexandrov'. Alexandrov was already quite sensitive about problems of attribution: this note manages to thank Eisenstein profusely and acknowledge his superiority and mastery, at the same time as it emphasizes the scenario as a product of Alexandrov primarily ('with your help'). Alexandrov well knew, of course, the scandal over the attribution of the scenario for *Strike* that had led, a year earlier, to Eisenstein's break with the Proletkul't (when Eisenstein had been unwilling to share authorship of the scenario). The 'pupil' here demonstrates a wily intelligence, but Alexandrov would eventually have to strike out on his own to secure artistic credit (see Chapter 6).

8. 'The scenario created by us in 1926 seemed out of date and the title of the film, *The General Line*, sounded somewhat pretentious. Stalin, having pronounced these completely reasonable considerations, proposed we change the title of the film. *The Old and the New* – those are his words, which became in the end the title of the picture.' GA 119.

9. Fond 1923, op. 2, e/kh 230, folder of notes dated May–August 1929, 1. 127.

10. *XIV s"ezd vsesoiuznoi kommunisticheskoi partii (b)* [18–31 December 1925] (Moscow; Leningrad: Gosizdat, 1926), p. 27.

11. Jay Leyda, *Kino*, p. 269.

12. *XV s"ezd vsesoiuznoi kommunisticheskoi partii-(b)* [opened 2 December 1927] (Moscow; Leningrad: Gosudarstvennoe izdatel'stvo, 1928), p. 71.

13. Fond 1923, op. 1, e/kh 134. Grisha Alexandrov, very concerned, as we have seen, with issues of 'priority' (who actually wrote that first literary scenario?) does not acknowledge, at any point, that he and Eisenstein were following a previously written book (*Maklochane*) as they constructed their film. This silence over origins leads to the rather disingenuous claim that the 'separator' idea came from a purely chance encounter: they happened to be in their model hamlet the day the cooperative got itself a separator and they waited for the miracle of cream along with everybody: 'The separator astounded the peasants and ourselves. Excitedly we began to film the whole process of the turning of milk into butter... The separator was our biggest find.' GA 91–92.

14. Review, *op. cit.*, p. 6.

15. Fond 1923, op. 1, e/kh 135, ll. 23–24.

16. My own grandmother, Elsie Bowen [Nesbet], who was raised on a farm in Ohio, chose as a topic for a school essay (in 1910 or so) the subject of the *Milk Separator*, the miraculously transformative powers of which she describes with evident wonder. Interest in separators as potentially symbolic objects was, apparently, not limited to Russia.

17. O Davydov, *Maklochane*, Biblioteka dlia vsekh (Leningrad: Priboi, 1926), pp. 12–13.

18. Ironic, then, that in *Maklochane* the machine must be lugged across roadless

countryside to its destination. The country is still too separate (in the negative sense) from the city.

19. SM Eisenstein, *Nonindifferent Nature*, trans. Herbert Marshall (Cambridge: Cambridge University Press, 1987), p. 38–58.

20. '[W]e must say to the whole peasantry, to all its strata: enrich yourselves, accumulate, develop your economy.' Nikolai Bukharin, *Bol shevik*, No. 9–10, 1925, pp. 4–5, as cited by Stephen Cohen in *Bukharin and the Bolshevik Revolution. A Political Biography. 1888–1938* (Oxford; New York: Oxford University Press, 1980), p. 177.

21. *Maklochane*, p. 16–18 (p. 17 is filled with a chart).

22. A *desiatin* is the equivalent of 2.7 acres.

23. *Maklochane*, pp. 56–57.

24. This title foreshadows the ending Eisenstein intended for his Mexican film a couple of years later: various government and business officials wearing 'Death Day' masks take them off – to reveal real skeletons beneath the masks...

25. This irony is also directed at Soviet policy during the NEP years; Davydov makes much of the fact that Malofeev has been aided and abetted in his profit seeking by Soviet authorities: 'After all, Soviet power depends on the peasant who runs his farm knowledgeably [*kul turno*]. And here there's only one such – Malofeev. All the rest are miserable wretches,' says one local cooperative official to the narrator, displaying a naiveté the narrator blames on the *kulak* s own propaganda efforts: 'With unnoticed steps Malofeev goes about the district, legally takes on a Soviet appearance. He sneaks into the cooperatives... and makes them talk the way the Party chairman of the factory cooperative spoke to this author.' (pp. 60–61) Only in the last lines of the section – and of the book – does the narrator finally find a minor official who sees the hazard posed by the kulak: 'You know, just between us, in the control commission they've written up a memo: it says something like give us more power, they're squeezing us, put more of our boys in the soviet – we'll get those no-good Ulanovs and Malofeevs under control and we'll put an end to all this "Malofeevizing". I just don't know how they'll take this, but really it's our last hope.' *Maklochane*, pp. 63–64.

26. Fond 1923, op. 1, e/kh 135, l. 140.

27. Jacques Aumont, for example, undertakes an extensive and exhilarating close reading of this section of the film in his *Montage Eisenstein*, trans. Lee Hildreth, Constance Penley and Andrew Ross (London: BFI; Bloomington and Indianapolis: Indiana University Press, 1987), pp. 75–107.

28. Fond 1923, op. 1, e/kh 135, ll. 28–29.

29. Fond 1923, op. 1, e/kh 136, ll. 11–12. This scenario is an interesting object. The title page reads: 'Staroe i novoe'/'General'naia liniia' Stsenarii v 6–ti chastiakh. SME. GVA. Moskva, Aprel' 1926 goda. (l. 1) However, this date (April 1926) is obviously wrong, since it clearly is a relatively late scenario (Evdokiia is already 'Marfa', etc.) and the filming had evidently already been done by the time the 'scenario' was written (thus the swimming pigs, the footage of which apparently was not planned beforehand). The archivists have dated the file (1926–1928), not wishing to flatly contradict the given date, but it must have been written in 1928 or 1929.

30. 'The task of the Party: to consolidate the achieved tempo of development of

socialist industry and strengthen it in the near future in the area of the creation of favorable circumstances, necessary in order to catch up to and surpass the advanced capitalist countries,' *XV s"ezd Vsesoiunoi kommunisticheskoi partii-(b)* [December 1927] (Moscow: Gosizdat, 1928), p. 55.

31.   *Pravda*, 15 June 1926, No. 135, p. 4.

32.   Eisenstein refers to the myth of Europa on the same scrap of paper on which he compares the separator to the Grail. Both apply 'an old schema to new material' (Fond 1923, op. 1, e/kh 145, 1. 8).

33.   Fond 1923, op. 1, e/kh 135, 1. 33, 22 June 1926. A sketch by Andrei Burov for the scene in the Sovkhoz laboratory features a lab table with a microscope, a retort hooked up to batteries and a set of test tubes – all the basic paraphernalia for the 'creation of new life'. Fond 1923, op. 1, e/kh 148. Alexandrov, says the following about Burov: 'In the film in the capacity of the New appeared a dairy farm constructed in the European style near Moscow. The architect Andrei Burov attempted to represent the dairy farms and pigsties of the future. His sketched projects lay at the basis of the 'model farms' built at that time out of plywood especially for the the film.' (GA, 97).

34.   Fond 1923, op. 1, e/kh 135, 1. 37.

35.   Fond 1923, op. 1, e/kh 146, 1. 11.

36.   Lenin, 'Doklad o kontsessiiakh na fraktsii RKP(b) VIII s'ezda sovetov' [21 December 1920], in *Polnoe sobranie sochinenii*, vol. 42, pp. 91–117; this quote from pp. 112–113.

37.   Such is the title that begins the eighth part of the June 1926 scenario (Fond 1923, op. 1, e/kh 135, 1. 54).

38.   Fond 1923, op. 1, e/kh 135, 1. 43.

39.   The incredible figure of 11 comes from William J Rosenberg's introduction to *Russia in the era of NEP: Explorations in Soviet Society and Culture*, ed. Sheila Fitzpatrick, Alexander Rabinowitch and Richard Stites (Bloomington and Indianapolis: Indiana University Press, 1991), p. 6.

40.   See Jeffrey Brooks, 'The Press and its Message: Images of America in the 1920s and 1930s', in *Russia in the Era of NEP: Explorations in Soviet Society and Culture*, ed. Sheila Fitzpatrick, Alexander Rabinowitch and Richard Stites (Bloomington and Indianapolis: Indiana University Press, 1991), pp. 231–252; p. 240.

41.   *The Old and the New* is very fond of its weddings. There is not only the mock-wedding in which Fomka is presented with his bovine bride, but also, at the end of the later version, Marfa (who is no longer a war widow) is rewarded for her efforts by being presented with a mate, a 'traktorist'). The 1926 scenario ends with a vision of general abundance and an old man inviting us to participate: 'Eat all you want!' reads the last title (1. 60). The later version (like the film) has Marfa driving the tractor in a leather jacket and goggles; the tractorist passes her in a wagon (role reversal); they recognize each other and we are (in the scenario) given the moral quite explicitly: 'And Marfa remembered her former dark life, swiftly the difficult scenes of the past went through her mind. And that is why she smiled so happily, because all that had ended and she, a Russian peasant, had become a new woman. And all because now she could not only not struggle under unrelenting labor, but also kiss a beloved tractorist'. (Fond 1923, op. 1, e/kh 136, 1. 22).

42.   SM Eisenstein, *Nonindifferent Nature*, p. 49.

Chapter 5

1. BTS 411.
2. 'Anyway, the swarthy Diego, photographs of his frescoes and his colorful tales all fanned the flames of my longing to get there and to see it all with my own eyes. And a few years later the dream became reality.' BTS 412. Diego Rivera visited the Soviet Union in 1927 to take part in its tenth-anniversary celebrations.
3. Sergei Mikhailovich Tret'iakov, six years Eisenstein's senior, was an avant-garde playwright who had been one of Eisenstein's chief collaborators during his days in the Proletkul't Theater (a partnership that led to *Enough Simplicity For Every Wise Man* and *Do You Hear, Moscow?* in 1923, *Gas Masks* in 1924). Tret'iakov's 1924 trip to China was the direct inspiration for Eisenstein's Chinese project. An inventive and multifaceted figure, a wide-ranging traveler in Europe and Asia and Brecht's Russian translator, Sergei Tret'iakov was responsible for Eisenstein's association with the Constructivists surrounding the journal *LEF*. Along with Vsevolod Meierkhol'd and Isaak Babel', Tret'iakov was one of Eisenstein's closest friends to perish in the Terror; he was purged in 1937.
4. Fond 1923, op. 1, e/kh 131.
5. Fond 1923, op. 1, e/kh 132, 1925–26. On one of these sketches Eisenstein has noted, 'We'll have to get rid of the moon; otherwise it will be necessary to sacrifice the lighting that's so advantageous.'
6. Fond 1923, op. 1, e/kh 133.
7. 'Statement on Sound', Eisenstein, Vsevolod Pudovkin and Grigori Alexandrov, SW1 113–114.
8. 'Conversation with Eisenstein on Sound Cinema', SW1 131–133: 132.
9. Alexandrov says that Joseph Schenck, President of United Artists, visited Moscow (with Douglas Fairbanks) and upon discovering that he was a distant relative of Eisenstein's through the maternal line, issued invitations to Eisenstein and his coworkers to visit America. While they were waiting for the US visas to come through, the three left for Germany (GA 128). Montagu's version credits the mediating influence of his 'Uncle Lionel [Montagu], the racehorse owner', who knew some important people at Paramount (notably Adolph Zukor, 'whom he had met at the gaming tables on the Riviera'): Ivor Montagu, *With Eisenstein in Hollywood* (New York: International Publishers, 1967), pp. 34–35.
10. Montagu, pp. 77–78.
11. Montagu, p. 96.
12. Jesse Lasky, head of production for Paramount, had met with Eisenstein in Paris, where preliminary arrangements for the Russians' stay in Hollywood had been arranged. A contract for six months was then signed in New York by Eisenstein and Amkino, Soviet cinema's trade representative in the USA (see Montagu, p. 41; p. 77).
13. See original text in *Close Up*, vol. 8, no. 1 (March 1931), pp. 3–16 and no. 2 (June 1931), pp. 91–4. Here, I am citing from SW1 206–218.
14. 'Why should a holy veneration for this mistaken 'golden section' persist if all the basic elements of this newcomer in art – the cinema – are entirely different, its premises being entirely different from those of everything that has gone before.' SW1 213.
15. See Montagu, p. 121.

16. Anita Brenner knew Diego Rivera, who may be the person who gave her book to Eisenstein.

17. RGALI, Fond 1923, op. 2, e/kh 250, 10 February 1943 (l. 4). These notes are headed by a few scribbled comments: 'Collective Farm of the First Five-Year Plan [his location at that moment]. Snow is falling. Filming is impossible. 10–Feb-43. I'm writing.' (l. 1b).

18. SM Eisenstein (1931), *The Film Sense* (London: Faber, 1943), p. 180.

19. Anita Brenner, *Idols Behind Altars*, (New York: Payson & Clarke, 1929), p. 15. In 'The Dynamic Square', Eisenstein had spent some time on picture scrolls – not 'Aztec history-scrolls', but 'the horizontal *roll picture*'. 'I would call it *unroll picture*, because unwound horizontally from one roll to another it shows interminable episodes of battles, festivals, processions...'. and its cousin, the 'vertical roll picture' (SW1 212–3).

20. See 'The Prometheus of Mexican Painting', in SM Eisenstein, *Film Essays and a Lecture*, ed. Jay Leyda (Princeton: Princeton University Press, 1968), pp. 222–231.

21. See Sergei Eisenstein, *Que Viva Mexico!* (New York: Arno Press, 1972); also in Inga Karetnikova, *Mexico According to Eisenstein* (Albuquerque: University of New Mexico Press, 1991), pp. 35–138.

22. *Mexico According to Eisenstein*, p. 39. Further citation as *Mexico* in the text.

23. The discovery of matriarchal Tehuantepec in the south, one of the first places Eisenstein's group traveled to (and the setting of the 'Sandunga' section), had been a major influence on the career of Diego Rivera, who traveled there in 1922 and dedicated a significant amount of wall space at the Ministry of Education to images of that region. See Desmond Rochfort, *Mexican Muralists. Orozco. Rivera. Siqueiros* (San Francisco: Chronicle Books, 1993), p. 34; p. 52. Thus Eisenstein's trip to Tehuantepec was very much an instance of following in Rivera's footprints.

24. Fond 1923, op. 2, e/kh 250, 10 February 1943, l. 18.

25. Fond 1923, op. 2, e/kh 250, l. 1. My emphasis.

26. Even the interiorities of the body (his relatives' intestines) became visible to the Square.

27. BTS 418–9, translation modified for accuracy. *Beyond the Stars*, like *Immoral Memories* before it, perpetuates the Russian edition's misreading of the manuscript in a key moment: 'external embodiment' (*vo vne*) is recast as the nonsensical 'embodiment in me' (*vo mne*).

28. Fond 1923, op. 2, e/kh 250, l. 34b.

29. As described by Marie Seton in *Sergei M Eisenstein* (London: Dennis Dobson, 1952 [rev. edition 1978]), p. 149.

30. This was Nikolai Chernyshevskii's Crystal Palace (the utopian vision at the center of his *What Is To Be Done?*, 1864) redrawn with a minus sign.

31. This took the idea behind the title of Anita Brenner's influential book – *Idols Behind Altars* – one step further, since in Eisenstein's conception the 'idols' and 'altars' coexisted on a single plane.

32. See the scenario for *An American Tragedy* in Montagu, pp. 207–341; the crisis in the boat is pp. 294–5.

33. BTS 583. The drawing habit stayed with Eisenstein when he returned home, but 'the most revealing and shamelessly frank drawings are torn into tiny shreds almost straight away, which is a pity'. BTS 583.

34. André Breton, 'Manifesto of Surrealism' (1924), in *Manifestoes of Surrealism*, trans. Richard Seaver and Helen R Lane (Ann Arbor, Michigan: The University of Michigan Press, 1969), p. 37.

35. Sigmund Freud, *Totem and Taboo* (1912–1913), trans. James Strachey (New York; London: Norton, 1950), p. 64. The original title under which Freud published these essays, 'Some Points of Agreement between the Mental Lives of Savages and Neurotics', reminds us that he, too, acknowledged that this 'primitive' ('narcissistic') view of the world persisted in the modern world, if only as a pathological condition.

36. MM Bakhtin, 'Forms of Time and of the Chronotope in the Novel', in *The Dialogic Imagination*, Trans. Caryl Emerson and Michael Holquist (Austin: University of Texas Press, 1981), pp. 84–258: 131–132.

37. Bakhtin says Rabelais can do all this 'without, of course, any poetic pathos, which is deeply alien to Rabelais' – but we must note that Bakhtin, in his look backward at Rabelais, himself suffuses Rabelais's surfaces with the 'poetic pathos' of nostalgia.

38. The motifs of people planted as seeds and of the Revolution as a 'growing', vegetal force, were central themes in another set of frescos by Diego Rivera that Eisenstein had seen, the ones decorating the walls of the Chapel of the Autonomous University of Chapingo (painted in 1926). In pictures such as 'The Blood of the Revolutionary Martyrs Fertilizing the Earth', 'Germination' and 'The Flowering', the comparison between the human and vegetable worlds was made strikingly literal.

39. Vsevolod Ivanov, 'Bronepoezd No. 14.69', *Krasnaia nov* No. 1(5), 1922, p. 110.

40. A Voronskii, *Krasnaia nov*, No. 5(9), 1922, p. 269.

41. Thus the dying peasant in Tolstoy's story 'Three Deaths': 'You take my boots, Serioga... Just buy me a stone when I die, y'hear?' AN Tolstoi, *Povesti i rasskazy v dvukh tomakh*, Vol. 1 (Moscow, 1978), p. 259.

42. Boris Pil'niak, 'Smert' starika Arkhipova', *Krasnaia nov* No. 1(5), 1922, p. 61.

43. Sergei Semenov, 'Tif', *Krasnaia nov* No. 1 (5), January-February 1922: 37–58, p. 57.

44. Immanuel Kant, *Critique of Judgment* (1790), trans. JH Bernard (New York: Hafner Press, 1951), p. 83.

45. From Kant's point of view, both enthusiasm and lack of affect could properly be termed 'sublime': 'The idea of the good conjoined with [strong] affection is called *enthusiasm*. This state of mind seems to be sublime, to the extent that we commonly assert that nothing great could be done without it... [A]esthetically, enthusiasm is sublime, because it is a tension of forces produced by ideas, which give an impulse to the mind that operates far more powerfully and lastingly than the impulse arising from sensible representations. But (which seems strange) the *absence of affection* (*apatheia, phlegma in significatu bono*) in a mind that vigorously follows its unalterable principles is sublime and in a far preferable way' (Kant, pp. 112–13).

46. Mikhail Bakhtin, 'Author and Hero in Aesthetic Activity', in *Art and Answerability. Early Philosophical Essays by MM Bakhtin*, trans. Vadim Liapunov (Austin: University of Texas Press, 1990), pp. 4–256; this quote p. 40.

47. SM Eisenstein, Fond 1923, op. 2, e/kh 251, ll. 26–27.

48. I take the chronology from Barthélemy Amengual, *Que viva Eisenstein!* (Paris: L'Age d'homme, 1980), p. 14; p. 638. Actually Amengual gives two different

versions of the dates involved, suggesting 7–17 September on p. 14 and 23 August-3 September on p. 638.

49. According to Alexandrov, Lazar Wechsler, who hoped to found a thriving Swiss cinema (although he himself was the son of Russian émigrés), invited the Soviet travelers to Switzerland to make the pro-abortion film. GA 133–134.

50. GA 134. Unfortunately for posterity, this shot did not make it into the final film, which contains a very graphic depiction of a c-section performed on what is certainly not Grisha Alexandrov's body.

51. Fond 1923, op. 2, e/kh 251, l. 26. He calls the fetus a 'souvenir' on the same page.

52. Fond 1923, op. 2, e/kh 251, l. 26.

53. Il'ia Il'f and Evgenii Petrov, *Odnoetazhanaia Amerika* [1935–6], *Sobranie sochinenii v piati tomakh*, Vol. 4 (Moscow: Gosizdat, 1961): 52–53.

54. Fond 1923, op. 2, e/kh 251, l. 26.

55. SM Eisenstein, *Que Viva Mexico!* (London: Vision, 1951), p. 27.

56. *Que Viva Mexico!*, p. 77.

57. Sergei Eisenstein, *Nonindifferent Nature*, trans. Herbert Marshall (Cambridge: Cambridge University Press, 1987), p. 362.

58. *Que Viva Mexico!*, p. 71.

59. *Mexico According to Eisenstein*, p. 132.

60. Isaac Babel, 'Salt', in *The Collected Stories* , trans. Nadia Helstein and Walter Morison (New York: Meridian, 1955), pp. 122–7. Originally published in *LEF* 4 (August–December 1924), pp. 73–75.

61. Babel', *Sol*, *LEF* 4, p. 75.

62. For a fuller account of the history of Eisenstein's Mexican project, see Harry M Geduld and Ronald Gottesman (eds), *Sergei Eisenstein and Upton Sinclair: The Making and Unmaking of* 'Que viva Mexico!' (Bloomington: Indiana University Press, 1970).

63. Kimbrough's observations as described by Upton Sinclair in a letter reprinted by Marie Seton in *Sergei M Eisenstein* (London: Dennis Dobson, 1952; revised edition 1978), p. 516.

64. Upton Sinclair, as cited in Seton, p. 515.

65. Upton Sinclair, as cited in Seton, p. 516.

66. Upton Sinclair makes this comparison in a very short film intended to be shown as an introduction to *Thunder Over Mexico*; the opening titles read 'Upton Sinclair Explains Thunder Over Mexico' and promise that Sinclair will 'tell you briefly the story of THE MOST CONTROVERSIAL MOTION PICTURE EVER PRODUCED'. This film is held in the Museum of Modern Art, New York.

67. These comments appear in 'Upton Sinclair Explains Thunder Over Mexico'.

68. 'In 1939 I tried to get the footage of *Que Viva Mexico!* into Sergei Mikhailovich's hands so that he might finally fulfill his creative vision of Mexico. Failing, I took the memory of what he had told me and attempted to reconstruct his dream in order that it might not be entirely lost. This became *Time in the Sun*.' Marie Seton, *Sergei M Eisenstein*, p. 300).

69. Some of the shots Seton incorporates into her film seem like the dregs of the footage barrel: on occasion, the actors are obviously giggling.

70. *Land and Freedom* and *Conquering Cross* are copyrighted 1941 by the firm Bell & Howell; *Spaniard and Indian* and *Mexico Marches*, in the prints held in New

York's Museum of Modern Art, contain no copyright dates or production information.

71. Isaak Babel's own first foray into film-work was apparently a cinematic version of 'Salt'. A short film, 'Salt', was made from the story in 1925 (415 meters, single reel). The film, which has since been lost and for which there is no synopsis available, was produced by VUFKU and directed by Petr Ivanovich Chardynin (1873–1934). See Jerry Heil, 'Isaak Babel and his Film-Work', *Russian Literature* XXVII-III (1 April 1990), pp. 289–416, especially pp. 291–6.

72. See illustration in BTS 109.

73. Fond 1923, op. 1, e/kh 396, 1. 35. This conversation is not dated, but the opis' suggests 1932–1933.

74. Fond 1923, op. 1, e/kh 397, ll. 1–2.

75. Fond 1923, op. 1, e/kh 397, 1. 5, dated 2 October 1935.

76. SW3 100–105.

77. Fond 1923, op. 1, e/kh 397, 1. 10.

78. Fond 1923, op. 1, e/kh 367, 1. 18.

79. Stepok's response: 'Judging by what I've heard about him, that sounds just like him.' (1. 18)

80. 'It's no coincidence that the topic of "Biblical themes" in the material was raised during the discussion. Judging from these segments, the image of Styopka's father and the image of the young arsonist are given traits from time immemorial: these aren't so much real class enemies, as they are characters out of mythology and ancient art... The scenario's situations are thus given an unrealistic emphasis.' Fond 1923, op. 1, e/kh 397, 1. 11, GUK, 27 September 1935. 'Styopka is given features that suggest doom and "saintliness," and not the features of a little boy Pioneer from the living young generation in the country' (Fond 1923, op. 1, e/kh 397, 1. 12).

81. Apart from the direct thematic connection, there is a pun tying together Babel's 'Pan Apolek' and Eisenstein's *Bezhin Meadow*, for one of the mythological characters to whom Eisenstein referred in his treatment of the Pavlik Morozov story was the god 'Pan'. 'The exaggeration of generalization, detached from a particular event and from concrete reality, inevitably sent a whole system of images flying in the only possible direction: towards figures and associations fashioned after mythology (Pan, Samson – the destroyer of the Temple – the "lad" in the first version). If, in the "rout of the church," this was done with conscious irony – biblical associations clashed with actions that were not characteristic of them (once I had abandoned the attempt at a realistic portrayal there was nothing for it but to work on a game of speculation) – in the serious part this sent the images and characters to their destruction without the author being conscious of it' (SW3 103).

Chapter 6

1. This telegram is reprinted in Marie Seton, *Sergei M Eisenstein* (London: Dennis Dobson, 1978), p. 517.

2. The decree of the Party Central Committee, 23 April 1932, contained a plank requiring that 'a similar change with regard to other art forms be carried out'; cited in *The Film Factory: Russian and Soviet Cinema in Documents*, ed. Richard Taylor and Ian Christie, trans. Richard Taylor (Cambridge, Massachusetts: Harvard University Press, 1988), p. 325.

3. The term 'socialist realism' first appeared in May 1932 and gradually became part of official cultural dogma; by the time of the First Congress of Soviet Writers in 1934, 'socialist realism', defined as 'the truthful, historically concrete depiction of reality in its revolutionary development', had found its place as 'the basic method of Soviet imaginative literature and literary criticism'; 'Ustav Soiuza sovetskikh pisatelei', *Pravda* and *Literaturnaia Gazeta*, 6 May 1934, as cited in Herman Ermolaev, *Soviet Literary Theories, 1917–1934: The Genesis of Socialist Realism* (Berkeley; Los Angeles: University of California Press, 1963), p. 197.

4. Although we do not know the exact terms used by Upton Sinclair to describe to Boris Shumiatskii his experiences with Eisenstein, we can get some of the flavor of that story from Sinclair's account in a letter to Marie Seton in 1950: 'When E first came to Hywd I paid him a call. He was polite but showed no special interest in me and did not ask to see me again. When he lost his job he sent some one to me and then came himself. He was good company and I liked him. He signed a contract to make a picture for $25,000 and we raised that. What first led us to distrust him was that when the money was spent he wrote us that we'd have to send more or w'd have no picture. He kept that up, over and over and we realized that he was simply staying in Mex at our expense in order to avoid having to go back to Russia. All his associates were Trotskyites and all homos. No doubt you know that and I'll be interested to see if it's in your book. Men of that sort stick together and we were besieged by them for several years... Some Russ officials said they wanted E and some not; one or two said he might be shot. The head of their film industry [Boris Shumyatsky] came from Moscow, a highly educated man and sat in our Pasadena home and heard the story of how he had treated us and at the end he smiled and remarked: "Well, he outsmarted you, that's all." And we had thought we were dealing with idealists and comrades!'. Cited in Marie Seton, *Sergei M Eisenstein*, Revised edition [London: Dennis Dobson, 1952; 1978), pp. 515–516.

5. Alexandrov's summary of the plot: 'The year 1917. On the eve of revolution. On the stage of the theater the ballet *Sleeping Beauty* is being performed. In the course of the story the fairytale beauty falls asleep. At that moment a worker/Red Guard soldier runs on to the stage and announces that the Revolution has triumphed in Petrograd. The bourgeois audience pelts the herald of the Revolution with opera glasses. But he continues to speak with a bloodied face. Through the theater roll the events of those stormy years... Finally it is clear from the events occurring in the building of the city theater that the revolution has triumphed definitively. The theater fills with a new audience – the people, triumphant. And on the stage, as if nothing had happened, the beauty awakens in her tutu and continues to dance.' GA 125.

6. Fond 1923, op. 1, e/kh 1029, 1. 3.

7. Fond 1923, op. 1, e/kh 1029, 1. 5. 'Wozu' means 'To what end' in German. The switch into another of Eisenstein's languages reflects the heat of his reaction. These notes are scribbled in a rough and in some places very dark hand, again reflecting the intensity of Eisenstein's criticism.

8. Fond 1923, op. 1, e/kh 1029, 1. 6.

9. The story of this project is rather interesting. When Eisenstein, Alexandrov and Tisse arrived in Europe in late 1929, they were pretty close to penniless. While Eisenstein traveled about giving lectures, Alexandrov and Tisse tried

to dredge up some paying hackwork in Paris. Finally they met a Mme Mara Gris, a Russian émigrée who had escaped her life of privation by landing on the doorstep of M Léon Rosenthal, known as 'The King of Pearls', who made Mara Gris his mistress and drowned her in rivers of diamonds. M Rosenthal, author of the 1924 book *Faisons fortune!* (*Let s Get Rich!*), was willing to pay the Eisenstein group to make one of his mistress's dearest wishes come true. She fancied herself a singer and she longed to star in a movie. The young Soviet visitors were only too willing to comply (see BTS 201–2). The final product was largely Alexandrov's doing, since Eisenstein, although he helped with the shooting, eventually had had enough of the 'white grand pianos floating in the clouds'. Although *Romance sentimentale* is basically a long music video, it has some interesting elements. The shots of trees and nature at the beginning of the film look almost like something out of *Dr Mabuse*; the film also has a number of elements reminiscent of *October*. The attention paid to a pair of fancy clocks reminds one of the gadgets and trinkets Eisenstein had found so entrancing in the Hermitage Museum. What's more, the group returned to objects that had played an important satirical role in *October*: the statues of Rodin. Here it is hard to argue that any of the satire remains; it seems to have been remade into kitsch. Some of this kitsch – the white pianos, the comic explosion of animated stars – would reappear in Alexandrov's work in the 1930s.

10. At first Alexandrov had a composer (Dunaevskii) but no lyricist. He went so far as to publish the music for the 'March of the Jolly Fellows' in *Komsomol skaia Pravda*, as a kind of contest for would-be songwriters, but that generated no usable lyrics, until Lebedev-Kumach appeared, perfect song in hand. See GA 198.

11. Alexandrov in his memoirs changes the fifth line here from 'The song helps us live and love' to the somewhat more sober 'The song helps us build and live' (GA 199).

12. Another contributor to the scenario (as to the play it was based on) was the writer Valentin Kataev, Petrov's brother.

13. See Il'ia Il'f and Evgenii Petrov, 'Pod kupolom tsirka', *Sobranie sochinenii*, Vol. 3 (Moscow: Gosudarstvennoe izdatel'stvo khudozhestvennoi literatury, 1961), pp. 476–512; p. 478. Sokolovskaia's comments can be found in a letter, dated 17 March 1936, held in RGALI's Fond 2450, op. 2, e/kh 1518, l. 34.

14. 'The original scenario, written on a theme taken from the life of a Soviet circus, took place on a low level and abounded with cheap comic devices of a low-minded sort and peculiarly 'Odessan' turns of phrase'; Fond 2450, op. 2, e/kh 1518, l. 8; this document not dated.

15. Fond 2450, op. 2, e/kh 1518, ll. 33–34; letter signed on behalf of Mosfil'm by Vice-Director Sokolovskaia and dated 17 March 1936.

16. In one scene from Il'f and Petrov's scenario that must have set Mosfil'm's collective hair on end, the director of the circus despairs to read in the paper that 'At a time when the organized spectator comes to the circus in order to work through a series of timely questions in an interesting way, he finds thrust upon him a ballet consisting not of middle-aged working women, typical for our epoch, but of young and even beautiful women (!) We must do away with such unhealthy eroticism' (*Pod kupolom tsirka*, p. 501). Horrified, the director races to reform his chorus line in accordance with what he

assumes is the political trend *du jour* until he takes another look at that column and discovers he has misunderstood; now it reads, 'The spectator demands from the circus healthy good spirits, healthy *joie de vivre* and a healthy eroticism. We aren't monks!' (*Pod kupolom tsirka*, p. 505). Quick! Another revision of the act. Although the final political moral of this scene – Soviets are no prudes and only bad readers would think so – is politically correct enough, the portrayal of a low-level bureaucrat dashing desperately to and fro in an attempt to fulfill what seem like oscillating political demands may well have been perceived as somewhat too daring.

17. *Pod kupolom tsirka*, p. 489.

18. 'And, finally, the "transparent shots," the essence of which consisted in being able to film any action essential to the film against a background filmed previously in the studio' (GA 208). Perhaps the opening sequence of *Jolly Fellows*, which features the gates of the collective farm 'Prozrachnye kliuchi' ('Transparent Springs') and is itself a 'transparantnaia s'emka', a 'transparent shot' (in Russian the two words for 'transparent' are calques, one with Latin and the other with Slavic roots) against a backdrop of snow-capped mountains, may be a subtle meta-reference to the technique so central to the production of this and all following Alexandrov films.

19. AV Lunacharskii, 'Il'f i Petrov', *Stat i o literature*, Vol. 2 (Moscow: Khudozhestvennaia literatura, 1988), pp. 163–170; p. 165. Lunacharskii criticizes Il'f and Petrov for not being poisonous enough in their depictions of class enemies and worries that foreigners may mistake the Russia depicted in Il'f and Petrov for the real thing (Lunacharskii, p. 167); these concerns illustrate how delicately balanced a weapon laughter could be. At any moment – through sheer misunderstanding, perhaps – the joke might turn and bite the wrong hand.

20. Evgeny Dobrenko characterizes this situation nicely with regard to *Volga-Volga* (Alexandrov, 1938): 'The popular culture of laughter survives under the most unfavorable conditions, under any ideological stamp of seriousness of authority, but it is powerless when faced with a laughing authority': 'Soviet Comedy Film; or, The Carnival of Authority', *Discourse* 17.3 (Spring 1995), pp. 49–57; p. 52.

21. This description comes from Rzheshevskii's revised scenario, April 1935, Fond 1923, op. 1, e/kh 367, 1. 44. Stalin's speeches are regularly interrupted by 'laughter' or 'general laughter' when he begins to attack factionalists and other enemies. See, for example, his speech 'On the Industrialization of the Country and On the Right Deviation in the VKP(b)' (19 November 1928), in IV Stalin, *Sochineniia*, Vol. 11, pp. 245–290, especially pp. 279–281.

22. A decade before *Volga-Volga*, Eisenstein and Alexandrov had found a page in some magazine that had captured their imagination enough to tear it out and add it to the pile of material they were collecting as they worked on *The Old and the New*: under the title 'Music of the Rivers' ('Muzyka rek') this page featured a large picture of a steamship (like the one Strelka and her friends would take to Moscow ten years later) and told the story of an old steamship mechanic who wished his ship could have a nice American whistle. See Fond 1923, op. 1, e/kh 155, 1. 109.

23. From the transcript of a discussion led by the Vice-Director of GUK (Dubrovskii), on 3 July 1939; speaking here is Comrade Zel'dovich, identified

as 'Consultant to GUK', Fond 2450, op. 2, e/kh 1295, 1. 32.

24. Fond 2450, op. 2, e/kh 1295, 1. 36.

25. Fond 1923, op. 1, e/kh 397, 1. 14.

26. Fond 1923, op. 1, e/kh 402, 1. 7, no date but must be 1936 or 1937.

27. There are signs also in *Circus* that Eisenstein, though by this time he and Alexandrov avoided each other as much as possible, was not forgotten by his former pupil. The very affection for circuses went back to the time Eisenstein and Alexandrov shared in the Proletkul't Theater, incorporating circus acts into theatrical performances. In *Circus* on occasion one spies what seem like mementoes of Alexandrov's Eisensteinian years: the 'Constructivist' diagonals of the tree shadows at the very beginning of the film, in shots that look more like *Strike* than like the rest of *Circus*; the Constructivist patterns on the parachute in the final, thoroughly electrified circus spectacle – one sees Popova's textiles in the parachute, the famous spiral of the 'Monument to the Third International' in the rotating multi-layered stage on which the Soviet dancers kick in Busby Berkeley-inspired collectivity. In the next chapter we will explore the ongoing Eisenstein-Alexandrov connection from the other side.

28. Fond 1923, op. 1, e/kh 348, 1. 7. This is a play on the Gospel of Luke, in which Elizabeth's unborn child 'leaps in the womb' as the pregnant Mary approaches. Eisenstein gives the Russian as 'i vzygrasha mladenets vo chreve ee' and then twists those words as the fresco animates to 'Mladenets nachinaet igrat' na skripke'.

29. Sergei Eisenstein, *Nonindifferent Nature*, p. 389.

30. Apparently Isaak Babel' helped Eisenstein with this important letter. See Naum Kleiman, 'On the Story of "Montage 1937"', in SW2 xvii–xx: xviii.

31. Kleiman, SW2 xix.

32. For instance, DI Vasil'iev was assigned to the film as Eisenstein's co-director throughout the autumn. See R Iurenev, *Sergei Eizenshtein. Zamysly. Fil my. Metod*, Vol. 2 (Moscow: Iskusstvo, 1988), pp. 135–138. Eisenstein had received the first version of the scenario from the writer PA Pavlenko in July 1937. At that point the project was still called *Rus* (Iurenev, 134–6).

33. Fond 2450, op. 1, e/kh 15, 1. 9. The discussion took place 3 December 1938.

34. See Russell Merritt, 'Recharging *Alexander Nevsky*: Tracking the Eisenstein-Prokofiev War Horse', *Film Quarterly*, Vol. 48, No. 2, Winter 1994–95, pp. 34–47.

35. 'Vertical Montage' (1940), SW2 327–399: 371.

36. 'P-R-K-F-V' (1946), in Sergei Eisenstein, *Notes of a Film Director*, trans. X Danko (New York: Dover, 1970), pp. 149–167; p. 156.

37. Sergei Eisenstein, *Nonindifferent Nature*, p. 33.

38. Sergei Eisenstein, 'True Ways of Invention' (1946), *Notes of a Film Director* (New York: Dover, 1970), pp. 43–52; p. 44.

39. *Notes of a Film Director*, p. 46.

40. Here is André Breton discussing the *trouvaille* in *Mad Love* (1937): 'It is a matter – in such a case – of a solution which is always superior, a solution certainly rigorously fitting and yet somehow in excess of the need... This object, in its matter, in its form, I more or less predicted. Now I have chanced to discover it, unique, doubtless, among so many other fabricated objects. It was obviously this one, it always differed in every way from what I had foreseen. You might have said that, in its extreme simplicity, which did not

keep it from answering the most complicated needs of the problem, it put the elementary character of my predictions to shame... In any case, what is delightful here is the dissimilarity itself which exists between the object wished for and the *object found*. This *trouvaille*, whether it be artistic, scientific, philosophic, or as useless as anything, is enough to undo the beauty of everything beside it. In it alone can we recognize the marvelous precipitate of desire. It alone can enlarge the universe, causing it to relinquish some of its opacity, letting us discover its extraordinary capacities for reserve, proportionate to the innumerable needs of the spirit.' André Breton, *Mad Love* (*L Amour fou*), trans. Mary Ann Caws (Lincoln; London: University of Nebraska Press, 1987), p. 13; p. 15).

41. *Notes of a Film Director*, p. 48. Prokofiev's genius stemmed from this effect: 'Prokofiev is a man of the screen in that special sense which makes it possible for the screen to reveal not only the appearance and substance of objects, but also and notably, their peculiar inner structure' (p. 162).

42. Eisenstein, *Nonindifferent Nature*, pp. 296–7.

43. SM Eisenstein, 'Vertical Montage', SW2 327–399: 381.

44. *Nonindifferent Nature*, p. 12.

45. See *Nonindifferent Nature*, pp. 18–19: 'Thus we see that this curve, which is actually present in all cases of growth – and is equally true for a section of a tree trunk as well as for the curve of a conch shell, for the structure of an animal's horn and for the section of human bones – is inseparable from this remarkable plastic image of the idea of growth and each of its three vectors of the type OA, OB, OC is found in a proportion that most closely embodies the mathematical image of the unity of the whole and its parts.

'Thus in symbols and proportions in the sphere of mathematics, the idea of organic unity is also embodied, which by all signs coincides with the process and facts of organic nature.

'Thus, in the area relationg to proportion, 'organic' proportions are the *proportions of the golden section.*'

46. *Nonindifferent Nature*, p. 354.

47. This effect is compounded by the citational nature of the scene: it is quite reminiscent of the emergence in *Strike* of the residents of the 'underworld' from barrels buried in the ground. In *Alexander Nevsky* the peasants are *too* organically linked to the landscape they inhabit.

48. The more traditional alternation between 'comic' and 'epic' strands is particularly salient at the end of the film, as the various marriages are arranged: Ol'ga has said she will marry the 'bravest' soldier; the men insist that honor goes to Vasilisa, who fought in the battle; logic would seem to require that the two women and the two men be confirmed in their status as couples, but of course they aren't.

49. Fond 1923, op. 1, e/kh 430, 1. 3.

50. In a bizarre twist on Eisenstein's role as a cultural educator, a 'Comrade D' announced that he had been inspired by Eisenstein's discussion of ecstasy to design a new 'rocket missile system of consecutive ejection of one rocket out of another' (*Nonindifferent Nature*, p. 155); the film director seems to have been tickled by the thought of having contributed, by means of philosophy, to the Soviet defense effort. These rockets would have been constructed on the ecstatic principle borrowed from an anecdote about kangaroo-smuggling: a sneeze at

the border and the kangaroos, packed neatly one inside the next one's pocket, discharge explosively (*Nonindifferent Nature*, p. 185; pp. 191–2).

51. VI Lenin, 'K voprosu o dialektike' (1914–1915, according to editors), in PV Alekseev (ed.), *Na perelome. Filosofskie diskussii 20–kh godov. Filosofiia i mirovozzrenie* (Moscow: Izdatel'stvo politicheskoi literatury, 1990), pp. 37–40; p. 39. Originally published 1925 in *Bol'shevik*, No. 5–6. See *Nonindifferent Nature*, p. 11.

52. SM Eisenstein, 'Montage 1938', SW2 296–326: 312–314.

53. 'Montage 1938' first appeared in *Iskusstvo kino*, No. 1, January 1939, pp. 37–49. See SW2 415.

Chapter 7

1. BTS 353.

2. Eisenstein places his first wrestling with the theme of Ivan in the Bolshoi Theater, January 1941, on the anniversary of Lenin's death: 'The first sketch of a scene is on the back of a ticket with the memorial silhouette [of Lenin]' (IP1 197). Eisenstein threw himself into the project, proposed to him by Zhdanov, wholeheartedly, enlisting LP Indenbom of the scenario division of Mosfilm to help him collect all possible references to Ivan the Terrible: R Iurenev, *Sergei Eizenshtein: Zamysly. Fil'my. Metod.*, Part 2, 1930–1948 (Moscow: Iskusstvo, 1988), p. 213. By 26 February 1941, Eisenstein had already put together a very preliminary version of the scenario (Iurenev, p. 215) and he continued to work feverishly on this project through the summer of 1941 (and the beginning of war in June, as Germany invaded the Soviet Union) and the autumn. On 14 October 1941, the entire Mosfilm studio, Eisenstein included, was evacuated to Alma-Ata, in Central Asia. This would be the city where, under sometimes trying physical circumstances, most of the footage for *Ivan the Terrible* would be shot. During 1942, preparations accelerated, with constant rehearsals and the arrival of Sergei Prokofiev as musical collaborator. By the time Mosfilm returned to Moscow, in the fall of 1944, Eisenstein was ready to work on the final editing of Part I, which premiered in January 1945 to great general acclaim. A year later Part II was completed. On 2 February 1946, having just finished his work on the second part, Eisenstein went off to a celebration of his having been given a Stalin Prize for Part I – and was stricken with a heart attack while dancing. Although this infarction didn't kill him, it did mark the end of Eisenstein's life as a film-maker. The last two years of his life would be marked by an ongoing struggle to rescue Part II from the gathering storm of criticism and by an intense dedication to the philosophical issues that had been of such great interest to him since the beginning of the 1930s.

3. EOD 7. The Russian edition can be found in AV Prokhorov, BV Raushenbakh, FS Khitruk (eds), *Problemy sinteza v khudozhestvennoj kul'ture* (Moscow: Nauka, 1985), pp. 205–284. The editor of the Eisenstein material for both editions is Naum Kleiman.

4. A more ordinary instance of condemnation of bourgeois drops of comfort appears in Lev Kuleshov's 1935 *Principles of Montage*, in the course of a directorial *mea culpa*: 'That is where our deepest mistake lay. Perceiving the petty bourgeois axioms of American montage and American morality in their entirety, we introduced elements of bourgeois art into our own films

unintentionally – a "consoling," bourgeois and so on; and that is why, along with a certain benefit derived from the uncritical study of American montage, came great harm.' From *Kuleshov on Film*, trans. and ed. by Ronald Levaco, (Berkeley: University of California Press, 1974), pp. 183–195.

5.   The invitation here to read Disney as an essentially Nietzschean phenomenon – and thus to short-circuit our present path and declare ourselves already in the company of Ivan the Terrible, whose position 'beyond good and evil' would seem beyond question – should perhaps be tempered somewhat by Eisenstein's next lines: 'Disney is simply "beyond good and evil." Like the sun, like trees, like birds, like the ducks and mice, deer and pigeons that run across his screen. To an even greater degree than Chaplin.' (EOD 9) This is a 'superman', in other words, drawn with big, lovable, infantile features.

6.   Eisenstein's passion for *Snow White* was shared by his collaborator Sergei Prokofiev, who had seen the film in Denver in 1938 more than once. Prokofiev deepens the 'vertical' axis of *Ivan*'s citational plundering of Disney in his score for Eisenstein's film, writing music that at times provides a melancholy Slavic echo of *Snow White*'s decidedly lower-brow ditties. Compare for instance the scene in *Snow White* that introduces us to the seven dwarfs as they 'dig dig dig dig dig dig dig' in the mines with the imitative 'mining' of Kazan' in *Ivan the Terrible, Part One*. Not only does the latter film provide a visual quotation (Ivan's men digging are framed by their cavern just as the dwarfs are framed by theirs), but it also plays this scene as a musical number, the dwarfs' work-song transformed into a minor key (but equally rhythmic) meditation on war preparation.

7.   This phrase is in English in the original (*Problemy sinteza*, p. 241); in the translation, for some reason, it appears as 'the most omni-appealing I've ever met'. Other critics who have been seen the appeal not only of Disney, but also of Eisenstein's analysis of Disney are Keith Broadfoot and Rex Butler. See their article, 'The Illusion of Illusion', in Alan Cholodenko (ed.), *The Illusion of Life: Essays on Animation* (Sydney: Power Publications in association with the Australian Film Commission, 1991), pp. 263–298.

8.   'The independently elongating contour is read as a "neck going out of itself." And then it skips over to a comical embodiment of the formula of pathos and ecstasy.' (EOD 58, November 1941); 'This is the plasmatizing of solid objects: the stretching of necks, legs, the rhythmical swaying of trees, of solid figures, etc.' (EOD 69, 1932); 'The necks of his surprised horses stretch the same way, or their legs become extended when running.' (EOD 10, 1940) As we'll see, the phenomenon of the stretched neck has significant consequences for the actors in *Ivan the Terrible*.

9.   For an extended discussion of the theme of 'fire' in Eisenstein's notes on Disney and in philosophy generally, see Keith Clancy, 'PRISTIR: The T(r)opology of Pyromania', in *The Illusion of Life: Essays on Animation*, pp. 243–262.

10.   His mention of 'silhouettes' in the notes from 1941 is quite brief: 'The *stroke drawing*, as a line, with only one contour, is the very earliest type of drawing – cave drawings.

'In my opinion, this is not yet a consciously creative act, but the simple automatism of "outlining a contour". It is a roving eye, from which movement the hand has not yet been separated (into an independent movement).

'This is preceded by the stage when simply the *whole* man *encircles* an object, making a drawing *with himself* (there is an element of this in the Acropolis).

'The silhouette drawing has its own attractiveness, evidently on the basis of this (cf. Japanese silhouettes as such in the book on silhouettes).' (EOD 43)

11.   One example of this has recently come into my hands: a little desk calendar for children from the year 1938, a curio mixing lessons in the history of Soviet aviation and treacly pictures of children hugging Stalin with advice on pleasant and edifying activities for indoors or out; on 2 February 1938, the child readers are given detailed instructions for the construction of a 'Teatr tenei', a 'Shadow Theater'.

12.   See Kristin Thompson, *Eisenstein's* Ivan the Terrible*: A Neoformalist Analysis* (Princeton: Princeton University Press, 1981), pp. 173–202, for a thorough discussion of *Ivan*'s 'Expressionistic mise-en-scène'.

13.   The dwarfs' cottage is a classic example of those magical structures which are distinctly larger on the inside than they are on the outside. Compare the view given 'externally' of this 'doll's house' of a cottage (as Snow White describes it) with the relatively cavernous spaces Disney reveals to us inside it. Where for example does that enormous antechamber/washroom come from? In a very *Einstein*ian gag, the space of the dwarfs' main room s-t-r-e-t-c-h-e-s as one of Sneezy's omnipotent blasts sends everyone sliding through it.

14.   This environmental component of *Ivan* and *Snow White* should also remind us of Eisenstein's ongoing interest in the effect of context on human life and activity. As he remarks in a strangely meandering note headlined 'Alma-Ata, 4.XI.1941': 'A new setting dictates a new modus in which to work: there is no material to quote from on hand. The modus is prompted by... *Ivan the Terrible*. There, it's done this way: episode follows episode and all the Beleg-Material [supporting material] of ideas is *als Anhang* [like an appendix]. Perhaps there is an outlet and salvation in this: in Moscow, I was "drowning" in citations. Perhaps this "new" approach will help to focus correctly the *essence* of the ideas and it will be possible to embellish in an appendix. It's funny – I'm writing in the same small handwriting that I used during... the Civil War! The identicalness of setting engenders, etc? Put more simply: no paper! Walt Disney's work is the most omni-appealing I've ever met.'

       This is a very rich quote: Eisenstein the inveterate researcher is in Alma-Ata not just without paper, but also without his library: material conditions change his handwriting. For Eisenstein, who was very tempted by the thought that handwriting encapsulates the personality. Thus he relates in an anecdote in *Nonindifferent Nature* how a German graphologist, Raphael Sherman, in 1929 was able to take one summary glance at him, grab a pen and *write with Eisenstein's own handwriting*; see Eisenstein, *Nonindifferent Nature*, p. 341. The very contours of the self must change as Eisenstein moves away from the Soviet center (he had just recently arrived in evacuation). Perhaps this shift in context would serve to reinforce the 'appeal' of the world of Disney, where evolutionary metamorphosis is super-Lamarckian and instantaneous.

15.   The theme of the emancipated shadow runs through the folk and fairy-tale traditions of many countries; ETA Hoffman, Hans-Christian Andersen, Chamosso; the most recent (with respect to the *Ivan* chronology) member of this genealogy being Evgenii Shvarts's short-running drama, *Ten* (*The Shadow*), in 1940.

16. 'Stalin says to Cherkasov that he can really transform himself and that another of our artists who can also transform himself is Khmelev.' This rather plodding bit of praise comes from the description of a meeting Eisenstein and Grigorii Alexandrov had with Stalin in February 1947; the 'transcript' was dictated right after the meeting to Sergei Agapov and signed by Eisenstein and Alexandrov. See GP Mar'iamov, *Kremlevskii tsenzor* (Moskva: Konfederatsiia soiuzov kinematografistov Kinotsentr, 1992), p. 88.

17. Later in his life, Nikolai Cherkasov would reflect more than once on the strain of literally embodying Eisenstein's graphic visions, as the endless drawings Eisenstein used as a sort of 'first draft' of *Ivan the Terrible* were brought to life ('animated') by the actors. The director's achievements, complains Cherkasov, came at the price of 'not infrequently constraining me within the cruel frames of his graphic and pictorial intent'; 'during the numerous rehearsals and shoots devoted to the mental anguish of Ivan, I thus was not once able to free myself from the sensation of physical constraint, which hampered to the highest degree my efforts as an actor'; NN Cherkasova and S Dreiden (eds), *Nikolai Cherkasov*, (Moscow: Vserossiiskoe teatral'noe obshchestvo, 1976), p. 101; p. 158).

18. See Marge Garber's interesting discussion of transvestism as a sign of 'category crisis' generally in *Vested Interests: Cross-Dressing and Cultural Anxiety* (New York: HarperCollins, 1992). She defines drag as 'the theoretical and deconstructive social practice that analyzes these structures from within, by putting in question the "naturalness" of gender roles through the discourse of clothing and body parts' (p. 151) and also cites Judith Butler: 'In imitating a gender, drag implicitly reveals the imitative structure of gender itself – and its contingency.' (*Gender Trouble: Feminism and the Subversion of Identity* [New York; London: Routledge, 1990], p. 137) I would argue that we may extend Garber's argument here to include as homologous boundary that between the 'real' and the 'animated' character, or for that matter, between 'animation' and 'inanimation' generally.

19. It might be interesting to consider here Wayne Koestenbaum's memory – as related in *The Queens Throat: Opera, Homosexuality and the Mystery of Desire* (New York: Poseidon Press, 1993) – of the role played by the strangely disembodied voice of Adriana Casselotti, as 'Snow White', in the development of his own identity as an 'opera queen' (see page 12).

20. Amusingly enough, some of the dwarfs' dance, though largely dominated by a sort of pan-Germanic kitsch (including a certain amount of yodeling), has a slight Slavic aura to it, as well. The dwarfs take turns with what in the Russian context would be called 'chastushki' (witty rhyming lines), punctuated by the 'Silly Song' refrain ('Ho Hum the tune is dumb, the words don't mean a thing/ Isn't this a Silly Song for anyone to sing?'); then at one point in the doubled dwarfs' dance with Snow White, the feet (Sneezy's) start doing a little Russian kick step as the rest of the dwarfs shout 'Hey! Hey!'.

21. This is one place where scenario and film do not quite match. In the scenario, the revelation of the real face behind the mask occurs in two dramatic stages: once to Ivan and 'us', the watching audience, as Fyodor overhears the sharp words exchanged by his father and the Tsar (IP6 347) and then finally to everybody at the end of the dance as he leaps on a bench and his fellow dancers strip off his costume (IP6 349). In the film, however, Fyodor plays a

cat and mouse game with the mask instead of symbolically holding back until a final revelation.

22. Eisenstein compares this blue blush to Disney's characters' exaggerated blushes; he mentions specifically the skunk in *Bambi*, but for the record we should also recall the blushing faces of several of the seven dwarfs and in particular the character who is 'all blush': Bashful. See SM Eisenstein, *Le Mouvement de l art*, trans. B Epstein, M Iampolski, N Noussinova, A Zouboff (Paris: Les Editions du Cerf, 1986), pp. 230–231.

23. As this scene continues, what happens? Dopey sees Snow White, mistakes her for a monster, runs. The other dwarfs see Dopey running, mistake him for a monster because he's covered with pots and pans and do their best to, well, 'assassinate' him with blows intended for another. Fortunately for Dopey, a few blows on the head from a pickaxe are no big deal for a cartoon character.

24. Fond 1923, op. 2, e/kh 268, 1. 3.

25. Fond 1923, op. 2, e/kh 268, 1. 3, dated 13 September 1947.

26. Fond 1923, op. 2, e/kh 269, 1. 24.

27. Fond 1923, op. 2, e/kh 231, 1. 4 (Folder dated December 1932–March 1934).

28. See Fond 1923, op. 1, e/kh 848, plans for *Ruka Moskvy*. On the second sheet of notes in this folder Eisenstein refers to the 'fifteen years' that have passed since the Revolution, giving us an approximate date for the project.

29. Could Eisenstein be playing here with the similarity between *fig* (the gesture) and *figliar*, the term for a 'circus acrobat, clown, buffoon'?

30. BTS 117. This reminiscence is dated 29 May 1946.

31. Fond 1923, op. 2, e/kh 268, 1. 20. This folder dated '13 September 1947–5 February 1948'.

32. Fond 1923, op. 2, e/kh 268, 1. 20. If we take that parallel seriously, then *Circus*'s blond Bolshevik hero becomes a stand-in for Grisha Alexandrov and Eisenstein must logically be played by the evil German, Von Kneischitz!

33. Fond 1923, op. 2, e/kh 268, 1. 30. (Dated 27 November 1947.)

34. Fond 1923, op. 2, e/kh 268, 1. 30. The 'conflict' with Alexandrov to which Eisenstein refers here would seem to be not merely the adolescent competition over Ianukova, but rather the betrayal Eisenstein felt when Alexandrov went off to make his own films in the early 1930s.

35. Fond 1923, op. 2, e/kh 268, 1. 30.

36. Fond 1923, op. 2, e/kh 268, 1. 30.

37. Eisenstein had already made explicit reference to this aspect of Freud's oeuvre in 1933, as we shall see below.

38. Sigmund Freud, *Beyond the Pleasure Principle*, trans. James Strachey (New York; London: WW Norton, 1961), p. 3.

39. Freud, p. 25.

40. Freud, p. 15. Freud does not insist that this rather 'optimistic' interpretation of the game (in that it is still tied to questions of 'mastery' and thus to 'pleasure') is necessarily the correct one.

41. See Fond 1923, op. 2, e/kh 268, 1. 22.

42. Fond 1923, op. 2, e/kh 416, 1. 9. This folder dated '20 January–7 February 1948'.

43. Fond 1923, op. 2, e/kh 416, 1. 23.

44. Fond 1923, op. 2, e/kh 416, 11. 3–6.

45. Fond 1923, op. 2, e/kh 416, 1. 15.

46. This advertisement held in Fond 1923, op. 2, e/kh 268, 1. 45.

47. Fond 1923, op. 2, e/kh 268, l. 41.
48. Fond 1923, op. 2, e/kh 268, l. 41.
49. Fond 1923, op. 2, e/kh 231, l. 17, dated 18 November 1933.
50. And, like various originary traumas, to be repeated and repeated, hence the 'oceans of cruelty' in his own work, he suggests. Other 'traumas', as we have seen, find their repetition in *Ivan*: the terror of watching a desired woman acting out perils he himself was directing in *Wise Man*; the betrayal later worked on him by his student and rival (and actor in *Wise Man*), Grigorii Alexandrov.
51. Eisenstein, *Immoral Memories*, pp. 32–33.
52. See SM Eisenstein, *Nonindifferent Nature*, p. 362, for one moment where these related images all come together.
53. For an interesting variation on this problem, see Valerii Podoroga's analysis of Eisenstein's desire to turn the 'face' into a 'mask' in 'Litso: pravila raskroia. Fiziognomicheskii opyt Sergeia Eizenshteina', a chapter in *Fenomenologiia tela. Vvedenie v filosofskuiu antropologiiu* (Moscow: Ad Marginem, 1995), pp. 282–326.
54. See Russell Merritt, 'Recharging *Alexander Nevsky*: Tracking the Eisenstein-Prokofiev War Horse', *Film Quarterly*, Vol. 48, No. 2, Winter 1994–95, pp. 34–47.
55. Susan Sontag, 'Notes on "Camp"' (1964), in *Against Interpretation and Other Essays* (New York: Delta, 1966), pp. 275–292.
56. The mother, seen briefly in flashback as she dies, poisoned by enemies, may be an unambiguous figure in white, but, then again, she does abandon (even if unwillingly) her small son to a world intent on dominating if not destroying him.
57. Ivan's identity – as well as the political meaning of the *Ivan* films – has been discussed with great energy since the 1940s (and since Stalin, dissatisfied with the portrayal of the character he and the Central Committee had commissioned as one of a series of the Soviet leader's historical forerunners, had criticized the Ivan of Part II as an indecisive 'Hamlet'). A good summary of the arguments surrounding the figure of Ivan is provided in Barthélemy Amengual, *Que Viva Eisenstein!* (Paris: L'Age d'Homme, 1980), pp. 347–394. A recent and interesting reading of *Ivan the Terrible* that stresses the congruences between 'SME's merciless poetic machine' and 'Ivan's vengeful cruelty' is provided by Alexander Zholkovsky in 'The Terrible Armor-Clad General Line: A New Profile of Eisenstein's Poetics', in *Wiener Slawistischer Almanach*, Sonderband 31 (1992), pp. 481–501. Zholkovsky is expanding here on Leonid Kozlov's famous suggestion that Ivan is partly modeled on the figure of Vsevolod Meyerhold, who had played Ivan on the stage at the end of the previous century. See Kozlov, 'A Hypothetical Dedication', in Lars Kleberg and Håkan Lövgren (eds), *Eisenstein Revisited: A Collection of Essays* (Stockholm: Almqvist and Wiksell, 1987), pp. 65–92.
58. Kristin Thompson, *Eisenstein s Ivan the Terrible: A Neoformalist Analysis* (Princeton, NJ: Princeton University Press, 1981), p. 295. See, in particular, Chapter 4, 'The Floating Motif' (pp. 158–72) and Chapter 9, 'Excess' (pp. 287–302).
59. Fond 1923, op. 2, e/kh 239, l. 2, dated 23 July 1940.
60. Fond 1923, op. 2, e/kh 239, l. 43.
61. Fond 1923, op. 2, e/kh 268, l. 37, dated 17 November 1947.
62. Fond 1923, op. 2, e/kh 268, l. 2.

63. Fond 1923, op. 2, e/kh 268, ll. 75–76.
64. See Chapter 4.
65. Fond 1923, op. 2, e/kh 228, l. 27.

Conclusion

1. Eisenstein cites VI Lenin, 'K voprosu o dialektike', *Filosofskie tetradi* (Moscow: Partizdat, 1933), p. 328. This essay, originally published 1925 in *Bol shevik*, No. 5–6, was one of that select number of Lenin's more philosophical writings that Eisenstein most liked to cite. See IP4 667.
2. Eisenstein cites Hogarth on the beauty of the spiraling contradance on p. 659. He calls the action of thinking 'the highest form of movement' on p. 85.
3. Eisenstein's students quickly identified the universal importance of 'recoil' as another instance of dialectical materialism's 'law of the negation of the negation'. See p. 85.
4. Cited in IP4 85, as from *Leninskii sbornik* XII, p. 229. Eisenstein adds the note that in the original the last phrase is in French: 'reculer pour mieux sauter (savoir?).' I have suggested already that Eisenstein gravitated towards Lenin when Lenin was writing most like Eisenstein. The multilingual nature of this citation may well have added to its appeal for Eisenstein, who liked to take notes in a shifting blend of four languages (Russian, German, French and English).
5. Sergei Eisenstein, *Nonindifferent Nature*, p. 188.
6. *Nonindifferent Nature*, pp. 188–189.
7. André Bazin, *What Is Cinema?*, trans. Hugh Gray (Berkeley: University of California Press, 1967), p. 36.

Bibliography

Films

Alexander Nevsky (*Aleksandr Nevskii*). Dir. Sergei Eisenstein. Phot. Eduard Tisse. Music Sergei Prokofiev. Mosfil'm, 1938

Bambi. Supervising dir. David Hand. Disney, 1942

The Battleship 'Potemkin' (*Bronenosets 'Potëmkin'*). Dir. Sergei Eisenstein. Phot. Eduard Tisse. Goskino, 1925

Bezhin Meadow (*Bezhin lug*). Dir. Sergei Eisenstein. Unfinished film. 1935–37. Surviving frames assembled by Sergei Iutkevich and Naum Kleiman

Bright Path (*Svetlyi put*). Dir. Grigorii Alexandrov. Mosfil'm, 1940

Chapaev. Dir. Sergei and Georgii Vasiliev. Lenfil'm, 1934

Cinema-Eye (*Kino-glaz*). Dir. Dziga Vertov. Phot. Mikhail Kaufman, ed. Elizaveta Svilova. Goskino, 1924

Circus (*Tsirk*). Dir. Grigorii Alexandrov. Mosfil'm, 1936

Conquering Cross. From footage filmed by Sergei Eisenstein, Eduard Tisse and Grigorii Alexandrov in Mexico. Bell and Howell, 1941

Death Day. Dir. Sol Lesser. 1934

Earth (*Zemlia*). Dir. Aleksandr Dovzhenko. Phot. Danylo Demutskii. VUFKU, 1930

The General Line/ The Old and the New (*General naia Liniia/ Staroe i novoe*). Dir. Sergei Eisenstein. Scen. Grigorii Alexandrov and Sergei Eisenstein. Phot. Eduard Tisse. Sovkino, 1929

Glumov s Diary (*Dnevnik Glumova*). Dir. Sergei Eisenstein. 1923

Ivan the Terrible, Part I (*Ivan Groznyi*). Dir. Sergei Eisenstein. Phot. Andrei Moskvin and Eduard Tisse. Music by Sergei Prokofiev. 1944

Ivan the Terrible, Part II (*Ivan Groznyi*). Dir. Sergei Eisenstein. Phot. Andrei Moskvin. Music by Sergei Prokofiev. Mosfil'm, 1946 (released in 1958)

Jolly Fellows (*Veselye rebiata*). Dir. Grigorii Alexandrov. Phot. Vladimir Nilsen. Music by Isaak Dunaevskii. Mosfil'm, 1934

Land and Freedom. From footage filmed by Sergei Eisenstein, Eduard Tisse and Grigorii Alexandrov in Mexico. Bell and Howell, 1941

Mexico Marches. From footage filmed by Sergei Eisenstein, Eduard Tisse and Grigorii Alexandrov in Mexico. No date, director, or distributor listed on the print held in MOMA

The Misery and Fortune of Women (Frauennot-Frauenglück). Collaborative direction: Eduard Tisse, Grigorii Alexandrov and Sergei Eisenstein. Phot. Eduard Tisse. Praesens AG, 1929

Moscow in October (Moskva v Oktiabre). Dir. Boris Barnet. Mezhrabpom-Rus, 1927

October (Oktiabr). Dir. Sergei Eisenstein, assisted by Grigorii Alexandrov. Phot. Eduard Tisse. Sovkino, 1928

Que Viva Mexico. Assembled by Grisha Alexandrov in 1978, with assistance from Esfir' Tobak and Nikita Orlov, from footage filmed in 1931 by Sergei Eisenstein. Phot. Eduard Tisse. Mosfil'm, 1979

The Skeleton Dance. Dir. Walt Disney. Disney, 1929

Snow White and the Seven Dwarfs. Supervising dir. David Hand. Disney, 1937

Spaniard and Indian. From footage filmed by Sergei Eisenstein, Eduard Tisse and Grigorii Alexandrov in Mexico. No date, director, or distributor listed on the print held in MOMA

Strike (Stachka). Dir. Sergei Eisenstein. Phot. Eduard Tisse; Vasilii Khvatov. Proletkul't; Goskino, 1925

Thunder Over Mexico. Prod. Sol Lesser and Upton Sinclair. From footage filmed by Sergei Eisenstein in Mexico. Sol Lesser, 1933. Print in MOMA is preceded by a short entitled 'Upton Sinclair Explains *Thunder Over Mexico*'

Time in the Sun. Assembled by Marie Seton from footage filmed by Sergei Eisenstein, Eduard Tisse and Grigorii Alexandrov in Mexico. 1939

Volga-Volga. Dir. Grigorii Alexandrov. Phot. V Petrov. Music by Isaak Dunaevskii. Mosfil'm, 1938

Print sources

Abbott, Edwin A, *Flatland: A Romance of Many Dimensions* (New York: HarperCollins, 1983)

Adorno, Theodor, 'Die Aktualität der Philosophie' (1931), in Rolf Tiedemann, with Gretel Adorno, Susan Buck-Morss and Klaus Schultz (eds), *Gesammelte Schriften*, Vol. I: *Philosophische Frühschriften* (Frankfurt am Main: Suhrkamp, 1973), pp. 325–44

——— 'Charakteristik Walter Benjamins' (1950), in Rolf Tiedemann, with Gretel Adorno, Susan Buck-Morss and Klaus Schultz (eds), *Prismen. Gesammelte Schriften*, Vol. 10.1: *Kulturkritik und Gesellschaft I* (Frankfurt am Main: Suhrkamp, 1973), pp. 238–53

Alekseev, PV (ed.) *Na perelome. Filosofskie diskussii 20–kh godov. Filosofiia i mirovozzrenie* (Moscow: Izdatel'stvo politicheskoi literatury, 1990)

Alexandrov, GV, *Epokha i kino* (Moscow: Izdatel'stvo politicheskoi literatury, 1983)

Altman, Rick, *The American Film Musical* (Bloomington: Indiana University Press, 1987)

Amengual, Barthélémy, *Que viva Eisenstein!* (Lausanne: L'Age d'Homme, 1980)

Aumont, Jacques, *The Image*, trans. Claire Pajackowska (London: British Film Institute, 1997)

———— *Montage Eisenstein*, trans. Lee Hildreth, Constance Penley and Andrew Ross (London: British Film Institute; Bloomington and Indianapolis: Indiana University Press, 1987)

Babel, Isaac, *The Collected Stories*, trans. Nadia Helstein and Walter Morison (New York: Meridian, 1955)

———— 'Sol'', *LEF* 4, August–December 1924, pp. 73–5

Bakhtin, Mikhail, *Art and Answerability: Early Philosophical Essays by MM Bakhtin*, trans. Vadim Liapunov (Austin: University of Texas Press, 1990)

———— *The Dialogic Imagination*, trans. Caryl Emerson and Michael Holquist (Austin: University of Texas Press, 1981)

Banchoff, Thomas F, 'From Flatland to Hypergraphics: Interacting with Higher Dimensions', in *Interdisciplinary Science Reviews* 15.4 (1990), pp. 364–72

Barna, Yon, *Eisenstein: The Growth of a Cinematic Genius*, trans. Lise Hunter (Boston: Little, Brown and Co., 1973)

Bazin, André, *What Is Cinema?*, trans. Hugh Gray (Berkeley: University of California Press, 1967)

Bekhterev, VM, *Kollektivnaia refleksologiia* (Petrograd: 'Kolos', 1921)

Bely, Andrei, *Petersburg*, trans. Robert A Maguire and John E Mamstad (Bloomington: Indiana University Press, 1978)

———— *Arabeski* (Moscow, 1911)

Benjamin, Walter, *Illuminations*, ed. Hannah Arendt, trans. Harry Zohn (New York: Schocken Books, 1968)

———— 'One-Way Street' (1928), in *Reflections*, ed. Peter Demetz, trans. Edmund Jephcott (New York: Schocken, 1978), pp. 61–94

Blachère, Jean-Claude, *Les Totems d André Breton: Surréalisme et primitivisme littéraire* (Paris: L'Harmattan, 1996)

Bonitzer, Pascal, 'Système de *La Grève*', in *Cahiers du cinema*, 226–227 (January–February 1971)

Bordwell, David, *Sergei Eisenstein* (Cambridge, Massachusetts: Harvard University Press, 1993)

Bowlt, John (ed.), *Russian Art of the Avant-Garde* (New York: Thames and Hudson, 1988)

Brenner, Anita, *Idols Behind Altars* (New York: Payson & Clarke, 1929)

Breton, André, *L Amour fou* (Paris: Gallimard, 1937), p. 36

———— *Mad Love*, trans. Mary Ann Caws (Lincoln; London: University of Nebraska Press, 1987)

———— *Manifestoes of Surrealism*, trans. Richard Seaver and Helen R Lane (Ann Arbor, Michigan: The University of Michigan Press, 1969)

Broadfoot, Keith, and Rex Butler, 'The Illusion of Illusion', in *The Illusion of Life: Essays on Animation*, ed. Alan Cholodenko (Sydney: Power Publications in association with the Australian Film Commission, 1991), pp. 263–298

Briusov, Valerii Iakovlevich, *Stefanos. Izbrannoe* (Moscow: Pravda, 1982)

Brownlow, Kevin, *Behind the Mask of Innocence* (New York: Alfred A Knopf, 1990)

Buck-Morss, Susan, *The Origin of Negative Dialectics: Theodor W Adorno, Walter Benjamin and the Frankfurt Institute* (New York: The Free Press, 1977)

Bulgakowa, Oksana, *Sergej Eisenstein – drei Utopien. Architekturentwürfe zur Filmtheorie* (Berlin: Potemkin Press, 1996)

———— *Sergej Eisenstein: Eine Biographie* (Berlin: PotemkinPress, 1998)

———— *Sergei Eisenstein: A Biography*, trans. Anne Dwyer (Berlin and San Francisco: Potemkin Press, 2001)

Butler, Judith, *Gender Trouble: Feminism and the Subversion of Identity* (New York; London: Routledge, 1990)

Carroll, Noël, 'For God and Country', in *Artforum*, 11.5 (January 1973), pp. 56–60

Charney, Leo, and Vanessa R Schwartz (eds), *Cinema and the Invention of Modern Life* (Berkeley: University of California Press, 1995)

Cherkasova, NN, and S Dreiden (eds), *Nikolai Cherkasov* (Moscow: Vserossiiskoe teatral'noe obshchestvo, 1976)

XIV s ezd vsesoiuznoi kommunisticheskoi partii (B) (18–31 December 1925) (Moscow; Leningrad: Gosizdat, 1926)

Clancy, Keith, 'PRISTIR: The T(r)opology of Pyromania', in *The Illusion of Life: Essays on Animation* (Sydney: Power Publications in association with the Australian Film Commission, 1991), pp. 243–262

Cohen, Stephen, *Bukharin and the Bolshevik Revolution: A Political Biography, 1888–1938* (Oxford; New York: Oxford University Press, 1980)

Commons, John R (ed.), *Trade Unionism and Labor Problems* (Boston, New York: Ginn and Company, 1905)

Davydov, O, *Maklochane*. Biblioteka dlia vsekh (Leningrad: Priboi, 1926)

Deutscher, Isaac, *The Prophet Unarmed: Trotsky, 1921–1929* (Oxford: Oxford University Press, 1959)

Dobrenko, Evgeny, 'Soviet Comedy Film; or, The Carnival of Authority', in *Discourse*, 17.3 (Spring 1995), pp. 49–57

Eisenstein, Sergei, *Beyond the Stars: The Memoirs of Sergei Eisenstein*, ed. Richard Taylor, trans. William Powell. Volume IV of *Selected Works* (London: British Film Institute, 1995)

———— 'The Dynamic Square', in *Close Up*, 8.1 (March 1931), pp. 3–16; 8.2 (June 1931), pp. 91–4

———— *Eisenstein on Disney*, ed. Jay Leyda and Naum Kleiman, trans. Alan Upchurch (Calcutta: Seagull Books, 1986)

———— *Eisenstein: Three Films*, ed. Jay Leyda, trans. Diana Matias (New York: Harper & Row, 1974)

———— *Film Essays and a Lecture*, ed. Jay Leyda (Princeton: Princeton University Press, 1968)

———— *Film Form*, trans. Jay Leyda (New York: Harcourt Brace Jovanovich, 1949)

————— *The Film Sense*, trans. Jay Leyda (London: Faber & Faber, 1943)

————— *Immoral Memories: An Autobiography*, trans. Herbert Marshall (Boston: Houghton Mifflin, 1983)

————— *Le mouvement de l art*, trans. B Epstein, M Iampolski, N Noussinova, A Zouboff (Paris: Les Editions du Cerf, 1986)

————— *Nonindifferent Nature*, trans. Herbert Marshall (Cambridge: Cambridge University Press, 1987)

————— 'Notes for a Film of *Capital*', trans. Maciej Sliwowski, Jay Leyda and Annette Michelson, in *October*, 2 (Summer 1976), pp. 3–26

————— *Notes of a Film Director*, trans. X Danko (New York: Dover, 1970)

————— *Que Viva Mexico!* (London: Vision, 1951)

————— *Que Viva Mexico!* (New York: Arno Press, 1972)

————— *Schriften*, Vol. 3, ed. H-J Schlegel (Munich, 1975)

————— *Towards a Theory of Montage*. Volume II of *Selected Works*, ed. Michael Glenny and Richard Taylor, trans. Michael Glenny (London: British Film Institute, 1991)

————— *Writings, 1922–34*. Volume I of *Selected Works*, ed. and trans. Richard Taylor (London: British Film Institute, 1988)

————— *Writings, 1934–47*. Volume III of *Selected Works*, ed. Richard Taylor, trans. William Powell. (London: British Film Institute, 1996)

Eizenshtein, SM, *Izbrannye proizvedeniia*, 6 vols, ed. PM Atasheva, IV Vaisfel'd, NB Volkova, Iu A Krasovskii, SI Freilikh, RN Iurenev, SI Iutkevich (Moscow: Iskusstvo, 1964–71)

————— 'Za kadrom' (Afterword), in N Kaufman, *Iaponskoe kino* (Moscow, 1929), pp. 72–92

Ejxenbaum, Boris, 'Cinema Stylistics', trans. Herbert Eagle, in *Formalist Film Theory*, Michigan Slavic Materials 19 (Ann Arbor: University of Michigan Press, 1981), pp. 55–80

Ermolaev, Herman, *Soviet Literary Theories, 1917–1934: The Genesis of Socialist Realism* (Berkeley; Los Angeles: University of California Press, 1963)

Fevral'skii, A, review of *Strike*, in *Krasnaia zvezda* (15 March 1925)

Fitzpatrick, Sheila, *The Cultural Front: Power and Culture in Revolutionary Russia* (Ithaca; London: Cornell University Press, 1992)

————— *Russia in the Era of NEP. Explorations in Soviet Society and Culture*, ed. Alexander Rabinowitch and Richard Stites (Bloomington and Indianapolis: Indiana University Press, 1991)

Freud, Sigmund, *Beyond the Pleasure Principle*, trans. James Strachey (New York; London: WW Norton, 1961)

————— *Sexuality and the Psychology of Love*, trans. James Strachey (New York: Collier, 1963)

————— *Totem and Taboo*, trans. James Strachey (New York; London: Norton, 1950)

'Gagen', review of *Strike*, in *Vecherniaia Moskva* (10 March 1925), p. 4

Garber, Marge, *Vested Interests: Cross-Dressing and Cultural Anxiety* (New York: HarperCollins, 1992)

Geduld, Harry M, and Ronald Gottesman (eds), *Sergei Eisenstein and Upton Sinclair: The Making and Unmaking of* 'Que viva Mexico! (Bloomington: Indiana University Press, 1970)

Goodwin, James, *Eisenstein, Cinema and History* (Urbana and Chicago: University of Illinois Press, 1993)

Gunning, Tom, 'Tracing the Individual Body: Photography, Detectives and Early Cinema', in Charney, Leo, and Vanessa R Schwartz (eds), *Cinema and the Invention of Modern Life* (Berkeley: University of California Press, 1995), pp. 15–45

Hegel, GWF, *Phenomenology of Spirit*, trans. AV Miller (Oxford: Oxford University Press, 1977)

Heil, Jerry, 'Isaak Babel and his Film-Work', in *Russian Literature*, 27–28 (1 April 1990), pp. 289–416

Henderson, Linda Dalrymple, *The Fourth Dimension and Non-Euclidean Geometry in Modern Art* (Princeton: Princeton University Press, 1988)

Hertz, Neil, *The End of the Line: Essays on Psychoanalysis and the Sublime* (New York: Columbia University Press, 1985)

Iampol'skii, Mikhail, *Pamiat Tiresiia* (Moscow: RIK 'Kul'tura', 1993)

Il'f, Il'ia, and Evgenii Petrov, 'Odnoetazhnaia Amerika, 1935–36'. *Sobranie sochinenii v piati tomakh*. Vol. 4. (Moscow: Gosudarstvennoe izdatel'stvo khudozhestvennoi literatury, 1961)

————— 'Pod kupolom tsirka'. *Sobranie sochinenii v piati tomakh*. Vol. 3. (Moscow: Gosudarstvennoe izdatel'stvo khudozhestvennoi literatury, 1961), pp. 476–512

Iurenev, R, *Sergei Eizenshtein. Zamysly. Fil my. Metod. Chast pervaia, 1898–1929* (Moscow: Iskusstvo, 1985)

————— *Sergei Eizenshtein. Zamysly. Fil my. Metod. Chast vtoraia, 1930–1948* (Moscow: Iskusstvo, 1988)

Iurenev, RN (ed.), *Bronenosets Potemkin* (Moscow: Nauka, 1965)

Ivanov, Viacheslav, *Ocherki po istorii semiotiki v SSSR* (Moscow: Khudozhestvennaia, 1976)

Ivanov, Vsevolod, 'Bronepoezd No. 14.69', in *Krasnaia nov* No. 1(5) (1922)

Jay, Martin, *Downcast Eyes: The Denigration of Vision in Twentieth-Century French Thought* (Berkeley; Los Angeles; London: University of California Press, 1993)

Kant, Immanuel, *Critique of Judgment* (1790), trans. JH Bernard (New York: Hafner Press, 1951)

Karetnikova, Inga, *Mexico According to Eisenstein* (Albuquerque: University of New Mexico Press, 1991)

Kleberg, Lars, 'The Audience as Myth and Reality: Soviet Theatrical Ideology and Audience Research in the 1920s', in *Russian History/Histoire Russe* (1982), pp. 227–241

Kleiman, Naum, 'On the Story of "Montage 1937"', in Eisenstein, SM, *Selected Works*. Volume II: *Towards a Theory of Montage*, ed. Michael Glenny and Richard Taylor, trans. Michael Glenny (London: British Film Institute,

1991), pp. xvii-xx

———— 'Vzrevevshii lev', in *Kinovedcheskie zapiski* 1 (1988), pp. 91–110

Koestenbaum, Wayne, *The Queen s Throat: Opera, Homosexuality and the Mystery of Desire* (New York: Poseidon Press, 1993)

Kozlov, Leonid, 'A Hypothetical Dedication', in *Eisenstein Revisited: A Collection of Essays*, ed. Lars Kleberg and Haken Lövgren (Stockholm: Almqvist and Wiksell, 1987), pp. 65–92

Kuleshov, Lev, 'Volia. Uporstvo. Glaz' (1926), in *Teoriia. Kritika. Pedagogika*, Vol. I of *Sobranie sochinenii v trekh tomakh* (Moscow: Iskusstvo, 1987), pp. 111–113

———— 'Znamia kinematografii' (1920), in *Teoriia. Kritika. Pedagogika*, Vol. I of *Sobranie sochinenii v trekh tomakh* (Moscow: Iskusstvo, 1987), pp. 63–85

Larionov, Mikhail, 'Rayonist Painting' (1913), in Bowlt, John (ed. and trans.), *Russian Art of the Avant-Garde* (New York, Thames and Hudson, 1988), p. 92

Lenin, VI, 'Doklad o kontsessiiakh na fraktsii RKP(b) VIII s'ezda sovetov'. 21 December 1920. *Polnoe sobranie sochinenii*. Vol. 42. (Moscow: Izdatel'stvo politicheskoi literatury, 1981), pp. 91–117

———— 'Konspekt Lenina k 'Nauke logiki' Gegelia'. *Leninskii sbornik* 9. (Moscow: Gosizdat, 1929)

———— 'K voprosu o dialektike' (1914–15), in *Na perelome. Filosofskie diskussii 20–kh godov. Filosofiia i mirovozzrenie*, ed. PV Alekseev (Moscow: Izdatel'stvo politicheskoi literatury, 1990), pp. 37–40

———— 'Ukazaniia o rabote agitatsionno-instruktorskikh poezdov i parokhodov', in *Polnoe sobranie sochinenii*, Vol. 40 (Moscow: Izdatel'stvo politicheskoi literatury, 1981), pp. 72–3

———— *What Is To Be Done? Burning Questions of Our Movement. The Iskra Period, 1900–1902. Book 2*. Vol. 4 of *Collected Works of VI Lenin* (New York: International Publishers, 1929), pp. 89–258

Levaco, Ronald (ed. and trans.), *Kuleshov on Film* (Berkeley: University of California Press, 1974)

Leyda, Jay, *Kino* (Princeton, New Jersey: Princeton University Press, 1983)

Lunacharskii, AV, 'Il'f i Petrov', in *Stat i o literature*, Vol. 2 (Moscow: Khudozhestvennaia literatura, 1988), pp. 163–170

Makovskii, Sergei '"Novoe" iskusstvo i "chetvertoe izmerenie".' *Apollon* (St. Petersburg) 7 (September 1913)

Malevich, Kazimir, 'From Cubism and Futurism to Suprematism: The New Painterly Realism' (1915), in Bowlt, John (ed.), *Russian Art of the Avant-Garde* (New York: Thames and Hudson, 1988), pp. 116–135

Mally, Lynn, *Culture of the Future: The Proletkult Movement in Revolutionary Russia* (Berkeley: University of California Press, 1990)

Mar'iamov, GP, *Kremlevskii tsenzor* (Moscow: Konfederatsiia soiuzov kinematografistov 'Kinotsentr', 1992)

Mayer, David, *Sergei M Eisenstein s Potemkin: A shot-by-shot presentation by David Mayer* (New York: Da Capo Press, 1972)

Merritt, Russell. 'Recharging *Alexander Nevsky*: Tracking the Eisenstein-Prokofiev War Horse', in *Film Quarterly*, 48.2 (Winter 1994–95), pp. 34–47

Michelson, Annette, 'Reading Eisenstein Reading *Capital*', in *October*, 2 (Summer 1976), pp. 27–38

———— 'Reading Eisenstein Reading *Capital*', in *October*, 3 (Spring 1977), pp. 82–89

Molochnoe khoziaistvo. Zhurnal vserossiiskogo soiuza molochnoi kooperatsii. No. 14 (37) (25 July 1926)

Montagu, Ivor. *With Eisenstein in Hollywood* (New York: International Publishers, 1967)

Moussinac, Léon, *Sergei Michailovitch Eisenstein*, Cinéma d'aujourd'hui 23 (Paris: Editions Seghers, 1964)

Nesbet, Anne, 'Babel"s Face', in *Russian Literature*, 42.1 (1997), pp. 65–83

Olesha, Yuri, *Envy*, trans. Clarence Brown, in *The Portable Twentieth-Century Russian Reader*, ed. Clarence Brown (London: Penguin, 1985), pp. 230–362

Petric, Vlada, *Constructivism in Film: The Man with the Movie Camera: A Cinematic Analysis* (Cambridge: Cambridge University Press, 1987)

XV s ezd vsesoiuznoi kommunisticheskoi partii-(b). (Moscow; Leningrad: Gosudarstvennoe izdatel'stvo, 1928)

Pilnyak, Boris, *Mother Earth and Other Stories*, trans. and ed. Vera T Reck and Michael Green (New York: Doubleday, 1968)

Pil'niak, Boris, 'Smert' starika Arkhipova', in *Krasnaia nov* 1(5) (1922), p. 61

———— review of *Dva mira* by Vladimir Zazubrin, in *Pechat i Revoliutsiia* 1 (4), (1922), pp. 294–296

Podoroga, Valerii, *Fenomenologiia tela. Vvedenie v filosofskuiu antropologiiu* (Moscow: Ad Marginem, 1995)

Prokhorov, AV, BV Raushenbakh, FS Khitruk (eds), *Problemy sinteza v khudozhestvennoi kul ture* (Moscow: Nauka, 1985)

Rochfort, Desmond, *Mexican Muralists. Orozco. Rivera. Siqueiros* (San Francisco: Chronicle Books, 1993)

Seton, Marie, *Sergei M Eisenstein* (London: Dennis Dobson, 1978)

Semenov, Sergei, 'Tif', in *Krasnaia nov* 1 (5) (January-February 1922), pp. 37–58

Shklovskii, Viktor, 'Oshibki i izobreteniia', in *Novyi Lef* 11/12 (1927), pp. 29–33

———— *O teorii prozy* (Moscow: Federatsiia, 1929)

———— *Za 60 let. Raboty o kino* (Moscow: Iskusstvo, 1985)

Shklovsky, Victor, 'Art as Technique', in *Russian Formalist Criticism. Four Essays*, trans. Lee T Lemon and Marion J Reis (Lincoln; London: University of Nebraska Press, 1965), pp. 3–24

Sinclair, Upton, *The Jungle* (1906), ed. James R Barrett (Urbana and Chicago: University of Illinois Press, 1988)

Sontag, Susan, *Against Interpretation and Other Essays* (New York: Delta, 1966)

Stalin, IV, 'On the Industrialization of the Country and On the Right Deviation in the VKP(b)' (19 November 1928), in *Sochineniia*, Vol. 11, pp. 245–290

Stites, Richard, *Revolutionary Dreams: Utopian Vision and Experimental Life in the Russian Revolution* (Oxford: Oxford University Press, 1989)

———— *Russian Popular Culture: Entertainment and Society since 1900* (New York: Cambridge University Press, 1992)

'Tak budet vsiudu, esli pobedit Kolchak', in *Voronezhskaia bednota* (26 April 1919), p. 3

Taylor, Richard, and Ian Christie (eds), *The Film Factory: Russian and Soviet Cinema in Documents, 1896–1939* (London: Routledge and Cambridge, Massachusetts: Harvard University Press, 1988)

Thompson, Kristin, *Eisenstein s Ivan the Terrible: A Neoformalist Analysis* (Princeton: Princeton University Press, 1981)

Tolstoi, LN, *Povesti i rasskazy v dvukh tomakh*, 2 vols (Moscow: Khudozhestvennaia literatura, 1978)

Tsivian, Yuri, 'Some Historical Footnotes to the Kuleshov Experiment', in *Early Cinema: Space/Frame/Narrative*, ed. Thomas Elsaesser (London: British Film Institute, 1990), pp. 247–55

———— *Istoricheskaia retseptsiia kino* (Riga: Zinatne, 1991)

Umov, Nikolai Alekseevich, 'Kharakternye cherty i zadachi sovremennoi estestvenno-nauchnoi mysli' (21 December 1911), in *Sobranie Sochinenii*, Vol. 3 (Moscow: Imp. Moskovskoe obshchestvo ispytatelei prirody, 1916), pp. 390–417

Uspenskii, Petr Dem'ianovich, *Chetvertoe izmerenie. Obzor glavneishikh teorii i popytok issledovaniia oblasti neizmerimogo*, fourth edition (Berlin: Parabola, 1931)

———— *Kinemodrama (Ne dlia kinematografa)* (Petrograd: Brianchaninov [Novoe zveno], 1917)

Verene, Donald Phillip, *Hegel s Recollection: A Study of Images in the Phenomenology of Spirit* (Albany: State University of New York Press, 1985)

Vertov, Dziga, 'Kinoki. Perevorot', in *LEF* 3 (June/July 1923), pp. 135–43

Voronskii, A, review of 'Bronepoezd No. 14.69' by Vsevolod Ivanov, in *Krasnaia nov* No. 5(9) (1922), p. 269

Vygotsky, L, *Thought and Language* (Cambridge, Massachusetts: MIT Press, 1962)

Wells, HG, *The Time Machine* (1898) (New York: Dover, 1995)

Za bol shoe kinoiskusstvo. Vsesoiuznoe tvorcheskoe soveshchanie rabotnikov sovetskoi kinematografii, 8–13 January 1935 (Moscow: Kinofotoizdat, 1935)

Zagorskii, M, 'Kak reagiruet zritel'?', in *LEF* 2(6) (1924), pp. 141–51

Zholkovsky, Alexander, 'The Terrible Armor-Clad General Line: A New Profile of Eisenstein's Poetics', in *Wiener Slawistischer Almanach* Sonderband 31 (1992), pp. 481–501

Index

27. April. 05

Coutts 60.45

25781